Links, Lore, and Legends

★

Links, Lore, and Legends

The Story of Texas Golf

Art Stricklin

TAYLOR TRADE PUBLISHING
Lanham • New York • Dallas • Boulder • Toronto • Oxford

Published by Taylor Trade Publishing
An imprint of The Rowman & Littlefield Publishing Group, Inc.
4501 Forbes Boulevard, Suite 200
Lanham, Maryland 20706

Distributed by National Book Network

Library of Congress Cataloging-in-Publication Data

Stricklin, Art.
    Links, lore, and legends : the story of Texas golf / Art Stricklin.— 1st ed.
      p. cm.
    Includes bibliographical references and index.
    ISBN 1-58979-240-8 (hbk : alk. paper)
    1. Golf—Texas—History. I. Title.
  GV982.T4S87 2005
   796.357'09764—dc22
2005007127

Contents

Foreword
Texas:
Golf's Most Historic State

I'VE OFTEN BEEN asked about why Texas golf and Texas golfers are so special, and I think the best way to answer that question is that we have the best intrastate competitions of any city or state. When I grew up, I played in an amateur tournament every single week. In Fort Worth, there were so many tournaments; the *Star Telegram* was the headquarters for all of them. We had to get a date so we wouldn't have a conflict with another tournament because we had so many events. We could play in a tournament every single week, all summer long.

We played on different golf courses, different putting surfaces: sand greens, Bermuda greens, bent greens, and rye greens. We played in wind conditions, heat conditions, hard ground and soft ground, everything golf has to offer.

When you learn to play here, you have some courses with wide fairways, some fairways that are as hard as a table. You have a wide variety of greens, great greens and sand greens. There is something about the competition and the background of

Byron Nelson (center), with
pro golfer Nick Price (left)
and Nelson's wife Perry (right).
(Photo courtesy of
Salesmanship Club Dallas)

golf in Texas that has produced the good players from 1928 on until now. It's almost like one generation is built upon the next.

I don't want to put myself up with Tiger, but any golfer who knows anything about golf at all knows that Tiger helped raised the level on Tour. The young players saw what he did, and now they are really good and playing for a lot of money. That's what we wanted to do when I played.

I've sometimes been asked what's been my role in Texas golf history. I was born and raised here and still live here. And the tournament that has my name on it raises more money for charity than any other tournament on the PGA Tour. I guess that says the way I feel about Texas golf and my role in it.

Byron Nelson
Roanoke, Texas

Preface
One Incredible
Texas Golf Journey

WHEN I THINK about all the great players, events, and history we've produced in Texas golf history, it's amazing to realize that decade after decade, year after year, the best, the most interesting, and the most historic players have come from the Lone Star State.

The greatest shotmakers that have ever played the game are from Texas because of the wide variety of courses we have here, differing weather, and varying conditions of our courses. I've always thought it was easier for players from Texas to go to the Northeast or elsewhere to play than for those same players to come down here. We're used to tough conditions and tougher courses, so when we went elsewhere, it seemed easier for us. When players from other states came here, they often had no chance.

The conditions we face on a daily basis force golfers to improvise and to learn lots of different kinds of shots for all different situations they will face. That's why I think Texas is a great place to live and learn and play golf and why I feel so fortunate to have grown up and played here and live here.

Lee Trevino. (Photo courtesy of Lee Trevino)

I've been asked before if Texas is really golf's most historic state, and to me there is no doubt that it is. Florida has more courses, the Northeast may have more of golf's beginnings, but no one can beat Texas for great players, great events, and great characters.

This book, which covers every historic decade of Texas golf's past and present history, should be a great background for those who have lived here for years and an interesting introduction for newcomers or Lone Star visitors. Heck, I'm even in here a few times, so enjoy it and educate yourself about this great golf state.

Lee Trevino
Dallas, Texas

Acknowledgments

Writing a book like this, which covers such a large time period and so much information, requires help from dozens of people for which I am very grateful. To mention some is inevitably to leave out others, and after talking to more than 100 Texas golf figures, that's a lot of people, but I want to give it a try anyway.

The first thanks goes to Texas golf historian Frances Trimble. I doubt there is anything she doesn't know about the Lone Star game. She was my first call regarding this project, quickly offering to buy me breakfast, getting me started on the right track, and keeping me there through this entire long process.

All of Texas' greatest living golf legends were extremely generous with their time and information. Byron Nelson arrived for a two-and-a-half-hour lunch just days after being bedridden with vertigo but was as interesting, helpful, clear in his memories, and graceful with his time as ever. Lee Trevino, an old friend from previous books, came through again for me. Jack Burke Jr. conducted a vividly interesting session in his office at Champions Golf Club complete with a handwritten chart, hands-on instruction of my grip, and words of wisdom to his wife Robin, all while recounting countless Texas golf tales.

Doug Sanders gave me a fast and interesting tour of his own Houston golf home/museum. Tinsley Penick met me for lunch at Austin Country Club with

Jackson Bradley. Joe Conrad met me at the San Antonio range, where he still gives lessons. Marty Leonard and Scott Corpening set up a fascinating lunch at Colonial to talk about Marty's dad and the tournament he founded. Fort Worth golf-writing legend Dan Jenkins gave me an interesting hour of information.

Steve Fallon of the Texas Sports Hall of Fame went out of his way to help with early Texas golf history. Frank Houseman of the Salesmanship Club and Joe Bendy of River Oaks Country Club contributed some great books. Burt Darden of the Houston Golf Association was a big help with Houston golf history, along with Paul Marchand at Shadow Hawk and Edward Turley at Houston Country Club.

Elsewhere, you'll see a list of the sources used for compiling the information and quotes for this book, but I especially want to note two outstanding books by the same Texas author: *Texas Golf Legends* and *Hogan*, both by Curt Sampson, a better golfer than I'll ever be and a writer I'm always working to equal. His books were very helpful in compiling history on previous Texas golf figures, as were so many other books I used.

Also, a special thanks to so many of Texas' helpful golf pros, players, and fellow golf writers who passed along photos and useful information, even if it wasn't at the most convenient time for them. A big thanks for tracking down so many historic Colonial golf photographs goes to longtime tournament manager Dennis Roberson.

My experienced and encouraging editor, Janet Harris, who's done this more times than I ever will, deserves a big thanks for helping me down this golf history path.

My ever long-suffering and wonderful wife Belinda read every word, and my great daughters Allison and Ashley hopefully understood when I told them for the two-hundredth time Dad had to work on his book again. Most important, all praise for my Lord and Savior Jesus Christ, who has given me this writing ability and whom I seek to honor every day.

Introduction
Texas Golfing Dreams

ALL BOB ESTES started out with was dreams. While growing up on the windswept, flat, some might even say just plain ugly eastern edge of West Texas known as Abilene, dreams were about all the young Estes had to sustain him during his frequent trips to the nine-hole Lazy Tee Par 3 golf course. Estes would always carry his clubs, often a favorite wedge and putter in his light canvas bag, dragging himself and his golfing tools around the small course, always alone with his dreams.

Estes's dreams were about joining his golfing heroes, guys like fellow Abilene golfer Billy Maxwell, who had achieved the amazing feat of winning 35 consecutive amateur tournaments in Texas during his high school and college years in the 1950s while helping lead North Texas State to four consecutive NCAA titles from 1949 to 1952. Estes also dreamed about joining in the footsteps of North Texas natives Ben Hogan and Byron Nelson on the PGA Tour, two players he said "set the standard" for competitive golfing in America. Nelson had done the seemingly impossible by winning 11 straight PGA Tour events in 1945, while Hogan achieved the incredible by overcoming a nearly fatal auto crash with a bus in 1949, not only surviving but thriving against golf's greatest players and capturing an additional five major championships in the years following the wreck. "The greatest accomplishment in golf is how Hogan came back to win five majors in the 1950s after the car accident," says legendary Texas golf writer Dan Jenkins.

Now living in Texas' capital city of Austin, Estes, a multiple winner on the PGA Tour himself and the former NCAA Golfer of the Year while playing for the University of Texas, still thinks about his juvenile golfing dreams, those that came true and those he has yet to achieve. "Texas helped lay the foundation for my game," he says. "All we need is a nine-hole course, a place to practice and a little imagination; we can conquer the world. It's not the money, but the history and the wins in Texas."

Looking at golf's ultimate honor, induction into the World Golf Hall of Fame, you'll see that's exactly what Estes's heroes past and present have achieved. Of the 104 people currently enshrined in the sport's ultimate showcase, 18 have some direct connection to Texas either through birth or longtime residence, a total which nearly doubles the next highest state represented.

The 2004 Hall of Fame honoree Tom Kite called his recent induction a dream come true for the latest in a never-ending line of great Texas golfers. "Texans are a breed unto themselves, and Texas golfers have made more history than any other breed the world has known," he said in the 1993 book *Texas Golf Legends*.

Jackson Bradley has been a Texas golf pro long enough to see multiple decades of great players, from Nelson and Hogan to Jack Burke Sr. and Jr. and University of Texas great Ben Crenshaw. He knows exactly what Estes is talking about when he mentions his Lone Star golfing dreams. "Everything in Texas is a dream," said Bradley, now in the midst of his eighth decade of Texas golf.

The longest of long-shot dreams is what brought the PGA Championship to the south in 1927 for the first time at Cedar Crest Golf Club in Dallas, thanks to the tireless work of early Texas golf promoters John Bredemus and Sol Dreyfuss. "The word pro means promoter. That's what we do for golf," says Houston's Jack Burke Jr.

Drive and dreams brought the U.S. Open south of the Mason-Dixon Line for the first time in 1941 at Colonial Country Club in Fort Worth, home of the first 18-hole course in the South and Southwest with bent-grass greens. In the ensuing decades, dreams persuaded Jack Munger, Graham Ross, and E. J. Burke to snare major golf championships for their beloved Texas courses when all were less than five years old.

Dreams are the only things that allowed Ben Hogan to escape the trauma of watching his father's suicide at home in Dublin, a nearly career-crippling hook off the tee box, and three failed attempts at the PGA Tour to emerge as the game's most feared and mysterious figure, even in death. They encouraged tenth-grade dropout Byron Nelson to persevere as a caddy, assistant pro, and head professional to become one of golf's greatest champions and its greatest gentleman.

Golf dreams, about the only thing Lee Trevino could afford for the first two decades of his life, allowed him to overcome a poverty-ridden childhood in a house without electricity or running water, a father he never knew, and a low-pay, blue-collar upbringing. He emerged as the first golfer to hold the professional golf championships in three different countries in the same year. "I broke the mold when I won because nobody with my background had ever won this much in any sport."

For Texas in the twenty-first century, golf dreams aren't merely for the history books. They are alive and well and teeing up for millions in prize money every week on the PGA Tour in the form of Dallas' Justin Leonard and Andrews native Chad Campbell. Leonard, almost the same size as Hogan, heard a thousand times as a kid that he was too small to succeed in today's high-powered world of professional golf. One of the few players who can match Hogan in on-course intensity, Leonard responded by hitting about a million practice balls under the watchful eye of mentor Randy Smith at Royal Oaks Country Club in Dallas. That led to national college and amateur honors for the Texas native who has never lived outside the state and never plans to. He captured a victory with the oldest prize in golf, the British Open Championship, along with a half dozen other prestigious pro golf victories and millions of dollars in prize money and endorsements.

Campbell prepared for golf greatness in the mold of Maxwell and Estes, often alone or with his older brother at the dubiously named Andrews "country club," a humble facility that had produced little but dust storms and two-for-one beer nights with overflowing ashtrays in its entire existence until Campbell honed his game there. He captured the season-ending 2003 Tour Championship at Champions Golf Club in Houston and added the 2004 Bay Hill PGA Tour title along with a spot on the 2004 U.S. Ryder Cup team, already making more in his brief career than most peo-

ple in Andrews will make in a lifetime. "I'm just happy we had a course in Andrews and an 18-hole one at that," Campbell said. "My past has made me the player that I am, and I like the way things have turned out."

Many of the state's golfers, both professional and amateur, are considered the greatest produced by the game. Their deeds are hard to believe in scope, nearly impossible to duplicate, and amazing to consider. Texas is the site of the nation's worst natural disaster, the 1900 Galveston hurricane, along with its greatest repeatable source, decade after decade, of golf champions and unforgettable characters.

In a 1940s Texas newspaper column, golf legend Gene Sarazen summed up the state's golfing heritage. "Ah, Texas. The golf capital of the world. It's the people and the golfers here who are responsible. They're friendly and thoughtful and loyal to their kids." Writing in the prestigious *New Yorker* magazine in the 1950s, author Herbert Warren Wind proclaimed the state "The New Scotland" for the large number of top players it had produced.

CBS golf analyst Lanny Wadkins, who moved to Texas three decades ago from Virginia, noticed the generational pull. "In Texas, it's just one solid generation after another," as Wadkins is now hopeful his own talented sons can contribute to the latest Lone Star legacy. "One generation inspires another," adds golf pro Buddy Cook, who grew up in the state's golf gambling hotbed, Odessa, and has served as head pro at some of the state's most prestigious clubs.

Longtime Texas historian Francis Trimble pauses when asked how the dreams of a state and its golfers could have started with nothing and wound up with just about everything they ever thought about. "Texas admires winners, they always have," Trimble said. "Rich men don't create champions. Winning and competition creates champions. We're so competitive in this state, it's a natural."

The Texas Golf Association helped launch the Lone Star golfing boom when it started in a Houston hotel in 1906. Its executive director, Rob Addington, says the state's golfers have built, embellished, and verified plenty of golfing myths. "A lot of that 'Tin Cup' stuff from the movies really existed in Texas."

What else to expect from a state that produced the forerunner of the modern electric cart and the sand wedge—a state that was the site of incorporation for the bylaws of the PGA Tour, the birth of the over-50 Senior Tour, and the one-time headquarters for the ladies' professional tour along with the home of its all-time most successful player, Kathy Whitworth, and its most colorful, Babe Didrikson Zaharias?

There is a century-plus trail of Texas golf dreams fulfilled, shattered, and yet to come with Lone Star golf glory still being built one dream at a time.

Texas Golf Beginnings, 1896–1919

The Dreams Turned into Links

5 Highlights of the First Decades

★ Dallas Golf and Country Club begins in 1896 as a six-hole crude homemade layout near downtown Dallas.

★ Galveston Country Club becomes the state's first officially chartered club in 1898.

★ Austin Golf Club begins in 1899 with Lewis Hancock and friends walking off the holes. Harvey Penick is hired as a caddy in 1913.

★ Brackenridge Park is founded as the first public course in Texas in 1916, featuring green-grass greens and A. W. Tillinghast as its architect.

★ John Bredemus arrives in San Antonio in 1919, serves as assistant pro at Brackenridge, and goes on to design 80 percent of the first courses in Texas.

The Story of the First Decades: The Father of Texas Golf

Of all the men who could be considered marked for success at an early age, John Bredemus should be at the top of almost any list. He was considered brilliant, yet he was a loner. Task oriented and highly productive, yet prone to wandering for hours without his shoes or telling anyone his destination, he would sometimes even enter into his golf clients' offices shoeless, as he did with banker Houston Jesse Jones when he was building Memorial Park in the 1930s. Bredemus might climb to the top of trees to get a better view of his latest golf course creation, according to an almanac listing.

"John Bredemus is the Father of Texas Golf, but nobody really knows who he is," said Tinsley Penick, the former head pro at Austin Country Club. Penick's father, Harvey, claimed to be Bredemus's closest friend after meeting him in 1919 when Bredemus came south from New York to teach high school math in San Antonio, looking for a place to play golf year-round.

While there are plenty of mysteries and gaps in his Texas career, what is not in doubt is that he was a huge factor in getting golf off the ground in the state. He built public facilities in Houston, Hermann, and Memorial Park, which he called his finest work. While serving as an assistant pro at Brackenridge Park in San Antonio, he helped spearhead the creation of the Texas PGA and the Texas Open, which began in 1922 and energized the dream of a regular professional golf tour with stops all through the South and Southwest during the winter months. He was also a part of the Texas contingent that helped land the PGA Championship,

the first held in the South, at Dallas' Cedar Crest in 1927. Near the end of his career, he helped create what is generally acclaimed as the state's finest overall layout, Colonial Country Club in Fort Worth, the site of the first U.S. Open held in the Southwest in 1941.

The son of hardworking immigrants from Luxembourg, he was born in 1894 and quickly earned acceptance into the finest East Coast schools. He began at the prestigious Phillips Exeter Academy in New Hampshire in 1904–1905, then on to Dartmouth College and later Princeton to study civil engineering, according to his published biography. But Bredemus was far from a book-smart, pencil-pushing academician generally removed from the real world—he was a gifted athlete as well. After one year at Dartmouth, he dropped out to prepare for the national Amateur Athletic Union (AAU) All-Around Competition, a grueling 10-event decathlon all performed in a single day in New York City. He captured the national AAU title as America's best all-around athlete and went to Princeton, where he was a star halfback for the Tigers football team, then a national powerhouse, according to a lengthy article on Bredemus in *Golfiana* magazine.

Bredemus graduated with a degree in Civil Engineering in 1912 and prepared to defend his AAU national title in New York against none other than Jim

John Bredemus, the Father of Texas Golf. (Photo courtesy of Institute of Texas Cultures/San Antonio Light Collection)

Thorpe. The king of Sweden had just acclaimed the legendary Thorpe as the World's Greatest Athlete after winning a pair of gold medals in the 1912 Summer Olympics in Stockholm, Sweden. In the national AAU competition held in New York under wet, sloppy conditions, both Bredemus and Thorpe broke the previous AAU decathlon scoring record with ease. The more experienced Thorpe gained the national title by a mere 175 points, according to the *Golfiana* article, but his landmark win would not last long. Less than six months later, Thorpe was stripped of his Olympic and AAU gold medals for having played semipro baseball, and his Olympic medals were placed in a bank vault and never returned. His gold AAU medals were given

to Bredemus, according to Penick, who carried them with him almost until the day he died.

In 1914, Bredemus discovered golf at America's first public course, Van Courtland Park, in New York City, learning the game well enough to play in several prestigious tournaments as an amateur. He helped build the Lido Golf Club on Long Island and was present for the founding of the PGA of America on January 17, 1916, in the Taplow Club at the Hotel Martinique in New York City.

After playing and working on the East Coast for a couple of years, Bredemus came to Texas in 1919, arriving in San Antonio. Since he was a man of few words, not given to lengthy speeches or detailed correspondence, there is little to indicate why Bredemus became such a proponent of the game and what drew him to Texas.

Penick was one of the first to introduce the name of Bredemus to the general golfing public in his best-selling *Little Red Book* in the early 1990s and says he never forgot the lessons of his legendary friend. "John taught me it takes the eyes of an artist to design a course, but the skills of an engineer to build one. He had both."

Bredemus was hired as an assistant high school principal in San Antonio for the 1919–1920 school year and also became a part-time assistant pro at Brackenridge Park, but his main profession was designing, building, and promoting Texas golf. He became the state's first professional, full-time architect, whereas well-meaning committees or traveling golf planners had done most previous Texas layouts.

His first design effort was San Felipe Springs in Del Rio in 1921, but he went on to build or renovate courses all over the state, including courses in Houston, Corpus Christi, Harlingen, Austin, all through the Hill County region, Fort Worth, and West Texas. He installed the first bent-grass greens on the nine-hole San Angelo Country Club in 1928 and had the distinction of never designing a sand-green course in Texas, according to golf historians, an extreme rarity for those times.

Texas historian Francis Trimble once wrote that Bredemus "saw Texas golf not as it was, but as it could be. He was goal oriented instead of people oriented." Prone to wandering the back roads of the state without telling anyone where he was going or what he was working on, Bredemus avoided all trappings of success. "I never knew what he was spending his money on," Penick said, and Bredemus strongly resisted any attempt to get him to visit the insides of the clubs once they opened.

He would often play checkers with members or with others who stopped by under the clubhouse trees for hours, but wouldn't enter the clubhouse. Bredemus told numerous pros who invited him inside, "I don't feel like I belong with the people inside there."

His tridesign of Colonial Country Club along with his protégé Ralph Plummer and architectural veteran Perry Maxwell in the mid-1930s is considered his greatest layout and has stood the test of time for golf architectural acclaim.

Penick appears to have the best insight into Bredemus's unseen genius temperament during a visit to Ridglea Country Club in Fort Worth, where he was working on the second 18 holes. "He said, 'There will be a tee and over there will be a green, Harvey.' He could picture all the holes in his head. All I could picture was we were knee deep in brush and I was getting covered in chiggers" (Penick's *Little Red Book*).

Bredemus died of a heart attack in Big Spring in 1946 while working on another course design. He is buried there under a simple gravestone that lists his name but not his many contributions to Texas golf. While alive, Bredemus indicated he cared little for money, lived in the sparsest possible facility, and carried all his possessions in a cloth sack. When he died, he was penniless, and his family, whom he hadn't seen in many years, wanted little to do with him. Longtime Brackenridge Park head professional Murray Brooks, at the course where the builder/dreamer got his Texas start, took up a collection among fellow pros for a proper service and burial, helping Bredemus avoid an unmarked pauper's grave, according to a *Golfiana* article.

When it was time for the funeral service, Texas pros and others lined up to see the gold medals from the man who was known to have kept Thorpe's AAU gold for more than 30 years. The medals were nowhere to be found, but Penick once said he thinks he knows what happened to them. "Not long before he died, John showed me the medals in a cigar box. 'You know what I'm going to do with them?' he asked. 'No. What?' I said. 'I think I'm going to melt them down.'"

Just one more mystery for the Father of Texas Golf.

Who Was First?

Looking to start a good 19th-hole argument among your Texas golfing friends on a slow, rainy afternoon? Just start talking about which course was the first golf course in Texas. There are all kinds of possibilities, all kinds of theories, and maybe a few hurt feelings, perhaps even a busted lip if the arguments run hot enough.

Start with the six-hole, crude layout designed by Welsh businessmen Richard F. Potter and H. L. Edwards in 1896 on a small street corner at Haskell and Cole near downtown Dallas. There was the nine-hole sand-green facility in central Austin that Lewis Hancock and friends walked off in 1898 and that began life as Austin Golf Club, then became Austin Country Club, and is now the public Hancock Park.

Add the 9- and 18-hole Dallas Country Club facilities, which followed Potter and Edwards's design at two different areas of Oak Lawn near downtown Dallas. Another possibility is the first 18-hole private club, Houston Golf Club, which opened in 1903 and has since moved to two different locations as Houston Country Club. Then there is Beaumont Country Club, which claims to be the oldest private club in the same location, not having moved from its 5355 Pine Street address since Alex Findlay designed and opened it in 1906.

There was even an article in the *San Antonio Daily Express* in 1887 that references a golfing exhibition by Scotsman Cumming Macdona. He arrived to explore the state but gave a demonstration of the new sport on the parade grounds at Fort Sam Houston thanks to the military permission given by Fort Sam commander Brigadier General David S. Stanley.

But for the oldest legally chartered club in Texas, the honor goes to Galveston Country Club. Unfortunately for this scenic Southeast Texas seaside location, the honor was short lived. Looking through the prism of Texas society, success, and prosperity at the end of the 19th century, a person can see how easily Galveston could claim to be the site of the first golf course in Texas.

While the game itself was less than 30 years old in America after coming over from Scotland, Galveston was a prime candidate for a top private facility. Because there were no effective methods of travel in Texas at the time, the state depended on sea waves, with some rail, to carry people, goods, and material in and out of state. Galveston was a booming seaport, 40 miles southeast of Houston, and in the late 1880s, the city was at the peak of its golden age. "We had more millionaires per capita than any place in Texas or in the Southwest," says club historian Margy Kelso. "It was a wonderfully sophisticated place." While not Texas' largest city, having been surpassed by Houston, Galveston was still a city of economic significance. The sophistication of life on the island was conducive to importing the gentleman's game from the East Coast.

With ships arriving daily from all parts of the world, but especially from Europe, Galveston was exposed to the best and most expensive of what the 19th century had to offer. The new visitors found a ready market among the many upscale citizens. Galveston had the first electric lights in Texas in 1884, the first national bank, the first real estate agency, the first nursing school in the South, and the first medical school west of the Mississippi. That the first private course as a home for "distinguished gentlemen" would take place in Galveston comes as no surprise.

The organization of Galveston Country Club took place in the spring of 1898 with an original membership of 30 men and an initiation fee of $50. On the first board of directors, according to club history, were Charles Fowlers as the first president; Frank Walthrew, vice president; Herb Lemonius, secretary; and businessman and philanthropist Charles Sealy serving as treasurer, all prosperous men who had been enriched by the booming Galveston commerce. They expressed a desire to experience the new game of golf with their closest friends and business associates.

Their new course was located on the beach overlooking the usually calm Gulf of Mexico waters, west of the U.S. Coastal Fortification, in an area known as the Denver Resurvey. To build the new course, the first to be designed by a professional architect in the state, they called on Scotsman Mungo Park. He walked off the Galveston course, personally designing the hole locations and staying around as the club's first winter professional, another first for Texas golf.

Early member Buzz Moore remembers that the first Galveston Country Club course certainly stood out for a number of reasons. "A peculiarity of this golf course was that all of the greens had two foot high barbed wire fences around them, the reason being cows were grazing on the golf course all the time people were playing golf," he was quoted in the official club history.

By all accounts, Park's design was scenic, with several of the holes offering direct views of the usually placid waters. But it was the location and the view that proved to be the course's and island's undoing that fateful fall. For four solid days, from September 8 to 11, 1900, the island was pounded by one of the fiercest hurricanes recorded in U.S. history. Despite some warning, the island was quickly cut off from the mainland and isolated from any help or escape.

After four days of dark skies, constant wind and rain, and record sea swells, Galveston awoke to the greatest natural disaster in U.S. history. An estimated 6,000 local residents were killed, and many thousands were injured. The island's buildings on the southern half of the island, including the new Galveston Country Club clubhouse, were wiped from the map, and Park's fine course was washed into the ocean.

The devastation was so great that it took days for the word to get out about the extent of the damage because of the lack of communication equipment and weeks for help to arrive from all over the country. When the rescuers arrived, they saw death and devastation few could imagine.

With the great loss of life, a destroyed golf course was the least of the city's worries, and the shell-shocked members rebuilt the best that they could. The club officially returned in 1910 safely off the island as Oleander Country Club, where an elegant interurban train brought golfers to the course from the mainland or the island. That course and clubhouse fell victim to a devastating fire and was later renovated by Bredemus. The Galveston Country Club moved back onto the island in the 1920s in the middle section of 61st Street, where it stood until 1946, when it was sold for a large profit, and the club moved to its current location on the west end of the island.

Through its years as a resort destination and Texas' first chartered course, Galveston Country Club attracted a number of top golfers, including Byron Nelson, Babe Didrikson Zaharias, Denny Schute, and Al Espinosa, all mindful of the course's original spot in Texas golf history.

Capital City Golf

Lewis Hancock's name usually is the first mentioned when talking about early Austin history. The personable Hancock was born in Austin in 1856, attended Austin High, founded the Hancock Opera House, and was co-owner of the elegant Hancock Building on Sixth Street. He served as a city alderman for two years and was elected Austin's mayor in 1896 and 1897. When the city's first golf course, Austin Golf Club, became a reality at the dawn of a new century, Hancock and his considerable means and influence were front and center again, and he would become known as the "pops of Austin golf," according to the club's official history book.

He often took his wife and two daughters on summer vacations to the East Coast, where he got his first exposure to golf. He was quite possibly at the first U.S. Open in 1895 at Newport Country Club in Rhode Island, not far from his annual vacation spot. On his return from one of his East Coast trips, Hancock gave a public golf exhibition in 1898 at a time when the overall Austin population was less than 30,000 and very few people had heard of golf, much less expressed an interest in it.

The next logical step, according to Hancock and some of his similarly minded friends, was to form a golf club. The first meeting to gauge interest for the new club, to be known as Austin Golf Club, was held on November 13, 1899, at the historic Driskill Hotel in downtown Austin. David Williams, an influential professor at the still relatively young University of Texas, was elected the initial chairman for the club. Hancock reported at the first meeting that he had already personally scouted five possible sites for the club. They eventually selected a tract of land just east of Hyde Park near downtown Austin and fairly close to the growing university. Hancock and his team initially rented 100 acres before purchasing it a few years later, the official club history reported.

Never one to wait when a project he favored was in the balance, Hancock went out to scrape dirt for the new course in the winter of 1899 with his own mule train and personally plot the holes. Without a background in golf course architecture, Hancock was far from an expert, but he was determined to bring the game he loved to the city he helped build, and the result was the first Austin golf layout. Austin's being the state capital meant one other thing to Hancock: they were closer to the state government to file official papers of incorporation. They did just that, making Austin Golf Club official on January 10, 1900, with the total value of the club listed on the incorporation papers at $150. The race to the state offices, a few miles' trek from the club, allowed them to get their papers in one week before Dallas Country Club officially incorporated.

The first official tournament at the newly opened Austin Golf Club took place on February 22, 1900, with Hancock, ever the promoter, offering a gold medal for the initial male and female champions. The *Austin Daily Statesman* recorded that Colonel Dave Harrell struck the first shot at the opening tournament, but the winner was Walter Bremond. A local businessman, he grabbed the first win with an opening score of 110 and a whopping 37 handicap. Pierre Bremond was second with a 129 and a 48 handicap, perhaps the first occasion of Texas tournament sandbagging.

Among the early female members were Hancock's two daughters and wife and Julia Pease, the daughter of former Texas governor Elisha M. Pease. In 1906, the club expanded to both sides of Waller Creek, purchased an additional 45 acres to expand facilities, and officially changed its name to Austin Country Club to better reflect its more varied offerings.

Just seven years later, the club achieved perhaps the most important milestone in its 100-year history. It hired 10-year-old Harvey Penick as a club caddy, at 20 cents a day, joining his brothers Tom and Tinsley in working at the club. That began an 81-year association for Penick with Austin Country Club, first as a caddy, then an assistant and head professional for 50 years, and then pro emeritus. His son Tinsley followed him by serving a two-decade stint as head professional.

Of course, the two pillars of Austin Country Club golf met as Penick caddied on occasion for Hancock. In one 1990 interview, Penick recalled his time together with Hancock. Penick said he was often eating candy while caddying for Hancock, who gave his blessing with the gentle warning, "It's all right to eat that candy while we go along. Just see that it stays in your mouth and doesn't get on my clubs." Hancock's clubs were not soiled and were promptly cleaned and stored after their historic first meeting.

The hiring of Penick, who would become head professional at age 18, was eventually hailed statewide and then across the nation for his golf teaching genius. He taught generations of future pros and eager amateurs, but Penick always insisted the credit should go back to the club and the game of golf. "My first job at Austin Country Club came in 1913. Since then, I've lived golf and nothing else. I've met people who have always been good to me. That's the thing I'm most proud of, the friends. When I watch people play, sometimes I feel like I've helped them, sometimes I haven't, but I get a pleasure out of this you wouldn't believe. Why would I want to do anything else?"

Golf legend Byron Nelson, born one year before Penick was hired at Austin Country Club, calls Penick one of the most influential men in Texas golf history for his teaching and help. "Every golfer in the country would like to take a lesson from Harvey Penick," Nelson said. "I'm proud to call him my friend." Tinsley Penick agrees on his father's legacy. "He lasted so long and helped so many people. They just loved and admired him."

Harvey Penick's first book of golf wisdom, the *Little Red Book*, became the best-selling sports hardcover of all time when it was released in 1992 with nearly a million copies sold, and two more books of Penick's teaching followed before he died three years later.

Harvey Penick, right, and his son Tinsley served as head pros at Austin Country Club for more than 70 years. (Photo courtesy of Tinsley Penick)

Austin Country Club had one more noted if disputed incident in its early days. President William Howard Taft was making a cross-country train trip in 1909 to meet the Mexican president and reportedly stopped in Austin for a rest after a long train trip. For decades the story has circulated that Taft stopped for a quick 18-hole round at Austin Country Club while security men on horseback patrolled the grounds resting shotguns on their laps. Texas golf historian Trimble claims the incident took place at La Quinta Ranch near Corpus Christi. Penick says his father was there at Austin Country Club when Taft played his presidential round. Regardless of the location, the fact remains it was the last visiting presidential round of golf played in Texas until Doug Sanders coaxed good friend President George H. W. Bush to Kingwood for a Senior Tournament pro-am nearly 80 years later.

Big D Welcomes Golf

While they may have been behind Austin Golf Club in filing their incorporation papers, the Dallas Country Club founders didn't allow anything to slow their love for the new game of golf. Along with original founders Richard F. Potter and H. L. Edwards, Colonel J. T. Trezevant served as the first president of Dallas

Country Club, from 1900 to 1907. He helped find enough land in their early Oak Lawn location near downtown to build 18 holes for the new private club.

The club's charter from the State of Texas says "to support and maintain the royal and ancient game of golf and other innocent sports." The club issued 320 shares of stock at $25 each with 34 stockholders and 10 playing members, the cream of the Dallas society, including Colonel A. H. Belo, founder of the *Dallas News*. Trezevant became the club's major promoter in its early days. "The purpose of building a first-class golf club has already been achieved," he wrote to prospective members in late 1904. "The construction of a modern, up-to-date country clubhouse would be the rallying point for social enjoyment."

The club hosted the first state golf tournament on May 8, 1903, which was won by original member Edwards by two shots over R. H. Connerly of Austin. Just three years later, Edwards promoted the formation of the Texas Golf Association, which took place in the winter of 1906 with seven member clubs hailing from Fort Worth, Waco, Dallas, Houston, San Antonio, Galveston, and Beaumont. He was elected the first president in their initial meeting at a Houston hotel.

The first Texas Golf Association state tournament took place in April 1906, when 60 golfers from the seven original clubs turned out at the Dallas Country Club. Edwards was again the winner, defeating Frank "Pops" Lewis of San Antonio for the championship flight title, giving him the distinction of winning the first two state golf tournaments ever held in Texas. The opening tournament survived a downpour of rain on the North Texas prairie that led Edwards to remark, "Nothing could top this since the previous big flood."

In appreciation for his hard work to get the organization started, the Texas Golf Association named its state amateur golf trophy the H. L. Edwards Trophy, a designation it still bears.

After a huge fire destroyed the new $25,000 clubhouse in 1908 but failed to derail the club's growth, the members begin to look north for additional land for their growing club. Today, Highland Park is a small enclave near downtown Dallas surrounded by the central city and clustered by million-dollar mansions. But in 1909, it was still considered far out in the rural countryside without any good roads to get there. The needs of a growing club and the aggressive lobbying from the newly formed city of Highland Park proved to be formidable pulls. After considerable discussion at the club, the decision was made to move to the new location with 115 acres purchased in the center of Highland Park and room for an attractive, two-story clubhouse.

In 1909, the club hired prolific course designer Tom Bendelow to lay out the new facility. He had already designed more than 500 courses in the United States and Canada, earning him the nickname "the Johnny Appleseed of American Golf" along with his "18 stakes on a Sunday afternoon" for what some felt was his rushed, unimaginative style. After touring the Highland Park site, Bendelow reported to the members that the land "had no superior in this country." He promised a course of more than 6,000 yards and produced one at 6,285 yards, huge by the standards of 1912, when it was finally completed.

The first tournament at the new site was held on February 22, 1912. C. H. Munger set the course record on the first day with an 81. The report in Belo's *Dallas*

Club Houses No. 1 and No. 2, above. Original home of "Dallas Golf and Country Club," at left, 1896-1904. At right, Club House No. 2 built 1904, burned 1906.

Club House No. 3, above, No. 4 below. No. 3 replaced No. 2, same location, 1906-1912. Present Club House, No. 4, 1912-1957; note barren prairie (1913 photograph).

Early view of the Dallas Country Club clubhouse. (Photo courtesy of Dallas Country Club)

News the next day was equally glowing: "The finest arrangement of hazards and play conditions in the South and the Southwest."

Dallas Country Club certainly was a far cry from the crude six-hole layout Edwards and Potter laid out by hand with string and metal cans just 16 years earlier.

Golf Comes to Houston

With the devastation in Galveston during the 1900 hurricane and the discovery of oil outside nearby Beaumont a year later, Houston quickly shot up as the largest city in the state with 100,000 in population by 1910.

With that type of growing population, golf seemed a natural for the city; the only question was when and where. Those questions were answered on March 21, 1904, when the organizational meeting of the Houston Golf Club took place for the purpose of building a new clubhouse and golf course for the like-minded citizens of Houston.

Houston civic leader A. W. Pollard was elected as the first president, and he presided over the awarding of a contract for $1,200 for the purpose of a new clubhouse. There were 15 individuals elected to the board of directors, including many of Houston's leaders, with Jesse H. Jones and William Rice among them.

The course acreage, known as the Mahan tract, was proclaimed as the "finest spot for golf links to be found in all of Texas," according to early club minutes. The Houston Golf Club's first charter read, "The object should be to promote interest in the ancient game of golf as well as other innocent outdoor games and sports and to acquire and maintain suitable grounds and buildings for the same." In 1904, one of the bylaws stated that no alcoholic drinks were permitted on clubhouse grounds, but that was quickly amended a year later to permit alcoholic drinks under the direction of the house committee from time to time.

The site for the first course was a 65-acre leased plot of land across the street from the Rice Institute on Buffalo Speedway. Club members laid out a small nine-hole facility with a length of 3,000 yards between Buffalo Bayou and West Dallas Street. Despite the lack of a known architect or any fancy facilities, the club quickly grew in size with an initiation fee of $25 and annual dues of $18. After a series of discussions at the local Thalian Club, the Houston Golf Club members decided the old club must cease and that a new and better location and name were needed.

The final meeting of the Houston Golf Club took place on May 5, 1908, when a motion was made to sell all buildings, fixtures, and memberships to the Houston Country Club for just over $4,000. The first meeting of the new Houston Country Club was held on May 19, 1908, at the Thalian Club, where Rice, namesake of the elite, private university he helped found, was named the first club president.

The club acquired 95 acres of land west of downtown known as the Wayside Property for the street that bounded the then open land. The club paid for the purchase by issuing 48 gold bonds of $500 each. Once again, the club used an unknown architect or perhaps a committee of members, but the results were a fine 18-hole facility, the first full 18-hole course in Texas, and play began in 1910 at Wayside.

The first golf pro for the new Houston Country Club was Willie McGuire, a Scotsman and one of the earliest of the full-time Texas golf pros. Among the early members was a young Howard Hughes who took over his family-owned Hughes Tool Company at the age of 20, and while earning $60 million a year at his company, he worked on his handicap at the club until he got it as low as a two.

Interest in the new Houston Country Club and its huge colonial-style clubhouse was immediate, with a membership of nearly 500 paying dues of $1.50 a month and an initiation of $25. Civic leader William Hogg raised $25,000 for the club and lavish clubhouse, setting the club apart as the standard for Houston luxury for years to come.

The Dream Catches On

While the game continued to grow in the metropolitan areas of Texas, it also caught on in the smaller towns as well. El Paso Country Club was opened on June 1, 1906, three months before the first paved roads appeared in this West Texas city.

Beaumont Country Club was designed by Scotsman Alex Findlay in 1906 in the same location it sits on today, close to the Spindletop Oil Discovery, which brought the black gold to Texas for the first time. The course was designed just one year before Findlay headed due west to design the San Antonio Country Club in 1907.

The Huaco Club in Waco at North 29th Street and Sanger Avenue opened in 1910 with a nine-hole golf course along with tennis courts and bowling alleys.

Among the early promoters of the new club were bankers Samuel M. McAshan, Mervyn B. Davis, and August Forest Smith. Eventually, the Huaco Club burned and was replaced by Spring Lake Golf Club in the early 1920s.

River Crest in Fort Worth, another Bendelow design, opened in 1911, as did Lakewood in Dallas in 1912. Other early courses of note were Sunset Grove in Orange, a Donald Ross design in 1912, and Glen Garden in Fort Worth in 1912, built on the site of the former O.K. Cattle Company. Amarillo Country Club was the first golf layout in the Panhandle with a 1919 opening to its William McConnell 18-hole design. Pinecrest Country Club in Longview was the first East Texas golf course, beginning construction in 1919 and opening two years later, with green fees of 75 cents.

The fast addition of courses in Texas prompted the birth of the Texas Golf Association, according to 2004 executive director Rob Addington: "In 1906 we were set up much like the United States Golf Association was in 1895 to promote and grow the game of golf," he said. They appeared to be doing their job well. At the beginning of the 1900s, Texas had only five golf courses, but by the end of the second decade of the century, the number had already grown to several dozen spread across the state. Initial member clubs were charged $20 to join the association. A similar organization, the Texas Women's Golf Association, was formed in 1916 to promote female advances in Texas golf, a goal the association fulfilled with gusto in the coming years.

While the clubs were beginning to catch on, the players who would one day dominate the golf world began to arrive as well. Both Byron Nelson and Ben

Hogan were born in 1912 in North Texas, and Jimmy Demaret was born in 1910 in Houston.

Finally, Power to the People

Until the early 1900s, the limited number of courses had all concentrated in catering only to the men and the most prosperous, privileged members of society. But an Alamo City twosome, the Laurel Heights Golf Club and Brackenridge Park Golf Club, was able to change all that. Laurel Heights Golf Club, located just north of downtown, near the current site of San Antonio College, was opened in 1911 by Will Symons Sr. He had gained valuable golf experience in the Midwest and put that to use running his privately owned daily-fee facility.

Located only a few miles from San Antonio Country Club, Laurel Heights attracted many of the top pros of the day from the Northeast who were down to play and visit during the winter months. Jack Burke Sr. and his brothers Tom and Edmond all paid visits to Laurel Heights before 1920, and Boston's Tom Lally was another regular visitor before becoming head pro at San Antonio Country Club. In 1913, San Antonio's first city championship was held at Laurel Heights with the *San Antonio Light* reporting that Will Symons Jr. slogged through wet weather to capture the first city title with clubs made by his father at the Symons Golf Shop.

The most significant development for the Symons family was the emergence of their eldest daughter Gertrude, who became the first female golf teacher in Texas in 1912, passing along the game she had learned from her father. Symons regularly made the rounds at the local San Antonio women's social clubs to explain the game to the potential players and drew a steady stream of female customers who wanted to learn the new game from a woman. Gertrude Symons's husband died in the great influenza epidemic of 1917–1918, leaving her with a small son to raise alone. She soon abandoned her role as Texas' first female teacher and never was involved in golf again, according to a *Golfiana* article.

Texas' first true municipal course didn't appear until the mid-1910s, when San Antonio civic leader and banker George W. Brackenridge donated some of his personal land to furnish the acreage for Texas' first city-owned golf course. Brackenridge had earlier sold some of his land to help give San Antonio Country Club the space it needed for their new club near Fort Sam Houston, but this was different. Brackenridge was donating part of the land he used for a hunting lodge because he felt his city, now at a population of 200,000, needed a place for recreation.

The one restriction he put on the deed for the land was that no alcoholic beverages could ever be sold on his land. Former Brackenridge pro John Erwin, who did extensive research of the Brackenridge Park facility, says Brackenridge was a reformed alcoholic and didn't want anyone to drink on his property and suffer the same problems he had experienced. Despite many legal challenges, his wishes still stand at Brackenridge, known as "Old Brack" to most San Antonio regulars.

Construction began in 1915 at Brackenridge with one of the most famous of golf architects, A. W. Tillinghast, doing the routing and building of the course in one of his many golf building trips from his headquarters on the East Coast. Tilley, as he was known, did a masterful job working around the San

Antonio River and the native Texas hardwoods. His first nine holes were open to the public in the spring of 1916, with the full 18 holes officially open for play on September 23, 1916. Just about everything associated with Brack was unique. It was open to anyone who wanted to play with green fees less than a dollar.

Unlike the hard-pressed sand common at the other Texas golf courses, Tillinghast had designed grass greens for the 18-hole course, a rarity most golfers had never seen. "I remember when I was 15, my parents and I got in our old car, and we went down to Brackenridge Park," Penick once recalled. "I paid a green fee and played on grass greens for the first time."

Brackenridge would later serve as the home of the Texas Open, the Texas State Junior Championship, and the home base for Bredemus, but just by opening on that fall morning in 1916, it provided true power to Texas golfers as a prime public facility.

"This is the most historic course in the state," Erwin said. "Anybody who is anybody has played here."

Texas' First Champion

In the early 1900s, golf was an amateur game. Professional golfers for the most part did not exist or, if they did, were regarded as con men or some similar lower class. The amateur golfer ruled, and in the early 1910s, no one ruled greater in Texas amateur golf than George V. Rotan. Like Bredemus, Rotan grew up as a child of wealth, but instead of resting on his family's fortune, he worked to make plenty for himself.

He was born in Waco, July 18, 1886, where his father was the first president of Waco National Bank,

the oldest bank in the city. Rotan attended Yale, where he was a member of the national championship golf team, graduating in 1907 with a business finance degree. Standing 6 feet 2 inches and weighing 172 pounds, he had a long, full golf swing, according to those who knew him, and progressed quickly in the game, becoming a member of Huaco and Spring Lake Country Club in Waco. He served at Kelly Field in San Antonio during World War I but moved to Houston in 1919 as a member of Neuhaus & Company, a brokerage company, and joined Houston Country Club, where he played until his death in 1943.

His new work didn't slow down his golf, as he won the Texas State Amateur Championship from 1912 to 1915, won the Texas Amateur again in 1919, and finished second in 1920. Rotan was a member of the U.S. Walker Cup team in 1923 and won the Houston Invitational at Houston Country Club a half dozen times along with a countless number of club championships. He won the Texas Senior Amateur title in 1939 and 1940 and was a runner-up in 1941.

He died of a heart attack at age 60, just a month after shooting 70 with some friends at Brae Burn Country Club in Houston. Golf legend Byron Nelson, one of the few to play with Rotan during his amateur dominance, remembers his overall contribution to early Texas golf and the dreams they fostered. "George V. Rotan was the first champion this state produced and a great overall player."

During the next decade, entire tournaments of great golf champions came to Dallas and San Antonio, spurring the state on its way to producing some superstars of its own.

The 1920s
The Dream Begins with Texas Tournament Golf

5 Highlights of the 1920s

★ "Lighthorse" Harry Cooper moves to Dallas from England when his dad gets the head pro job at Cedar Crest Country Club in 1920 and becomes Texas' first professional golfing star.

★ First Texas Open under the leadership of sports editor Jack O'Brien and architect John Bredemus staged in 1922, paving the way for the modern PGA Tour.

★ River Oaks Country Club opens in 1924, with Jack Burke Sr., the first head pro, bringing a wealth of East Coast golf professional knowledge with him.

★ PGA Championship held at Cedar Crest in Dallas in 1927 with Walter Hagen winning his fourth straight title.

★ PGA Tour bylaws and framework incorporated by golfer Tommy Armour in 1928 during lengthy rain delay at the Texas Open.

The Story of the Decade:
The Birth of PGA Tour Golf

By the 1920s, Jack O'Brien had been sports editor long enough that his routine at the *San Antonio Evening News* was down to a familiar science. He would arrive early in the South Texas morning, settling back in his office to read over any other regional newspaper he could find and looking over the still newfangled Associated Press Teletype copy. But one morning in the winter of 1921, he read a story that made him sit straight up in his seat.

The Denver-born O'Brien read something he had trouble believing, that two prizefighters had recently been paid $25,000 each for pounding each other's

brains out. But golf, O'Brien's new favorite sport since moving away from the wintertime snows in the Rocky Mountains, awarded only $500 for its national championship, the U.S. Open. That got the civic-minded O'Brien to thinking. San Antonio, which had a population of 200,000 and was the 37th-largest city in the

San Antonio sports editor Jack O'Brien came up with the idea of the Texas Open. (Photo courtesy of Institute of Texas Cultures/ San Antonio Light Collection)

country at the time, already had plenty of mild winter weather. It also had the newly opened Brackenridge Park golf course, Texas' first public golf facility, where O'Brien often played.

O'Brien reasoned, why couldn't golf's best players, almost all amateurs with some traveling professionals mixed in, come to San Antonio during the winter months to play a tournament at Brackenridge for record prize money? "Californians sell their whole state to the world," O'Brien wrote in one of his sports columns. "Why can't we sell San Antonio as the city where the sun goes for the winter?"

In the early 1920s, San Antonio was a far different place than the tourist mecca it has become today. There was no River Walk with its shops and restaurants lining the canals or boats bringing through another load of visitors. The Alamo was less than 100 years from its climactic battle and not the powerful draw to visitors worldwide. Why not bring top golfers to the South Texas warm winter sunshine and a great municipal golf course for a sporting activity the likes of which San Antonio had never seen? O'Brien reasoned.

O'Brien was accustomed to supporting athletic causes in his regular newspaper columns in his adopted hometown. Among his previous efforts were ball fields for children without a place to play and touting the area as a winter oasis for northerners, long before the term "Snowbirds" had been invented.

"It takes the President of the United States four years to earn as much as it takes a man of fisticuffs to earn in 10 minutes," he wrote in a column. Fortunately for his new golf tournament effort, O'Brien encountered John Bredemus, the new assistant pro at Brackenridge Park Golf Club. Bredemus, known as the Father of Texas

Golf for his architectural efforts, had already started on his first design in Del Rio but knew O'Brien from his rounds at Brackenridge Park and shared his passion for a "National Open," as Bredemus called it to showcase their city and course in the wintertime.

More important, Bredemus, who had been in New York City for the founding of the PGA of America in 1916, still had plenty of contacts on the East Coast with the top golfers and knew what it took to stage a professional event. O'Brien also had plenty of local friends and contacts. His tournament committee was led by *Express* and *News* publisher and general manager Frank Huntress, early San Antonio golf pro Frank "Pops" Lewis, and Mayor O. B. Black. According to a *Golfiana* article on the founding of the Texas Open, the *Express* and *News* papers were among the first tournament patrons along with the St. Anthony, Menger, and Crockett hotels as well as the City of San Antonio and the Junior Chamber of Commerce.

As summer turned to fall, the committee was hard at work, and O'Brien and Bredemus held regular meetings for the tournament without a name, a date, or any committed players. Bredemus was in charge of all golf-related details, and he regularly reported to committee members the extent of work that remained if they were going to pull off their wintertime golfing dream. Banker George W. Brackenridge's hunting lodge, which had served as the original clubhouse, had burned down, and the current accommodations were substandard even by the reduced standards of the day.

The condition of A. W. Tillinghast's design at Brackenridge were uneven at best, depending on the weather and number of players tramping across the grass. There was no caddy master, no starter's shack, and no starter for that matter, a position O'Brien personally volunteered to fill during the tournament. Most important, the tournament had no players, and with a projected early February tournament, there was only a scant three months to attract them.

O'Brien's hard work and business connections finally paid off. His committee raised $14,000, a huge amount of money in the early 1920s, and was prepared to offer a first-place prize of $5,000, 10 times more than what U.S. Open Champion James M. Barnes had received for winning the Open in 1921. Bredemus made a late 1921 trip to New York to lobby personally his golfing friends to come to Texas for the tournament. O'Brien was still nervous whether the top players of the day would make the lengthy trip to San Antonio in the winter of 1922, but according to Austin Country Club pro Harvey Penick, he didn't have to wait long to get an answer. "For that money, we'd play in a pasture," Penick recounted leading star Gene Sarazen as saying.

O'Brien and Bredemus had to wait on players to respond to the cable they had sent out in early December inviting them to the first Texas Open at Brackenridge Park. One by one, the top players committed to come south, and by the end of January, almost all of them had arrived in San Antonio. Included in the first field were Sarazen and "Wild" Bill Mehlhorn. Texas players included Willie McGuire (the cofounder of the Texas PGA), Cyril Walker, and amateur star George V. Rotan. He had grown up in Waco but moved to Houston, where he was the five-time Texas Amateur state champion.

The *Express* and *News* blanketed the area with coverage of the upcoming tournament, including daily updated reports on which golfers had arrived and what hotel they were staying in. Even the national golf media, such as it was for the times, had arrived in the form of Craft Higgins, editor of *Golfer Magazine*, who wrote glowingly about the San Antonio weather and the fine Tillinghast design at Brackenridge. "None of the places have better weather or a better course than you have right here," he wrote. O'Brien, ever the promoter, reported that much of the Northeast was locked in a fierce snowstorm while visitors to the first Texas Open were playing golf in warm sunshine.

Longtime San Antonio Country Club pro Tod Menefee attended the first Texas Open and played in them himself through four decades. He said in a 1992 interview that the first event still brought back plenty of memories. "I remember the winner and knew a tournament was born here. Can you imagine the pros are still playing there today?" Harvey Penick did not attend the first Texas Open because his job as head pro at Austin Country Club took up all his extra time but said today's pros don't realize how significant that first event staged in the winter of 1922 was. "Some people still don't realize this is the tournament which helped start the PGA Tour," Penick said in a 1992 interview. "They played in San Antonio and then moved on to Los Angeles or over to Shreveport, New Orleans, and Florida."

Current PGA Tour golfer Tommy Armour III won the 2003 Texas Open with a record low score, nearly 70 years after his grandfather, the "Silver Scot" Tommy Armour, competed in several early tournaments. "The Texas Open is very special because of what it made possible," he said.

Walker held the first halfway tournament lead with a 36-hole total of 138, one shot better than Bob MacDonald, a Scot credited with helping to invent the modern stance. In the final two rounds, it was MacDonald who rallied for the win with a 281 total, including a final-round 70. He was one shot better than Walker, who missed an eight-foot putt on the last hole, and five shots ahead of Leo Diegal. MacDonald took home the first-place check of $1,633.33, the largest payout on the still young professional tour. O'Brien passed the hat among the estimated 4,000 spectators on the final day to make up for sponsors who had not fully fulfilled their commitment, but in almost every way possible the first Texas Open was considered a huge success.

The players were treated to liberal doses of South Texas hospitality with lavish dinners at local hotels, and Sarazen was so appreciative that he announced at a players' dinner, "Instead of going to Florida to get in shape for the Texas Open next year we are coming directly to San Antonio for a month, at least." Two events in that first decade helped ensure that the Texas Open would remain strong and viable 80 years after the initial tournament. The first came in the 1923 tournament, which still offered the same enlarged purse thanks to a $1,500 contribution from the San Antonio Junior Chamber of Commerce. Walter Hagen, one of golf's early stars, rallied from a six-shot deficit on the final day with rounds of 65, a new course record, and 71 to catch Bill Mehlhorn and defeat him in a brief playoff. Not only did Hagen collect the largest tournament

Action at the 1929 Texas Open, with the Brackenridge Park clubhouse in the background. (Photo courtesy of Institute of Texas Cultures/ San Antonio Light Collection)

check of his career, but his amazing comeback was picked up by all the large newspapers on the East Coast as validity that the new tournament in Texas could be accorded major status.

The second incident occurred in 1928 and made the tournament more famous off the course than on, where Mehlhorn scored his first Texas Open victory over Dallas' Harry Cooper. Almost from the beginning, the 1928 tournament was plagued by bad weather. The Thursday pro-am was played in a steady downpour, and the Friday round was washed out entirely. The tournament scheduled for the following week in Hot Springs, Arkansas, was pushed back to allow the San Antonio event, which was moved to the public Willow Springs golf course, to finish in wet and frigid conditions.

With all the time to wait out the weather, Tommy Armour called a players' meeting. He had recently been elected president of the Professional Touring Golfers' Association of America and used the weather-mandated break to tell the players he wanted to adopt articles of incorporation for the organization that would emerge as the PGA Tour. Armour introduced a local attorney who explained how this would make their new organization legal and introduced some basic guidelines. A year later, Armour again used his time in San Antonio to announce the progress in the new tour, which now included stops in half a dozen cities. He announced a series of requests for players that seem positively modest by today's perk-laden standards, including no backtracking on the winter routes and help from the railroad stewards with the players' baggage.

A new clubhouse for Brackenridge, looking like a stone castle on the outside, was built before the 1929 tournament and still stands today. So does the Texas Open, which is the fifth-oldest stop on the professional circuit and the only tournament held in the same city for more than 80 years. "The winner's list is like a who's who of golf," Armour III said—thanks to a local sports editor with a drive and a dream and a golf pro/architect with friends in high golfing places.

Big-Name Architects for a New Game

John Bredemus has been given proper credit for the dozens of golf courses he designed in the early decades of Texas golf, but the Lone Star State also attracted plenty of big-name architects in its early years. The 1920s and 1930s have been called the golden years of golf architecture for the many classic designs created during this period, and two of the most commonly mentioned famous designers were A. W. Tillinghast and Donald Ross, both with Texas golf courses to their credit. Tillinghast and Ross would often have a dozen different projects under various stages of construction but visit only once every three months because of the time required to journey to the various sites. Ross's first visit to Texas came when he laid out Sunset Grove in Orange in 1912. He returned in 1923 to design one of Texas' first master-planned communities, River Oaks Country Club in Houston.

River Oaks is today surrounded by million-dollar mansions, but early planners included houses in the initial planning stages to entice golfers to travel the long distance from downtown Houston. Local builder T. W. House Jr. came up with the idea of building houses in the 200-acre Country Club Estates, the area near Westheimer and Buffalo, then known as Four Mile Place. Despite being told by two of Houston's leading businessmen, Will Hogg and Jesse Jones, that his project was doomed to fail because of its distance from the central city, according to the official club history book, House persevered by teaming with Houston congressman Thomas H. Ball to sell homesites and memberships for a golf course not yet established.

Ball is credited with the idea of hiring Ross in 1923 to design the 18-hole course. Ross had already gained national acclaim for his courses, and his presence in Houston was enough to secure the viability of River Oaks, at least in the early stages. Ross was famous for saying that God created golf holes and that his only chore was to discover them. On April 9, 1923, Ross and his construction team broke ground and began construction on the River Oaks site discovering the 18 finest holes. "We have as fine a course as can be built," Ball said. Although construction was basically done by the end of 1923 and the club began collecting its $80 annual dues, the par-71 layout wasn't actually open for play until July 1924 to give the course a chance to mature.

At the grand opening in July 1924, Ross explained how every bunker and green was designed to play naturally and showed players where they had various options to approach the greens, succeeding through strategy instead of power. During the presentation, he included some of his other favorite sayings, including, "Golf should be a pleasure, not a penance" and "You don't see a straight line in nature," explaining his many dogleg holes.

Albert Warren Tillinghast had first come to Texas to design Brackenridge Park in 1916, then moved north to build Cedar Crest Country Club for businessman Sol Dreyfuss in southern Dallas in 1919 and Brook Hollow Golf Club in Dallas in 1920. Club founders purchased approximately 160 acres from local families in the only sandy loam area near downtown to plot the Brook Hollow layout and clubhouse. The club founders had contacted Tillinghast to work on their property after seeing the high-quality design done at Cedar Crest.

During the period between 1919 and 1924, Tillinghast had more than a dozen properties on the drawing board, but he was very positive about the Brook Hollow project when he first walked the property. Ground was broken on May 1, 1920, and with construction costs of $300 to $400 dollars a week, work was under way with nine holes ready by early 1921.

By spring of that year, Tillinghast was on the move in Texas again, this time returning to San Antonio, where he would design and construct Alamo Country Club just north of downtown. The founders had acquired 155 acres from the J. M. Nix Ranch and were determined to build a club that would rival San Antonio Country Club, along with Brackenridge Park, Willow Springs, and Riverside, a trio of public layouts all near the center city. Tillinghast was in his architecture heyday during this period, exhibiting a huge ego and living a flamboyant lifestyle while at home in New York and on the road. According to club minutes, in a move that smacks of Texas brashness and challenge, Alamo Country Club founders hired Tillinghast for $1,700 and kept him supplied with endless quantities of tequila at the posh Menger Hotel.

When the Tillinghast course officially opened in November 1921, it had the finest of whatever the club founders could imagine as part of a $145,000 budget for land, course, clubhouse, and improvements. It boasted one of the longest holes in America, the 605-yard, par-5 fifth hole, along with a 240-yard carry over a steep ravine from the first tee box to the fairway. A review in the October–November 1921 issue of *Texas Today* lavished praise on the new Tillinghast design and his unique lay-out: "With green grass of velvety softness and smooth, well-kept fairways that await the golfer, and by way of a brand new feature, even the tee boxes are made of grass for greater conveniences to the player."

Perhaps the course and clubhouse were a bit too grand for the times, as Alamo Country Club lasted only 10 years until it succumbed to the Great Depression and closed its doors in 1931. The course sat idle for 16 years and was almost sold and used for other purposes before reopening in 1946 as Oak Hills Country Club, still with its timeless Tillinghast design in place and still used today for championship golf.

Texas' First Professional Star

Although amateurs still dominated the game in the early 1920s, Texas' first professional star came from a most unlikely place: Leatherhead, England. Harry Cooper first came to Dallas at age 10 when his dad, Sid, accepted his first head professional's job at the newly opened Cedar Crest in Dallas. The senior Cooper was the adventure-some sort, and after serving as an assistant for the leg-endary Old Tom Morris at St. Andrews Golf Links in St. Andrews, Scotland, he took off for America, where he heard of the head pro's opening at the Cedar Crest course, which had been designed by Tillinghast and backed by prosperous Dallas businessman Sol Dreyfuss.

Not only was Cooper a fine teacher and pro, but his wife Alice was also a top teacher and worked in the Cedar Crest shop giving lessons much like Gertrude

Symons had done in San Antonio in the previous decade. Their son Harry turned out to be the best of them all. He truly was a child golf prodigy, winning the Texas State Open in 1923 at age 18 and then repeating his victory the following year. He captured his first PGA Tour title in 1926 when he won the Los Angeles Open with Austin Country Club pro Harvey Penick in the field. "I was playing some fine golf, but Harry Cooper was better," Penick said in a 1992 interview. "He was a tremendous player."

Fort Worth native Byron Nelson, who faced Cooper in both professional and amateur matches, said he was an unknown quality. "Not many people had heard of him because he wasn't born here or grew up in Texas, but he was a great player in those days. He beat me several times, so I certainly knew him."

During the 1926 victory in the Los Angeles Open, he picked up the nickname he would carry the rest of his career, "Lighthorse." Famous sportswriter Damon Runyon came up with the name for the speed in which Cooper played and the nimble way he carried himself around the Los Angeles Country Club layout. Playing with George Von Elm, who would finish second, he finished the final round in 2 hours, 30 minutes, while his caddy carried the 26 clubs he used, long before the 14-club limit was instituted.

Cooper won an amazing 30 times between 1926 and 1941, including eight times in 1937, when he cap-tured the first Vardon Trophy for low stroke average, but he never captured a major championship. He was second in the Masters twice and second in the U.S. Open twice and in the semifinals of the PGA Championship, but he could never grasp one of the coveted titles. "First you've got to be good, then you've

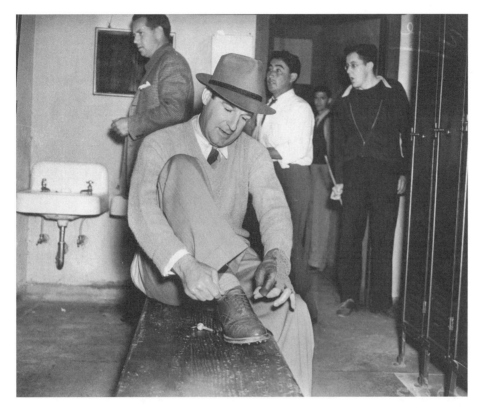

"Lighthorse" Harry Cooper was Texas' first professional golf star. (Photo courtesy of Institute of Texas Cultures/San Antonio Light Collection)

got to be lucky," Cooper was fond of saying of his near misses. Harry and Sid both competed in the first Texas Open in 1922 at Brackenridge Park, where Harry would finish second in 1928, and also competed in the 1927 PGA Championship at his home course at Cedar Crest.

Still, Cooper's Texas-sized pro golf success set the stage for an entire stampede of homegrown golfing talent.

The Arrival of the Little Pro

Much like Austin Country Club's hiring of caddy Harvey Penick proved to be the club's most successful decision, the opening of River Oaks in 1924 wasn't the best thing that happened to the club even with a Donald Ross–designed course. The most fortunate thing that happened to River Oaks was the hiring of its first head professional, Jack Burke Sr.

Burke, a native of Philadelphia who had worked at some of the top courses on the East Coast and in the Midwest, brought a generation of golf knowledge and teaching ability when he was hired at new golf territory at River Oaks Country Club. "My dad was the first second-generation golf pro in the state," said Jack Burke Jr., the longtime president/owner of Champions Golf Club in Houston. "That means he came from a generation of knowledge and was able to spread that around when he came here. Everyone else here was basically a first-generation pro, but my dad taught many of the pros in the state like Harvey Penick and Tod Menefee." Two things made Burke such an overwhelming success for River Oaks and the state of Texas: his open and friendly nature, giving him the nickname "Smiling Jack," and his golf teaching knowledge resulting from his East Coast background.

"I can't tell you the number of nights I came home to dinner and there was Texas pros at the table, talking with my father about golf and just sharing stories and learning about the game," Burke Jr. said. Known as the "Little Pro" for his small stature, Burke Sr. would teach anyone and share his thoughts with whoever came to River Oaks. He was also an outstanding player, defeating Cooper to win the Texas PGA Championship and finishing tied for second in the 1920 U.S. Open behind British Champion Ted Ray.

Burke had been coming to Texas for a number of years to serve as the winter professional at Glen Garden Golf Club in Fort Worth when snow and cold made it impossible to teach up north. There he met Quo Vadis Quayle, whom he married in 1921. Their first son, Jack Jr., was born in Fort Worth in 1923. Deciding that a family and full-time warm climate were two important priorities in their life, the Burkes began looking to move south permanently, and when the opening came up at River Oaks in 1924, they jumped at the chance.

Among the players Burke taught and encouraged was Glen Garden assistant Jack Grout, who eventually made his way to Ohio, where he taught a pretty fair junior, Jack Nicklaus. Penick helped teach decades of pros; Menefee was at San Antonio Country Club for 40 years,

while Burke's son helped found Champions Golf Club with another Houston native and Burke disciple, Jimmy Demaret. "Jack Burke Sr. deserves a large amount of the credit and influence for the golf teaching in this state," said Nelson. "Because not only have we always had good players, we've had good teachers." Burke Sr. stayed at River Oaks until 1946, when he passed away.

Demaret was the caddy master and the starter at River Oaks and met both Burkes for the first time after coming over from public Hermann Park. The elder Burke would be a lifetime mentor, the younger Burke a lifelong friend and business partner—just another legacy of Smiling Jack, the Little Pro.

More Golf for the Masses

Brackenridge Park had been a major success when it opened as Texas' first public and first green-grass course in 1916, and it was far from the last. By the mid-1920s, more public courses had begun to open all over the state, giving more options to the Texans who wanted to try the new game of golf for the first time.

Among the first new public layouts was Willow Springs in San Antonio, another John Bredemus design that featured the longest municipal course hole in the state, the 600-yard, par-5 second hole, which stretched the length of the property. Another early San Antonio public course addition, Riverside Golf Course, was famous for another reason. The course opened in 1919, only 21 years after being used as the staging ground for Teddy Roosevelt's famous charge up San Juan Hill. On his way to Puerto Rico, Roosevelt stopped in San Antonio to recruit more volunteers for his fabled charge. He stationed himself in the bar of the downtown

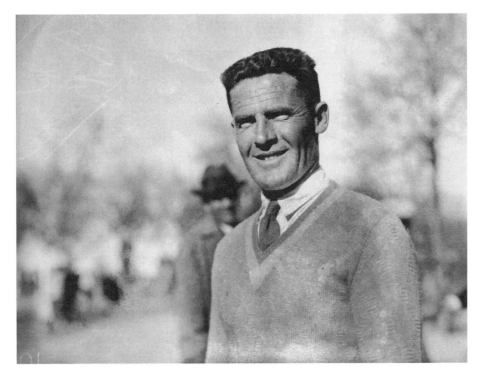

Jack Burke Sr., the first head pro at Houston's River Oaks Country Club. (Photo courtesy of Institute of Texas Cultures/San Antonio Light Collection)

Menger Hotel where eager locals, looking for a chance for glory, arrived to join his small army. After fortifying their courage at the Menger bar, they were sent to the camp staging area near downtown, which just happens to be the location of today's sixth hole at Riverside.

In Houston, the first public course was opened in 1922, named Hermann Park in honor of civic leader George H. Hermann, who donated the land across the street from Rice University. Hermann was an immigrant to America who arrived penniless but made a fortune in business and wanted to give back to those who began life with little economic wealth, just as he did. One of the first employees of Hermann Park, which was built by a committee led by Bredemus and George V. Rotan,

was Demaret. He was hired as an assistant club maker, cleaning and repairing the clubs of the Hermann Park players worn after several weeks of use.

Dallas' first public course was Tenison Park, built in 1924 in East Dallas. It was another Bredemus-designed course on 105 acres of land donated by Dallas banker Edwin O. Tenison, who wanted it as part of a park to honor his son, Edward, who had died in World War I.

Stevens Park in Oak Cliff was another public course that opened in Dallas in May 1924. Walter Stevens and his sister donated 40 acres of their estate as a way to honor their parents, and the City of Dallas leased part of the acreage to complete room for the 18-hole public facility, according to a 1940s report prepared for *The*

Texas Golfer by Dallas Director of Parks L. B. Houston. All Dallas public courses charged $1 to play on the weekend, 75 cents during the week.

The Austin golf scene went public for the first time when the Lions Municipal course opened nine holes in October 1924. A Lions Club finance chairman and founding member was quoted in the *Austin American* newspaper as saying, "This course is for all of Austin," as Lions club members had pledged $25 each for the project. The architect for the course is in dispute. Several stories connected with the Lions Club identify the architect as Tom Penick, the longtime head pro and Harvey's brother. Others think the designer was likely Bredemus, who was doing some renovation work at Austin Country Club at the time, or perhaps they worked together to build Lions. Whoever was responsible, Lions remains a highly popular course today with nearly 80,000 rounds a year and still a large, white lion statue presiding in front to represent the builder, who officially turned it over to the City of Austin in 1929.

Another factor in the state's fast-paced public golf scene was the beginning of the Texas State Junior Championship at Brackenridge Park in San Antonio and held there from 1927 to 1974 before being rotated around the state. Scores of future Texas golfing stars have captured the state junior title, but for nearly the first 50 years the attraction was getting to come to San Antonio and play at Brackenridge. "For a Texas kid from a small town like me, you can't overestimate what a big deal that was," said Fort Stockton native and PGA Tour winner Blaine McCallister. "It was huge just to get to come there and play where all my heroes had played."

Fort Worth's Caddy Kingdom

While amateur golf ruled the 1920s only to be eclipsed eventually by the professional game, another 1920s staple, caddies, hung around much longer. In the 1920s, all private clubs employed a large number of caddies. Almost every serious golfer of the day began his golfing career as a caddy. Such was the case at Fort Worth's Glen Garden Golf Club, which employed dozens of caddies for their members but none who would become more famous than John Byron Nelson and William Ben Hogan.

Although the two boys wound up caddying at the same club and were linked together during their entire careers, they came from very dissimilar backgrounds. Nelson was born in Waxahachie and enjoyed a fairly stable family life, moving to Fort Worth when he was still in grade school and settling near the Glen Garden course. Nelson dropped out of school midway through the tenth grade "because there wasn't much need for school back then," he said, but worked happily at Glen Garden, perfecting his game with head pro Ted Longworth and honing the consistent swing that would one day rule the golfing world.

Hogan was born in Stephenville and grew up in Dublin, where his father, a local factory worker, committed suicide at the family home with Hogan in the same room. According to Hogan's superb biography by Curt Sampson, the family moved to Fort Worth after the father's death, and while both Ben and his brother Royal worked hard to help support their mother, Ben also found time to caddy at Glen Garden.

Nelson first became aware of Hogan during December 1926, according to his autobiography, when the Glen Garden members put on a caddy boxing match. "Ben liked to box and so did another caddy we called Joe Boy," said Nelson. "I was just watching. I never liked to box or fight." By that time, Nelson was engrossed in caddying at Glen Garden and working on his own game.

"I remember we would get 50 cents a bag for caddying and the members might give us something extra at times as well," said Nelson in a 2001 interview. "I remember I was caddying for a doctor in Fort Worth one day, and he promised me an extra 25 cents if I didn't lose a ball. That was really big money back then. On the first tee he hooked his tee shot into the woods, and I never found it. After that I made sure I never lost another ball."

Nelson took every opportunity to practice his golf, but Longworth had strict rules that caddies could not practice on the course and could not play the course when members were there. The young Nelson was as honest and as rule-abiding as any caddy who likely ever lived, so he didn't make up a phony story the one time he was confronted by the club manager. "He asked if I had been practicing on the golf course and I said 'Yes, sir,'" Nelson recalled. "He said, 'You know you can't practice out here,' but that was the only time I ever broke the rules." Nelson even took to practicing at night at Glen Garden, putting his white handkerchief over the hole to allow the moonlight to show him where the hole was.

The only time caddies were allowed to have a real tournament was the annual caddy outing, where Hogan and Nelson squared off in December 1927. It was the first time the two Glen Garden caddies had

ever faced off in their lives, one of only three head-to-head competitions in their careers, but it was the first of three close matches. It was clear to anybody who was paying attention that Hogan and Nelson were two of the best players the club had to offer, and both caddies, dissimilar in personality but joined in talent, shot 40 on the par-37 course. The Glen Garden members were clearly enjoying the show and determined there was still enough playing time, so they decided a playoff was in order.

Hogan won the first hole, according to Sampson's biography, and the format was not sudden death but an extra nine, so Nelson took the match when he sank a long putt on the 18th hole. The prize for each boy was a club, a 5-iron for Nelson and a 2-iron for Hogan, which they promptly traded to help complete their own individual sets.

Nelson certainly progressed faster, moving into the pro shop working with Longworth, then moving on to Texarkana in the early 1930s to turn pro and begin winning tournaments. Hogan struggled with his hook off the tee and financial woes in the beginning, but neither ever forgot their Glen Garden caddy beginnings. "You always heard Hogan say he dug it out of the dirt," Jack Burke Jr. said. "I can promise you there was no grass in the caddy yard where he was."

This pairing that began in Texas continued around the country for nearly three decades. Nelson achieved golf's most unbreakable record, with 11 straight wins. Hogan is golf's most mysterious and mystique-filled player even in his death. "If you say Texas golf to me, I close my eyes and see Hogan and Nelson. That's Texas golf to me," said Bruce Lietzke, a professional golfer who moved from Kansas to Texas as a young child and never left.

Golf's Magic Tool

Texas has produced not only great players and teachers but top-quality equipment as well. Such was the case in the late 1920s, when Houston Country Club golfer E. K. MacClain came up with the idea for an early forerunner of the sand wedge. MacClain, an avid golfer who spent more time than he wanted in the bunkers, began experimenting with a niblick, making changes in the face of the club, giving it a concave face, and reinforcing it at the bottom, resulting in a total club head weight of 17 ounces. He gave one to amateur legend Bobby Jones, who was in Houston to receive an honorary membership at River Oaks, who proclaimed it "one of the greatest trouble clubs I've ever used," according to a story in the *Houston Press*.

First Masters champion Horton Smith was playing an exhibition round at Houston Country Club and was given a copy of MacClain's invention. He was so pleased that he promised to take it on the Tour with him. Club pro Willie Maguire, who cofounded the Texas PGA with Bredemus in 1922, marketed the club to members and pros who were passing through, and it became quite popular, especially in traveling exhibitions.

The Young Company, which was later bought by Wilson Sports, started marketing the club nationwide in 1929 as the Walter Hagen Sand Wedge, capitalizing on Hagen's popular name at the time but leaving the mistaken impression that Hagen had invented the club, an honor that should go to Houston Country Club member MacClain. Unfortunately, the honor was short lived, as the United States Golf Association (USGA) banned the club as nonconforming in 1931, and it was replaced by today's wedge featuring a non-concave back. MacClain's new club aided generations of early Texas golfers seeking perfection in a nonperfect game.

Texas' First Major

Ask Texas golfers or golf fans, and they'll sadly tell you that the Lone Star State, for all its history, tradition, and pedigree, has not received nearly its share of golf's major championships. Of the two U.S. majors that rotate every year, the U.S. Open and the PGA Championship, Texas has received a total of six: three U.S. Opens and three PGA Championships and none since 1968. But the common denominator for each championship that was awarded to a Texas course was that each boasted a dynamic, driving individual who was pushing the event at every turn. Such was the case for the 1927 PGA Championship at Cedar Crest with course owner Sol Dreyfuss. A fan of all sports, Dreyfuss had personally seen to the smallest of details when he began to lay out the course in the mid-1910s.

The club, Dallas' third private facility after Dallas Country Club and Lakewood Country Club, was located just south of downtown in Oak Cliff with stunning views of the city skyline. Dreyfuss, the vice president of the Dreyfuss Paper Company and secretary and treasurer of Dreyfuss and Son, a clothing store in downtown Dallas, had hired noted architect Tillinghast to design his 18-hole facility.

The results were spectacular, and Dreyfuss turned his attention to professional golf tournaments at his new course. He staged the first Dallas Open there in 1926, which was won by Scotland's MacDonald Smith, who also captured the Texas Open by a single shot in San Antonio in February of that same year.

That got Dreyfuss thinking of bigger things for his new course. The PGA Championship, which was begun in 1916, had never been played in the South or the Southwest, but Dreyfuss came up with a $15,441 purse, the largest ever offered at the time and the largest the PGA pros would play for in the next 20 years, and combined with Bredemus to personally lobby his PGA friends on the East Coast to bring the tournament to Texas.

That was enough to get the PGA Championship headed south for the first time and give Texas its first major championship. In the late 1920s, mention of the PGA Championship meant only one thing: Walter Hagen, who had won three straight titles and was known for his impeccable dress and impeccable play. The problem for the PGA and especially the Dallas golf fans and promoters is that Hagen had loudly announced his retirement from golf after his third consecutive PGA title at Salisbury Golf Links in Long Island, New York, and famously given away his clubs. According to early golf historian Stephen Lowe, Hagen began to pursue other interests, including bass fishing and the purchase of a minor league baseball team, the Rochester (New York) Tribe.

Dramatically at the last minute, as Hagen was prone to do, he changed his mind and announced he would come to Dallas to see the new Cedar Crest course and attempt to gain his fourth straight title. "All of a sudden it dawned on me that unless I defended my title whoever won would not receive the credit that would have been coming to him. Many would have said, 'Well, if Hagen had been here, it would have been different,'" Hagen was quoted as saying in the PGA Championship history book *The Season's Final Major*.

He arrived at the Dallas train station on Monday afternoon to face a field of 65 other players, which included Gene Sarazen, Jack Burke Sr., Tommy Armour, Tony Holugen, and Al Espinosa. The players were housed at several fashionable downtown Dallas hotels, an easy ride from the course, and were treated to mild fall weather for October 31–November 5, 1927. Although crowds were expected, golf was still fairly new to the majority of Dallas sports fans. "We had pretty good crowds, but it's like you would see for a junior tournament now," remarked Nelson, one of the few men alive who attended the tournament and still has excellent recall of the events nearly 80 years later.

In typical Hagen style, he trailed in four of his five matches but rallied in each for the win. In the first round, he was four holes down to Johnny Farrell, only to rally for a 3-and-2 win in the 36-hole match. The expected feature of the tournament was anticipated to be Hagen versus Armour, but Hagen overcame an early deficit for an easy 4-and-3 win.

In the semifinal match against Espinosa, Hagen again trailed on the back nine and was squinting into the sun on the par-4 18th when he announced loudly, "This is one time I wish I had a hat," according to published reports. At that, 15-year-old Byron Nelson, who had been trailing his hero Hagen the entire day, stepped up to offer the schoolboy hat he was wearing. Hagen thanked the future PGA Tour superstar for the hat, without ever knowing who he was, and proceeded to knock his approach shot to eight feet, according to Nelson, to win the hole and capture the match on the first extra hole in a playoff.

Nelson, who was attending his first professional event as the guest of Longworth, was amazed by the skill and the ability of the players but learned something else that day from watching Hagan. "He had a personality which could aggravate you without being disagreeable," Nelson said. "He would hit his tee shot on the first cut of rough and Espinosa would be in the middle of the fairway, but Hagen would walk over to inspect Espinosa's shot and his lie. When they got on the green, Hagen was about 30 to 40 feet and Espinosa was closer. He walked up to Espinosa's ball and looked at it and was playing mind games. Of course, Espinosa three-putted, and Hagen won the match."

In the finals, Hagen overcame shooting an 80 in the morning round and was only two down. He captured the win in the afternoon over Joe Turnesa one-up when he rallied with three birdies and Turnesa missed several makable putts. Milt Saul reported in his November 6, 1927, story for the *Dallas News* that "after the tumult and shouting of a week of a PGA Championship play ended, the captain and the king of all golfers, Walter Hagen departed."

Hagen, who was gracious in victory, walked away with $1,000 in cash for first place along with four diamond-studded gold medals for his four straight PGA Championship wins. Of course, with Hagen's lavish off-course lifestyle, there were always strings attached. In a 1986 *Golf Digest* article, author Ross Goodner claims Hagen asked to be awarded his cash prize in the basement of Cedar Crest, as there were men upstairs looking to attach his winnings for alimony payments.

The week proved to be a highlight for both Cedar Crest and Hagen, who was defeated the following year in his bid for his fifth straight title by Leo Diegel. Hagen never won another PGA Championship. Money troubles, hastened by the stock market crash and the Great Depression, caused Dreyfuss's prized Cedar Crest course to fail, and the G. H. Schoellkopf family ultimately purchased it in 1930. The course was basically closed and used very little from 1930 to 1946 until it was purchased in 1946 by the City of Dallas for $135,551 from the Schoellkopf estate as a municipal golf addition. Cedar Crest had one more moment in the spotlight when it hosted the USGA National Public Links Championship in 1954 but gradually fell into disrepair.

Texas' new golfers had seen the best golf the world had to offer playing in their home state; they had their first Texas-based star and had seen the birth of the PGA Tour. In the next decade, home-state golfers would jump to the top of the leaderboard as never before.

The 1930s
Texas' Late-Blooming Dreamer

5 Highlights of the 1930s

★ Marvin Leonard opens Colonial Country Club in 1936 with bent-grass greens, a first for the South and the Southwest.

★ Houston's Memorial Park opens in 1936 on a public course designed by John Bredemus and built by Works Progress Administration labor.

★ Dallas' Ralph Guldahl wins the 1937 and 1938 U.S. Opens and the 1939 Masters before suddenly and unexplainably losing his game.

★ Byron Nelson wins the first major ever won by a Texas-born and -bred player, the 1937 Masters tournament.

★ Dallas native Gus Moreland becomes a multiple amateur champion in Texas and nationwide.

The Story of the Decade: A Belated Convert to Texas Golf

When a person approaches a sport or endeavor late in their life without having grown up in the activity, they often approach it with an intense or "missionary" zeal as if to make up for lost time. Never has that principle held truer than in the case of Texas businessman and native John Marvin Leonard.

Poor health couldn't slow down Leonard, the son of the tiny East Texas town of Linden. The Great Depression couldn't stop him; floods, fires, or pressing civic commitments wouldn't deter him from his newly found mission of advancing Texas golf.

When the longtime Fort Worth businessman and golf leader died in 1970, he deserved to be held in the same lofty esteem as John Bredemus and Jack Burke Sr. and Jr. as true Texas golfing visionaries. "He just wasn't going to let the Great Depression or anything else slow him down, that's just the way he was," said daughter Marty Leonard.

Leonard, who was soon joined by his brother Obie, moved to the Fort Worth area in 1914 and worked in a series of merchandising jobs learning retail sales in deep-discount general stores. In 1918, he opened his own discount store, Leonard's, which would eventually evolve into the seven-block Leonard Brothers complex in downtown Fort Worth. It offered just about anything a North Texas shopper could want or need. "There wasn't anything you couldn't find at Leonard's," said longtime Colonial Country Club member Scott Corpening. "It really was the first superstore back then."

TEXAS GOLF FACT

Harold "Jug" McSpaden fired a historic practice round 59 before the 1939 Texas Open with Hall of Famers Sam Snead, Ben Hogan, and Paul Runyan in his foursome, 40 years before the first sub-60s score was recorded in an official PGA Tour round.

With his brother's help and sharp, talented shop assistants whom Marvin personally hired, the Leonard Brothers store quickly became a success for the family. The money Leonard earned was invested back into his growing store and lavished on his newfound hometown. He even offered to cash payroll checks for all locals during the Bank Holiday at the height of the Great Depression in 1933.

But all this business activity began to take a toll on Leonard's health. Golf had first been suggested as a recreational outlet in 1922, when he joined Glen Garden Country Club. He knew little more about the game than that he stocked golfing equipment in the store and soon soured on the sport. "I found it took about four hours to get around the course. I thought that was silly. How could anyone stay away from work that long?" he said in his biography, *Texas Merchant: Marvin Leonard and Fort Worth.*

He put away the clubs and plowed himself back into work with a renewed vigor, but his single-minded fervor didn't do anything to solve his health problems, including chronic fatigue and stomach trouble. "I woke up one morning in 1927 feeling so low that I went to the family doctor and he said, 'Start playing golf or

Marvin Leonard, left, and Ben Hogan were close friends for nearly 50 years. (Photo courtesy of Colonial Country Club)

a great putter, but seemed to make every putt he needed."

While playing at Glen Garden, Leonard, who was friendly and talkative by nature, struck up a friendship with caddy and pro shop worker Ben Hogan. It was a classic case of opposites attracting, as Hogan was as closed and tight-lipped as Leonard was upbeat and open. Leonard had already made a sizable stake of his fortune in the early years of his store, while Hogan was almost always broke and would stay that way for another decade, often kept financially aloft by Leonard's generosity. But they formed a deep friendship that lasted more than 40 years.

With a membership in two Fort Worth private clubs while building his own local business empire, Leonard did not to sit idly by even in his recreation time. In the early 1930s, he became a director at Glen Garden and was involved in the first test of a new putting surface, bent-grass, a smooth, carpetlike surface compared to the hard, bumpy Bermuda grass that had replaced sand greens on most Texas courses.

One thing Leonard liked to do as much as play golf was travel, and he often took his family on extended vacations to California with stops in Colorado and Arizona. "While he was out there, he played on a few courses with bent-grass greens and became convinced that was the best type of putting surface and that is what we should have here," Marty Leonard said.

Anyone who ever saw Leonard in business or any other pursuit knew that once Leonard was convinced about something, changing his mind was nearly impossible. At Glen Garden he actually had the 18th green carpeted in bent grass, while the other 17 were Bermuda.

prepare for a crackup.'" Faced with that grim prospective, Leonard, 32, made a second, more determined try at golf, paying his back dues at Glen Garden. He started slowly, playing nine holes on Saturday morning and then returning home for a full breakfast. After a few months of fresh air and exercise at Glen Garden, he noticed his health problems faded and his general outlook greatly improved.

He also joined Rivercrest Country Club, which opened a year before Glen Garden in 1912 as Fort Worth's oldest course and began to play every Sunday, Tuesday, and Thursday, not averse to an on-course wager at either course. "Mr. Leonard worked very hard to become a better golfer," said Corpening. "He got his handicap down to single figures," his daughter Marty added. "He was very straight off the tee and wasn't

It was a unique arrangement to say the least, but "Marvin was determined to have his bent-grass green," Byron Nelson said.

The acclaim for bent grass in Texas was far from universal. Many Glen Garden members thought it was too fragile to stand up to the Texas heat, too expensive, and too prone to failure. Leonard didn't get much further with the powers that be at Rivercrest. Bermuda was the proper grass for Texas; bent grass was only an expensive folly, the majority said. "We have the hardheads here to thank for the starting of Colonial," said longtime Rivercrest head pro Mac Spikes. "Finally they just got tired of talking to him about it and told him to go build his own course."

The official Colonial history book relates the conversation between Leonard and the Rivercrest board. "Marvin, if you're sold on bent grass, why don't you go build your own golf course and put them in." Leonard replied, "Thank you very much. I may do just that."

While he was a genius at marketing and merchandising, Leonard knew very little about building his own golf course, especially at the height of the Great Depression, when established courses were going under almost every week. "Marvin Leonard was just a great man with great vision," said longtime Texas golf writer Dan Jenkins, who grew up in Fort Worth. "My dad was very positive and very visionary to be able to do this thing at Colonial," Marty Leonard recalled. "I remember when we had a big flood one time and we literally had workers hanging from the trees. My dad came out here, and we had all the hoses and pumps everywhere, and he just said, 'Well, it looks like we got a whole bunch of new topsoil.' That's just the type of person he was."

To build his "championship course" with bent-grass greens, Leonard first had to find the land. He had his eye on a scenic 157-acre parcel in southwest Fort Worth near Forest Park and Texas Christian University, next to the Trinity River and some old rail yards. He used his business skills to acquire the property and some of his proceeds from Leonard Brothers to help fund early construction, which would begin in late 1934.

Leonard next had to find the golf architects, and he handled the job in typical Leonard fashion. "I don't think daddy really knew who any architects were, but he determined to get the best, find out the best way to do it and go about it," Marty Leonard said. In Texas in the mid-1930s, the best architects were John Bredemus, who had been building courses in the state for more than 15 years, and Perry Maxwell, who had just finished building his masterpiece at Southern Hills in Tulsa. Leonard demanded each man produce five routing plans for the new, still-unnamed course, a bit of a rude awakening for two such esteemed architects, and then demanded five more after reviewing the initial drawings.

Bredemus brought in his protégé Ralph Plummer to help with the design, and the three men with 15 plans and Leonard walking with them every step created one of the true Texas golf masterpieces, one that has stood the test of golfing time since it opened on January 29, 1936. To develop his prized bent-grass greens, the construction crew used a combination of seaside bent grass mixed with sand and fertilizer. To combat the heat, the avowed enemy of bent grass, the greens were regularly watered, with Leonard keeping a close eye on the proceedings. "Mr. Leonard was such a visionary and a risk-taker he was determined to make it work when others didn't think it could happen," longtime Colonial head

Colonial Country Club in Fort Worth was Marvin Leonard's crowning vision. (Photo courtesy of Colonial Country Club)

pro Dow Finsterwald Jr. says. "It's just a great old course. A huge part of Texas golf history."

The course took its name from the massive white colonial columns that grace the front of the stately clubhouse. Leonard had little trouble selling memberships to his new course, with 100 Fort Worth residents already signed up by the time the club opened its doors. Total cost for Colonial was about $250,000, according to *Texas Merchant*, but it turned out to be the steal of the century.

The par-72, 6,800-yard course used water from the Clear Fork of the Trinity River to keep the greens in good shape, and the course looked better than anything most local players had ever seen. Leonard's new club welcomed golfers from all backgrounds, includ-ing top women players like Aniela Goldwaite and Babe Didrikson Zaharias as well as the leading Jewish members of the community and anyone who could "pay their bills and act decently," according to the club records. There were no stated dues when the club opened, with members being asked to put up only a $50 security deposit against club charges. The Great Depression was still going strong when the club opened, and it suffered through a few tough years, but slot machines proved to be very successful in turning the financial tide.

Leonard was thrilled his new members liked the club and the course and was very satisfied that he had been proven right on the bent-grass greens, which were thriving with the special treatment they had been given. By the end of the 1930s, Leonard had a plan to showcase his new course to the entire country. His background shows he always had a plan, one that was usually two steps ahead of his competition and one that was usually proven right, visionary, and ultimately successful. His plan involved showcasing his new course to the United States Golf Association (USGA) officials in New York, and in the next decade his plan would change Texas golf forever.

Golf Comes to the Valley

In the late 1920s and early 1930s, Texas' Rio Grande Valley didn't possess today's publicity about lush vegetation, 80-degree winters, and endless golfing opportunities. When Harlingen Country Club opened in 1931 as the first golf course in the Valley, the area had a population of only 25,000, and no winter Texans had yet arrived late each fall to stay through another balmy South Texas winter.

Perhaps it's no surprise that Texas' first golf promoter, John Bredemus, built the nine-hole Harlingen Country Club, foreseeing a time when the southernmost part of Texas would boast of dozens of courses and thousands of tourists. The course was not long by today's standards, just over 3,000 yards, but it required strategic thinking as almost all Bredemus courses did and featured green-grass greens that quickly adapted to the tropical climate.

Golf legend Water Hagen was on hand for the opening exhibition match in 1931 at Harlingen Country Club. While the Texas golfing resort population may have been slow to find this South Texas winter vacation sport, the top professional golfers of the 1930s were not.

The first Harlingen Open Golf Tournament, held on February 7, 1931, attracted a variety of top professional and amateur talent. Included in the field were brothers Tom and Harvey Penick, former Texas Open champions Wiffy Cox and Denny Shute, and Tony Butler, who was then the head professional at Corpus Christi Country Club. Also included were Dallas' "Lighthorse" Harry Cooper, future Colonial U.S. Open champion Craig Wood, and Al Espinosa, who lost in the finals of the 1928 PGA Championship.

While Bredemus built the first course in the Valley, the man most associated with golf there in its early stages was Tony Butler. He was born in South Texas in 1908 but moved as a kid to Austin, where he became Harvey Penick's next-door neighbor. The pair formed a friendship that would last decades and grew up playing golf together. "We hit a lot of shots into my parent's backyard," Penick said. Butler attended the University of Texas in 1928 and took his first head professional job at Corpus Christi Country Club later that summer, dropping out of the university to pursue his golfing dreams. He won the Texas PGA amateur title in 1931 and advanced to the PGA Championship that year in Rhode Island, where he was defeated in match play by runner-up Denny Shute.

After a couple of years of playing on the professional tour, Butler accepted the head pro's job at Harlingen Country Club in 1933 and began to work tirelessly to promote the area as a prime winter vacation spot. Among the events Butler promoted were the Rio Grande Valley Open and the Life Begins at Forty Tournament. When Butler accepted another job in 1937 that would move him out of the area, hundreds of Valley golfers signed a petition begging him to stay, which he did until he finally retired as pro emeritus in 1975. The City of Harlingen showed its appreciation for Butler's longtime work and promotion of the Rio Grande Valley game by changing the name of the city's municipal golf course to Tony Butler Municipal Golf Course on June 30, 1973. Butler became the first local golfer inducted into the Rio Grande Valley Sports Hall of Fame in 1998.

Another famous course in the Valley in the 1930s was the Casa Blanca Golf Club in Laredo, built in 1936. The first course in Laredo played host to the Border Olympics Shootout golf tournament, which has been won by such players as Billy Maxwell, Tom Kite, and Ben Crenshaw, before moving over to Laredo Country Club in the 1980s. The University of Texas at Pan American became another early promoter of golf in the area, fielding a competitive team. The Broncos advanced to the National Association of Intercollegiate Athletes playoffs several times in its early years. Today there are dozens of fine courses in the Valley, but all owe a debt of gratitude to Butler and his tireless work to promote the area's golfing charms.

Nelson and Hogan Begin Their Pro Careers

Just as Ben Hogan and Byron Nelson's amateur backgrounds vary greatly before being brought together on the caddy yards of Fort Worth's Glen Garden Country Club, so did the start of their respective professional careers.

Nelson turned pro in late 1932 just before he accepted the head professional's job at Texarkana Country Club, a position he had been recommended for by his mentor and former Glen Garden pro, Ted Longworth. "Back then, your goal was to play well enough to catch the eye of a club and get a professional's job." Nelson said. "Texarkana was a wonderful place to start." It was a start in many ways, as Nelson played his first tournament there at the invitation of Longworth. The former Fort Worth pro, who had been replaced by brothers Dick and Jack Grout at Glen Garden, was getting ready to take his dream job at a course in Oregon, but he staged one more professional event before leaving. He invited Nelson to participate as an amateur, and with no other means of transportation, Nelson rode a Greyhound bus up to Texarkana, carrying his small suitcase with his set of golf clubs and bag by his side.

On the long bus ride from Fort Worth to Texarkana, Nelson began to think about turning pro and collecting whatever money he could win at his friend's course. "When I got up to the tournament, I told him I'm playing for the money," Nelson said. "All the heads turned my direction, and they asked if I was turning pro. I said I was playing for the money and that's what I did." Nelson's decision to turn pro paid off when he won $75 for finishing third, quite a handsome sum for that day.

When Nelson took the job at Texarkana Country Club, the country was still in the most dismal days of the Great Depression, and the supply of national hope was in short supply. "In those days, no man played golf during the week; they were too busy trying to earn a living. Saturday afternoon was when they really came out," Nelson said in his autobiography. "Texarkana was a fine course, but nobody was there, so I'd hit my sack of range balls on one end of the range, walk down and

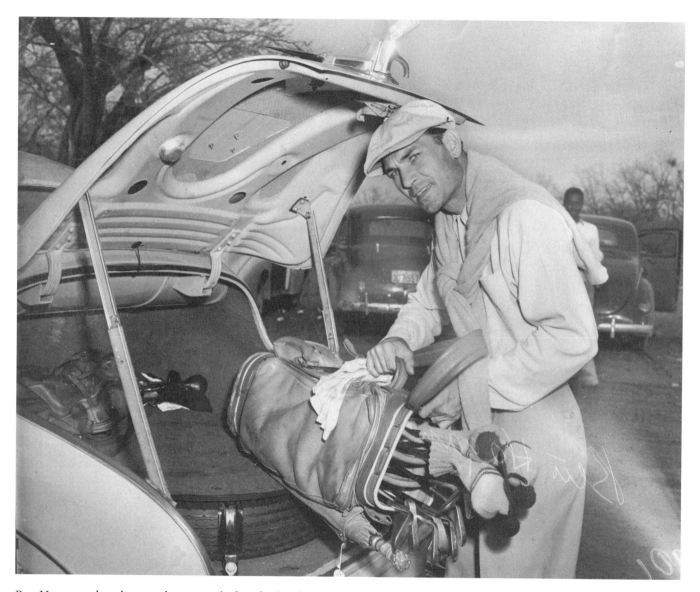

Ben Hogan endured many slow starts before finding his place in Texas golf history. (Photo courtesy of Institute of Texas Cultures/San Antonio Light Collection)

pick them up, and hit them again," Nelson said. "You can say that's where I really learned to play my game was in Texarkana."

He progressed through the professional ranks quickly, playing in the second Masters tournament in 1935, where he finished ninth, and he became a dominant player on the PGA Tour in the 1930s, winning his first major at the 1937 Masters. He traveled throughout the country playing the new Tour schedule with his wife Louise alongside, winning what little money there was for players back then. "If you turned professional back then, it just meant you wanted to starve," said longtime Texas golf pro Jackson Bradley, who was head professional at River Oaks Country Club in Houston before moving to Austin, where he still teaches with his daughter Tina.

Ben Hogan was another matter altogether. Just as he had to overcome tremendous roadblocks just to begin his career in golf, Hogan had another decade of struggle ahead of him. "I don't know why Hogan was the way he was, I don't know if anybody did, but I'm sure it had something to do with the way he grew up," said Nelson, who knew his fellow caddy longer than any professional golfer. After his caddy tournament success with Nelson in 1927 and other assorted amateur victories, Hogan rode down to the 1930 Texas Open with Longworth and Dallas amateur star Ralph Guldahl. Typical of his self-sustaining ways, Hogan decided to turn professional at age 17 without telling a soul. The local San Antonio paper carried a large photo of Hogan and Guldahl as future golfing stars on the front section of the Texas Open preview, but in truth Hogan was far from that at the time.

Typical of his early struggles, Hogan got off to a bad start, shooting 78 in his first professional start. Ray Mangrum, another Dallas golfer whose brother Lloyd would achieve greater fame in the 1940s, had the best local score with a 71 at historic Brackenridge Park. Guldahl shot a 74, and first-round leader Denny Shute fired a 68, leaving Hogan 10 shots behind. The second round wasn't much better, as Hogan shot a 75 and departed as quickly as he arrived, not even coming close to making the 36-hole cut. "I found out the first day I shouldn't even be there," Hogan said in his biography. He hitchhiked home, back to Fort Worth and the rest of his professional career.

Unfortunately for Hogan, that began a dismal pattern in his early career: a slow start, a string of missed cuts, and eventually the loss of his meager bankroll and his forced return to Fort Worth. Hogan was very different from the pros of that era in many ways, especially with his lack of social skills. The golf professionals of those days were a friendly lot. Without corporate jets or any other modern means to get to each tournament stop, they often traveled together or in one large pack, stopping for meals or overnight stays at humble accommodations. "Texans always looked out for each other," one traveling pro said. Upcoming Texas stars like Jimmy Demaret, Guldahl, and Nelson thrived in this style of atmosphere. Hogan preferred to travel, practice, and play mainly by himself. He liked to say he dug out of the dirt with his golf game, but mainly he did it by himself, alone on the range with his dreams, whacking endless practice balls—a kind of Vijay Singh practice clone of the 1930s. "If you walked on the range and Hogan was practicing, he might sit down and smoke a cigarette so you wouldn't watch him practice," Nelson said.

Hogan's one true friend in Fort Worth was the visionary Leonard. "I don't really know the first time they met," Marty Leonard said 70-plus years after the two future Fort Worth legends hooked up. "They just got together at Glen Garden and were friends ever since." Leonard, ever the visionary and encourager, told Hogan he could make something with his struggling professional career. Hogan, ever the private brooder, would doggedly go back out after another failure to the next tournament on the schedule.

In 1931, after his solo appearance at the Texas Open a year earlier, Hogan borrowed $225 from Leonard to go along with the $75 he had saved. The money didn't last long, as Hogan failed to make a mark on the Tour and by early 1932 was back at home. "Daddy wanted to help him get going, and he would loan a little money every now and then," Marty Leonard recalled. After a series of pro jobs in the Fort Worth area, including Nolan River Country Club in Cleburne, Hogan was back on the pro tour again in 1934, but the results were depressingly similar. "I was always last if I got any money at all. As I said, I was a terrible player," Hogan said in a famous and well-paid interview with CBS-TV in 1983.

After marrying his wife Valerie, another North Texas native, in 1935, Hogan stayed close to home, working on his game at Nolan River and playing at Leonard's new course, Colonial, which opened to great fanfare in 1936. He made one more try for the PGA Tour in 1938 with his wife, life savings, and worldly possessions in tow.

The results were similar as he failed week after week with his confidence and his bank account growing ever smaller. But with his wife as his encouragement and Leonard's belief still ringing in his ears, Hogan pressed on to California, eating stale sandwiches and oranges he picked from roadside trees. In Oakland, the rear tires of his car were stolen, and he had to bum a ride to the course with Nelson, but still he wouldn't quit, making the largest check yet of his career, $285, just enough to keep him going. "I was sure that was the biggest check I'd ever see," he said in the CBS interview. Hogan continued in the 1938 season and stayed on the Tour for 1939, finally capturing his first victory, partnering with Vic Ghezzi to win the Hershey (Pennsylvania) Four-Ball in 1939, his first PGA Tour win after a decade of trying. It was certainly not to be his last. He had finally gotten his game off the ground, but there was one other Texas golfer who overshadowed him, along with everyone else in the game of golf in the 1930s, until he became golf's first fast-falling meteor.

Texas' First Shooting Star

In the early half of the 20th century, especially in the decade of the 1930s, nobody ruled the game of golf more absolutely than Ralph Guldahl. Born on November 22, 1911, in Dallas, Guldahl grew up in the area of Dallas now known as the "M Streets" for the grouping of streets all with the same first letter in their names. As a boy, he caddied at the long-since-abandoned Bob O Link Golf Club in Dallas and would practice hitting balls across Glasgow Avenue from his front yard to a neighbor's, according to longtime Texas sports writer Denne Freeman, who had family living in the area.

Dallas native Ralph Guldahl was golf's dominant player during the 1930s before losing his game. (Photo courtesy of Institute of Texas Cultures/San Antonio Light Collection)

His parents came from Norway, and Guldahl wasn't overly talkative as a player, but he grew to 6 feet 2 inches, had a fast, jerky swing, and could he hit the ball straight!—a fact Nelson found out early in his own amateur career. "I knew Ralph Guldahl very well," said Nelson. "One year I was considered the Fort Worth amateur champion, and Ralph was the Dallas amateur champion." The owner of both Katy Lakes in Fort Worth, where Nelson played, and Bob O Link, where Guldahl started, proposed a 36-hole match between the two amateur stars. The result is still memorable to Nelson nearly 70 years later. "We started out at Bob O Link, and we were supposed to play 36 holes, but he gave me such a beating, I don't think we even played much of the final 18. I beat him a few times on the pro tour, but I still remember the beating he gave me as an amateur."

Demaret, the Houston native who would later go on to plenty of fame and fortune of his own, spoke for most of the Lone Star professional golfers shortly after Guldahl turned pro in the early 1930s. "Ralph Guldahl might have been the greatest golfer ever for a short period of time." Big Ralph, as he was known for his tall Texan frame, won his first tournament at the 1932 Phoenix Open, but after a near miss at the 1933 U.S. Open, he abruptly left the Tour for three years, selling used cars on Ross Avenue in Dallas and working by himself at Bob O Link.

After being asked to design a nine-hole course in Kilgore and restoring his confidence, he returned to the game with a vengeance. Guldahl used his trademark straightness off the tee to win the 1936 Western Open and finish eighth in the U.S. Open. In 1937, he won the Western Open again and the U.S. Open at

Oakland Hills. "I would consider Ralph Guldahl the best player in the world for five years," said writer Dan Jenkins. "He won the Western Open two years in a row when it was a major." Before the Masters was established as the legendary event it is today, the Western Open in Chicago was considered the fourth major by most golfers.

With his first Open victory over Sam Snead, Guldahl displayed his trademark air of confidence and calm that Nelson, who was in the gallery, had seen many times while growing up in Dallas. "He had two putts to win the Open, and he put his first putt there really close. Before he putted to win, he stepped back, eyed the cup then pulled out a comb to brush his thick black hair."

Guldahl continued his mastery on the links in 1938 with another Western Open title and another U.S. Open victory at Cherry Hills in Denver, where he became the last Open champ to win sporting a necktie and still combing his hair before putting for victory. "It helps check my pace and helps me retain a confident composure," he explained. Guldahl became the first player to win the Western and U.S. Open in the same year, the latter tournament with a scoring record that stood for 11 years. Golf Writer Charles Price called Guldahl the original deliberate player, so slow that the crowds would often check their watches while he lined up a shot. But when he hit the ball, Sam Snead called it the most perfect motion he had ever seen. Nelson called him a player without weakness. "Nothing really stood out, but he was very steady in everything he did."

Guldahl captured the season's first major by winning the 1939 Masters and appeared ready to roll over his competitors for another year. His Masters scoring record stood for 14 years along with his 33 on the back nine of Augusta National. Hogan and Nelson appeared to be battling for little more than the title of second-best player in North Texas, not best player in the world. But just as quickly as the golfing magic appeared to make Big Ralph the most dominant golfer of his or any era, the magic left him. After his thrilling Masters win in 1939, he never won another individual pro event. Except for a partnership win with Snead in 1940, Guldahl never won another event and was seldom close to victory.

His driving, which had been straight and strong, lapsed into a pattern where he couldn't even hit the fairway. A host of theories emerged as to what factor was responsible for causing the Dallasite to completely lose the game he had once dominated. The most popular centered on a book that was published in 1939 by Wilson Sporting Goods titled *From Tee to Cup*, which Guldahl cowrote and which featured foldout pictures of him posed to demonstrate certain shots. "The most celebrated victim of paralysis by analysis," according to *Golf Digest* senior editor Guy Yocum, who said the book forced Guldahl to think about a game that had come naturally, forever altering his efforts.

Other ideas were that he simply lost his competitive fire for championship golf and had burned out after a brief but brilliant career. "Behind my so-called poker face, I'm burning up," he once stated. The reason favored by his family and many close friends was that his love for his West Texas wife, Laverne, and his son, Ralph Jr., caused him to be homesick on the road. He called his wife one time from a California Tour stop almost in tears. "I don't know if we should be apart like this. How are you holding up?" Guldahl was quoted in *Texas Golf Legends*.

Dallas' Gus Moreland
was golf's outstanding
amateur player in the
1930s and 1940s.
(Photo courtesy
of Institute of Texas
Cultures/San Antonio
Light Collection)

Nelson says he naturally wonders about his fellow Texas pro, who once dominated him so thoroughly, but prefers to keep his thoughts to himself. "I think I know what happened, but I don't want to say anything because of the people involved. He didn't lose it all at once, but it was pretty quick, to be sure." Guldahl quit the Tour in 1942 at age 34 and, except for a brief comeback seven years later, never played again. He became a well-respected pro at Braemar Country Club in Southern California, where he and his wife became involved in racing horses and giving golf lessons.

Depression Diamonds

The Great Depression remains one of the greatest non–war-related calamities to ever hit the United States, and its effect was no less severe in Texas. Dozens of golf courses went out of business or changed hands during the 1930s, including Cedar Crest in Dallas, Alamo Country Club in San Antonio, and Spring Lake in Waco. People of all income levels and professions, including golf pros, bounced from place to place looking for work.

During this troubled time, smart men and innovative government programs found ways to advance the growth of golf in Texas. With millions of people were out of work, one of the first acts of the Franklin Roosevelt administration was the creation of the Works Progress Administration (WPA) to give the many unemployed gainful employment while helping the general society at large. Golf courses were prime targets for the WPA because they put plenty of people

to work and aided the local community's need for recreation and happier times in the dismal era. Among those courses in Texas still open today are the then-nine-hole Lost Pines in Bastrop and Tyrell Park in Beaumont. Another course built during the Depression was Conroe Country Club, a Bredemus design that brought golf to the Southeast Texas area for the first time, along with a similar course layout in Huntsville near where the new Texas state prison was being built.

Lone Star Amateur Greats

While professional golf was steadily taking over the state in the 1930s, amateur golf would not go away without a few parting shots. Naturally, two of the best amateurs in the nation came from Texas. With the retirement of Bob Jones in the early 1930s after capturing his historic Grand Slam, the cry went out to find the country's next great amateur. That search ended with a former Dallas caddy, Gus Moreland, who grew up playing at Oak Cliff's Stevens Park and won just about every worthwhile amateur title. In the 1930s, he was twice named to the U.S. Walker Cup team, then a much higher honor than the professional Ryder Cup, and posted an undefeated record against Great Britain.

He was a two-time winner at the 1932 and 1933 Trans-Mississippi Amateur tournament and finished second in the 1932 Texas Open to professional legend Gene Sarazen. Moreland went by two nicknames on the course: "The Texas Walker" or "Gus the Walker" for his habit of walking after putts that were headed straight into the hole and "The Next Bobby Jones" for his outstanding amateur record. He didn't turn pro early because of the meager wages offered and once gave back a new car he won at a tournament because he feared it would damage his amateur status. That didn't stop Moreland from regularly beating the best players of his day. He defeated Nelson on the 18th hole to win the Glen Garden Championship in Fort Worth on Nelson's home course. He won the Southwest Invitational, the Western Amateur in Chicago, the Texas Open, and the Houston Invitational in 1932, defeating Johnny Goodman, who would go on to win the 1933 U.S. Open.

Nelson, who saw plenty of top golfers, both amateur and professional, in his career, summed up Walker's career simply: "Best amateur golfer I ever saw. I don't want to say he was cocky, but he was confident. He had Jack Nicklaus confidence." Tinsley Penick, who succeeded his father Harvey as head pro at Austin Country Club, said his dad had the same opinion. "During the 1930s who was the best player you saw?" Tinsley once asked his father. "Gus Moreland," answered Harvey Penick.

Moreland played professional golf eventually, at the grand age of 53, but his great golfing skills were already in a decline. Quoted in his father's written obituary, Steve Moreland said his dad, who died at the age of 86 in Grapevine in 1998, never regretted the fact that his glory years were as an amateur. Moreland's full-time job was owning and operating a very successful North Texas printing company. "Using golf to enhance printing sales, he could make more money romancing all those big company executives than Byron

Nelson did in winning 11 straight tournaments," Steve added.

Moreland eventually won amateur championships in several other states, including a 1932 California match where he defeated Charlie Seaver, the U.S. Amateur semifinalist and father of future baseball Hall of Famer Tom Seaver. Moreland's play even attracted the attention of noted hustler Alvin "Titanic" Thompson, who was making Texas his headquarters at the time. Thompson tried to interest Moreland in a national tour where they would fleece the unsuspecting golfers by pretending Moreland was a humble caddy "randomly" selected by Thompson for high-stakes matches. It was one of the few golfing challenges Moreland would turn down, not because he felt he couldn't achieve it but because he felt such a venture was not befitting of a gentleman amateur.

While David Goldman's career wasn't as spectacular as Moreland's, it was more consistent and longer lasting. He was nicknamed "Spec" at an early age because of his freckled complexion enhanced by long practice sessions in the sun. The Dallas native and member of Dallas Country Club won 165 amateur tournaments on two continents in his seven-decade amateur career. He won the World Seniors twice, along with the USGA Seniors twice and the Life Begins at Forty event. He captured the Texas state title as well as the Mexico national title. Goldman went to the finals of the Trans-Mississippi tournament at Oklahoma City Golf and Country Club, where he lost to Moreland, who fired a course record 63 in their match. While becoming a prosperous Dallas businessman with a longtime Dallas Country Club membership, he traveled nationally and internationally, playing the game he loved with great amateur success.

Memorial to Memorial

John Bredemus has received much credit for his role in building Texas golf courses, most of it well deserved. His work with Colonial Country Club has been almost universally praised as his finest effort, but whenever the subject came up, Bredemus himself referred to Memorial Park in Houston as his "best work."

Memorial Park didn't start life with that name; in fact, it was originally Camp Logan Army Hospital in the 1920s with a nine-hole sand-green golf course developed by a Houston citizen committee. The nine-hole course and hospital had been built on land donated by one of the founding families of Texas, the Hoggs. When the hospital closed in 1923, it opened its course to the public, making it one of the first public courses in the Houston area. In one of its first reports in Texas in 1934, the WPA announced that Memorial Park would be a prime area for a new golf course.

The WPA announced that Bredemus, who had already begun work at Colonial, would be the architect on the course. The project would employ nearly 500 men with a $184,166 total cost. The best thing for the cash-strapped City of Houston was that its portion would be only $29,601. With financial terms like that and backing from local business leaders like banker Jesse Jones, the city could hardly say no and approved the project by an overwhelming vote in late 1934. Bredemus and his government-paid crew began construction in early 1935, building the first holes with one tractor and 20 teams of mules. True to the

Bredemus tradition, he built skill and strategy into his course with dozens of bunkers, a rarity at the time, and true green-grass greens. The course itself was fairly flat, but Bredemus used the natural steams and trees to create "the finest municipal course in the nation," according to city documents.

When the course finally opened with a grand exhibition on June 18, 1936, Memorial Park was a municipal golf marvel for all to see. It covered 600 acres, making it the largest course in the city if not the state. It had four natural water areas, 96 traps, and some of the longest fairways in the city for the par-72 layout. Among the first foursomes was Houston native and local golf pro Jimmy Demaret and Jack Burke Sr., the pro at River Oaks Country Club. Green fees were 35 cents on weekdays and 50 cents on the weekend, with caddies getting 70 cents a bag, a perfect economic tonic for the troubled times.

Former Rice University quarterback King Hill was one of the hundreds who grew up at Memorial Park and said that the Bredemus design was a magnet for anybody who owned a set of clubs and that playing the course was a Texas golfing dream. "Eventually everybody came through Memorial Park one time or another." "Our front porch," was the report of another local pro. In the most dire of economic times, Memorial Park had been built with less than $50,000 from the city, provided relatively debt-free city services, and would be used by the tens of thousands over the next several decades.

Jug's Practice Round Record

One thing that has changed very little with PGA touring pros is the ritual of the practice round. Most of the players got onto a certain course only early in the week, coming off the road briefly from a previous destination and looking to explore that week's tournament setting. The round itself was a casual affair. As they played with their friends, there was plenty of good-natured bantering, and likely a few dollars changed hands according to the low score. So in that sense, there was little to suggest that Jug McSpaden's early week practice round before the 1939 Texas Open would be any different. Historic Brackenridge Park was again the setting, and the par-71 layout featured rubber mats on the tees because of the trouble of getting enough grass to grow in the wintertime with the amount of play the course received. McSpaden, who would later team with Nelson in enough partnership events to be known as the Gold Dust Twins, was paired in this round with friends Ben Hogan, Sam Snead, and Paul Runyan.

But once the round started, fans knew this would be no ordinary 18 holes, as McSpaden was on fire with all parts of his game. He shot a 30 on the front nine at Brackenridge and came home with a 29 on the back

side for the first 59 score at the course and the first recorded 59 on the PGA Tour. Since it was a practice round, the record-low mark never went into the PGA record book. But that didn't keep Jug's low number from being the talk of the tournament, which was eventually won by Arkansas native Dutch Harrison. McSpaden posted a 63 in the third round of the 1939 Open, but it wasn't enough to get him to the pay window on his record week in San Antonio. To commemorate the record-breaking round, the San Antonio Golf Association, which had recently taken over the organization and promotion of the Texas Open, mounted a jumbo scorecard inside the Brackenridge clubhouse of Jug's record 59 signed by all four future World Golf Hall of Fame members; the scorecard still hangs there today. "I still remember Brackenridge Park every well," McSpaden said in a 1992 interview. "It's a great old course." For one magical practice round of golf at the 1939 Texas Open, it certainly was for McSpaden.

In the following decade, the magic for Byron Nelson lasted several months, but it established golf's most lasting and amazing record.

The 1940s
Golf's Unreachable Record

5 Highlights of the 1940s

★ Byron Nelson and Ben Hogan face each other in playoffs at the Texas Open in 1940 and the Masters in 1942.
★ The first U.S. Open held in the South is staged at Colonial in 1941.
★ Byron Nelson wins 11 straight tournaments in 1945.
★ Dick Jackson patents first motorized golf cart in 1948 at Houston Country Club.
★ Houston native Jimmy Demaret becomes only Texas three-time Masters champion.

Story of the Decade:
Byron Nelson's 11 Straight Wins

Sports have always been fixated with numbers: 56 for Joe DiMaggio's baseball hitting streak, 49 for Peyton Manning's touchdown passes in a season, or 100 for Wilt Chamberlain's points in a single basketball game. For golf, the number is and likely will always be 11. In 1945, the number 11 represented not the number of tournaments in a single season (more than 20), not the number of wins for a single golfer (that would be 18), but the number of tournaments won in a row by one golfer in one single season. In the spring and summer of 1945, Texan John Byron Nelson entered 11 tournaments and won all of them. Nelson had 11 starts and 11 wins in one glorious streak—golfing dominance that has never been approached before or since and likely never will again.

"Byron Nelson's 11 straight wins is the 50-foot pole vault or the 40-foot long jump of golf," says PGA Tour superstar Tom Watson. "To see what Byron did in that one season is almost too incredible to believe." But for any golfing doubters, the record is clear, and they can look it up.

In the mid-1940s, Nelson had already established himself as a dominant force on the PGA Tour. Of course, there had been Ryder Cup appearances and various exhibitions to aid the American war effort, which had limited or curtailed many of the professional tournaments in the early 1940s. But for those who want to diminish Nelson's 1945 landmark by saying he competed against only weak, war-depleted fields, they will have to explain away the fact that his two biggest rivals of the time, Ben Hogan and Sam Snead, had both returned from military service and played more than 15 times during that historic season, with Snead having won four times prior to April. Traveling with his wife Louise via car or with other professionals to save money, Nelson banked every possible dollar he made and found ways to cut his expenses at every stop. "It was a happy time back then, very happy. I was winning and finally making some money, which you didn't do much back then," he said.

There was little to indicate that Nelson was about to begin his historic streak when he teed up in the Miami International Four-Ball with longtime partner Jug McSpaden on March 8, 1945. The twosome had played together so much in the 1930s and 1940s in the four-ball format common to the Tour that they earned the nickname "Gold Dust Twins" for the amount of prize money they had won.

The 1945 season had already been a typically consistent one for Nelson. Although World War II had canceled the season's first major, the Masters, as it would the U.S. Open and the British Open that year, Nelson had already won three times. Still, he was coming off his worst performance of the year, finishing tied for sixth behind Snead in Jacksonville, when he arrived at Miami Springs Country Club in Miami Beach, Florida. He teamed with McSpaden to take the tournament title, defeating Sam Byrd and PGA Champion Denny Shute, 8 and 6, in the final.

Nelson stood on the 18th green at Miami Springs, smiling broadly when he was handed the winners' trophy. The next week, the same scene was repeated at the Charlotte (North Carolina) Open, where Nelson outlasted Snead in a playoff, and the week after that at the Greater Greensboro Open with Nelson over Byrd

Byron Nelson is the holder of golf's most unbreakable record. (Photo courtesy of Institute of Texas Cultures/ San Antonio Light Collection)

following that you have today," Nelson said. "There was one writer at every event, but no TV, little radio and no way to really get the news out."

In fact the, "S" word, streak, didn't even appear in any copy about Nelson until the fourth or fifth straight victory. "I was too busy concentrating about the next tournament, and nobody else was talking about it because they hadn't seen me play except that week," said Nelson. Finally, at the 1945 PGA Championship, the season's only major, at Moraine Country Club in Dayton, Ohio, with Nelson going for his ninth straight victory, the news had finally gotten out. Nelson was greeted by six writers from around the country at his pretournament press conference. "I looked up before the tournament and saw six writers, and I had never seen six reporters before at a golf tournament, so I knew it must be a pretty big deal," he said.

Nelson excelled in the unpredictable match play format that was the PGA Championship with his consistent game wearing down opponents if he trailed early. In the first round, Nelson bested golf legend Gene Sarazen, 3 and 2, then downed longtime pro and tournament winner Mike Turnesa in the second round. "People think it's easier in match play than stroke because you're only playing one person, but they forget that most of the matches were 36 holes and there was a lot of pressure," Nelson said. Denny Shute, a two-time PGA champion who had already defeated Nelson in this type of format, was his next victim, followed by Claude Harmon, the one-time pro at River Oaks Country Club who later would send sons Butch and Dick to Texas as top golf club professionals.

In the finals, Nelson, who had won eight out of his last nine PGA Championship matches dating back to

by eight shots. A trend was forming, not that Nelson or anybody else in the golfing world really cared. Exactly one journalist showed up at most of Nelson's 1945 victories, sometimes with a radio reporter in tow, sometimes not. They knew only that the local golf tournament was in town and that that Nelson guy had proven hard to beat. "There wasn't the national golf

1944, faced off against old friend Byrd. He got off to a hot start and had Nelson down by two holes after the morning match. He added to his lead on the front nine of the afternoon matches, but once again Iron Byron rallied for the victory, 3 and 2, in the finals for his second PGA Championship, his ninth straight win.

Finally, at long last, after nearly five months of unbelievable golf, the streak was on top in the public sports arena. While Nelson's achievements weren't exactly shouted from the rooftops, he had at least become the dominant sports story of the year and had his records broadcast from coast to coast, at least for those who could afford a newspaper or knew somebody who had a radio. "No one ever said a word to me until I finished the final match with Sam and I was completing my final press conference at the PGA," he said. "As I got up to leave, somebody asked me if I had forgotten I had now won nine tournaments in a row. 'No,' I said, 'I just thought you people in the press had forgotten.'"

After the PGA Tour took the next week off, Nelson was back in action the following week at the Tam O' Shanter All-American Open in Chicago. Backed by wealthy Midwestern businessmen, the Tam O' Shanter boasted a total purse of $60,000, the largest on the PGA circuit, and the 1945 tournament attracted a stellar field. They were no match for a hot Nelson, who defeated his longtime golf colleague Hogan in second place by 11 shots. After months of consistently brilliant golf, the ever-increasing media and fan attention, along with all the pretournament publicity that revolved around Nelson, started to wear on him. "I was so sick of it, before I went to the first round of the Tam, I told Louise, 'I hope I blow up today,'" Nelson said in his autobiography. Several hours later he returned and was asked by his wife if he did indeed rupture his streak with a sky-high round. "Yes," Nelson replied. "I shot 66."

The following week, Nelson headed north of the border again for the Canadian Open at Thornhill Country Club in Toronto. The Royal Canadian Golf Association had gone public with its plans to make the course the toughest ever for the Texan and be the event where his streak ended. Nelson took a large lead into the final round and wound up winning by four shots over Herman Barron.

With the streak now at 11, Nelson's next event was the Memphis Open, where the streak indeed came to an end as amateur Fred Haas, an Arkansas native, captured the surprising victory, with Nelson tied for fourth. Nelson's late-round rally was ended when his perfectly struck tee shot on a back-nine par 3 hit the large wooden pin and bounced into the rough, costing Nelson a double bogey. "It was a fun time for me, but I can't say I was sorry to see it end," a weary Nelson said. Instead of being devastated by the end of his streak or being relieved and satisfied that his incredible record had come to an end, Nelson won the following week by 10 shots in Knoxville, Tennessee, collecting another $1,033 in war bonds.

By the end of the year, Nelson had collected 18 wins, including a then–PGA Tour 72-hole record at Seattle, breaking Hogan's new mark, which had lasted all of two weeks. Nelson says the 18 wins total will last even longer than the 11 straight victories "because today's top pros don't even play 18 times a year, much less win that many."

In one incredible season, Nelson had gone where no man had ever gone before in golf. He set the record for lowest scoring average at 68.33, which stood for 45 years until broken in 2000 by Tiger Woods, and the most consecutive rounds under 70 at 19. He did it all while driving from tournament to tournament on bad roads and playing courses in uneven conditions, while still incredibly playing the stymie, with balls on the green unable to be moved if they were in the way of another golfer's putt. His total winnings for the unmatched season were just over $52,000 in prize money and war bonds.

Most important to Nelson, he had saved the money he needed to buy his beloved ranch, combining his savings, prize winnings, and war bonds on his North Texas spread, which he purchased following the 1946 season. "I was never rich enough to hang onto the war bonds until they matured. I needed the money too badly, but I got my ranch, and that was enough for me," he said.

In 1946, there were six more wins, including three of the first four tournaments of the year, but then Nelson was gone. No medical condition forced him from the game; it was not pressure or stress that caused him to leave at age 34. He simply had his ranch, his majors, his streak, and his place in golf history. Most important, he had one singularly spectacular season that will likely never be topped.

The Open Comes to Texas

Marvin Leonard had already done the incredible by proving to one and all that bent-grass greens would work in the heat of North Texas and that his new Colonial Country Club could become a success locally and statewide. So doing the impossible with his next golf mission didn't seem that difficult.

Almost from the time Colonial opened in early 1936, Leonard had a bigger idea to showcase his course nationally. The U.S. Open, golf's national championship, would be the perfect showcase for his new course. The U.S. Open, run by the United States Golf Association (USGA), had never been held in the South or Southwest, being the exclusive province of the elite Northeastern clubs. Bent-grass greens had never been tried in this area, and that worked, so what was the difference in the daunting tasks? Leonard reasoned. "Colonial really helped put Texas golf on the map," said CBS executive golf producer Lance Barrow, who grew up in Fort Worth.

Not only did Leonard offer golf's governing body a $10,000 check, a hefty sum, to make the trip Southwest but he also offered them a chance to expand golf's national tournament to a part of the country where it had never ventured before. To aid in his quest, Leonard enrolled local heavy hitters like Amon Carter Sr., who knew many of the leading sports writers and sports figures of the day, along with Dr. Alden Coffey, the president of the Fort Worth Golf Association, who had plenty of national contacts. "Daddy kept after the USGA to bring the U.S. Open down here," Marty Leonard said. "He kept saying they needed to try someplace new, somewhere they hadn't gone before."

According to the official Colonial club history book, Leonard was relentless on the telephone as well, spending 60 minutes with USGA president Harold Pierce extolling the virtues of Colonial and Texas golf in general. Finally, a weary Pierce told Leonard the call was getting pretty expensive for the Texan. "That's OK," Leonard snapped. "This is important."

Unlike today's major championships, where a decision is made years in advance to allow a club to prepare properly, there had been no decision made by early 1940 for the 1941 tournament. Before the USGA executive committee would approve the new site, they sent their site inspection committee to Fort Worth to view the course still not even five years old. They reported that they liked the course, designed by John Bredemus, Perry Maxwell, and Ralph Plummer, but that the fourth and fifth holes were not tough enough to be considered championship caliber. "No problem," was the quick Leonard reply, "we will toughen both holes including the par-3 fourth." That helped seal the deal once USGA committee members George V. Rotan of Houston and Charles Dexter of Dallas visited the course to give their approval. The final report was issued by the USGA executive committee on April 26, 1940.

In typical bold Leonard, Texas-sized fashion, he fulfilled his bargain to toughen the front nine by purchasing a new section of property on Roger Road near the course, paying the owner several times the assessed value for the additional land he needed. He brought back Maxwell to shape the renovated holes, which would be dubbed the "Horrible Horseshoe" for their difficulty. They lengthened the par-4 third hole by 50 yards and extended the par-3 fourth to its current 225-yard length, but their greatest change was on the par-4 fifth. The new hole wrapped around the Trinity River, which ran all along the right side; at more than 440 yards from the back tees, it required a combination of accuracy, length, and the right amount of daring. "I consider it a great hole because sooner or later you must play a tough shot," Arnold Palmer was quoted in the club history. "Nearly every great player has experienced the rigors of the hole and many wish they hadn't."

Leonard showed off the proposed new holes in late 1940 to USGA executive director Joe Dey, who expressed serious doubts that the changes would be ready for the 1941 Open, only six months away. Obviously, he didn't know that once the Texas golfing dreamer set his mind to something, there was no holding him back. Golf's greatest players began to arrive in Fort Worth in early June 1941 to see Leonard's master stroke, what the *New York Times* titled "The Southwest Invasion." Crowds of 10,000 on the weekend swarmed the Fort Worth course to see the players and the new layout. Much of the pretournament publicity focused on Fort Worth natives Hogan and Nelson along with defending champion Lawson Little. A total of 169 players turned out for the first Texas-based U.S. Open, including a pair from Brazil who arrived late and were granted special entry by the USGA officials. Unfortunately, the long trip jangled the nerves of one Walter Ratto, who shot rounds of 90 and 100 to become the last player in U.S. Open history to fire a triple-figure score in Open competition.

Denny Shute fired a one-under-par 69 to lead after the first day, with Vic Ghezzi and Dutch Harrison a shot back, but after the end of the second round, New York's Craig Wood took the lead and never looked back. Wood had been a runner-up in the U.S. Open, the British Open, and the PGA Championship already but was determined to shed his bridesmaid's label. His dominating three-shot victory over Shute was capped by a birdie on the 18th hole. Hogan was tied for third, while Nelson finished in a distant tie for 17th. Dallas' Harry Todd, the first head pro at the Northwood Club

(Dallas), was the low amateur and finished tied for 13th. A total purse of $6,000 was paid, with Wood taking home the top money of $1,000. "The people of the Southwest more than lived up to their reputation for being hospitable," wrote national PGA president Tom Walsh in reviewing the tournament. Wood would remain defending champion for a long time. Six months after the Colonial Open, Pearl Harbor was attacked by the Japanese, and the USGA suspended all national championships for the duration of the war. The Open wouldn't return to Texas for another decade, but once again, Leonard had shown the way with his golfing vision.

Texas' Three-Time Master

Fans can argue for hours about who truly was the best Texas golfer, but as to who enjoyed it the most, there is little doubt that that title belonged to Jimmy Demaret. After a series of amateur successes, the Houston native turned professional in 1928. He will be remembered for many things both on and off the golf course, but perhaps none is stronger than what his biographer John Companiotte referred to in his 2004 book on Demaret as "a decade bordered in green."

Demaret had already captured a couple of PGA Tour victories before the start of the 1940 season, but he began the year on a roll, winning five times, including three times in a row and once in Houston, before the Tour even got to the season's first major, the Masters at Augusta National Golf Club. The part-time golf coach at Rice, who led the Owls to the 1939 Southwest Conference title, was clearly at the top of his game when the Masters arrived and he showed it by winning his first major championship. But typical of Demaret, he did it his own way, cracking jokes and one-liners all along the fairways. "He was the most underrated golfer in our game," Hogan once said. Sportswriter Grantland Rice called him the "Swinging Texan" and the "Singing Texan" for his abilities on and off the course. Sam Snead said he was the most liked pro on the Tour.

Demaret came back to win the Masters again in 1947 and 1950, making him Texas' only three-time Masters champion. After serving as head pro at Brae Burn Country Club in Houston for five years in the 1930s and 1940s, he became head pro at River Oaks from 1943 to 1946. Despite more than a dozen victories on the PGA Tour, Demaret became more prominent in later decades for building landmark courses in both Houston and Austin, but whatever he did in his 73 years of golfing life, he always did it with a smile and a laugh.

Hogan's Fifth Open

In any golf record book, Ben Hogan's name is tied at the top of the list for the most U.S. Open victories with four. To legions of Hogan fans and followers, that record has always been incorrect. They insist, with ample evidence and justification, that Hogan won his fifth U.S. Open in 1942, the Hale America Open.

The tournament, held in Chicago in June, was cosponsored by the USGA, the PGA, and the Chicago Golf District Association partly as a fund-raiser for the war effort and to serve as a national tournament for all interested professional and amateur golfers. The issue of it being the true U.S. Open for that year has long been debated.

Houston's Jimmy Demaret, second from left, a three-time Masters champion, is pictured with, left to right, pros Elroy Marti, Ben Hogan, and Byron Nelson. (Photo courtesy of Brae Burn Country Club)

"The reason Hogan didn't win the U.S. Open that year is because there was no U.S. Open," said Marty Parkes, senior director of communications for the USGA. "The USGA executive committee voted to suspend all national championships at the start of the war and you cannot be the U.S. Open champion when there is no U.S. Open."

To that, Hogan defenders simply ask, "What about the medal?" Hogan won five exactly similar USGA medals for his four Open titles and one victory at the Hale America Open. Although the front of each medal is the same, the back of the 1942 event reads "Hale America Open Champion Ben Hogan." Furthermore,

writer Dan Jenkins and others, including Hogan himself, argue that the tournament was played according to all USGA rules; there were four 18-hole rounds like the Open, and there was regional and national qualifying like the Open.

After his victory, which was broadcast nationally on radio just like the Open, Hogan shook the hand of USGA president Pierce, just like at the Open, and gave an Open victor's speech. After being paired with Bob Jones, who came out of retirement for the event, for the first round, Hogan shot a 62 in the second round to separate himself from the field just like so many Opens he had won. "There is no doubt that was his fifth U.S.

Open win because of the way it was played and set up just like an Open," Jenkins said. "It was just one more mark of Hogan's greatness."

Loveable Lefty Stackhouse

Texas has never had much trouble producing golf champions, but it has also produced plenty of colorful and unusual characters as well. Lefty Artist Stackhouse would certainly be near the top of the latter list. Born in Atoka, Oklahoma, Stackhouse moved to Texas as a child and quickly impressed his friends and teachers as a talented golfer. He excelled in the amateur ranks, beating players twice his age, but had a rough childhood, as both his parents died when he was a teenager, leaving him to fend for himself.

Golf was to become Stackhouse's salvation and his greatest curse. He played professionally through the 1930s and 1940s, doing well enough to finish in the top 10 twice at the Western Open and playing in the 1941 U.S. Open at Colonial. But he had two problems on the golf course, drinking and an explosive temper, a troubling combination for anyone making his living on the course. His son, Wayne Stackhouse, confirmed in the book *Texas Golf Legends* that most of the stories about his dad, even those of the outlandish variety, are accurate. Stackhouse himself wrote in his memoirs, "If anybody had more alcoholic pass outs on the golf course than I did, I certainly feel sorry for them."

Stackhouse drank only two times on the golf course, to celebrate a good round or to commiserate a bad one, which is to say pretty much all the time. His temper was another thing. Stackhouse was prone to do himself bodily harm after a shot below his lofty stan-dards. He would cause himself physical pain as if to punish himself for such a woeful effort. The most famous story was reported by Hogan and his North Texas caddy Shelly Mayfield in the *Atlanta Journal*. After hitting a poor shot during a pro-am one day, Stackhouse raked his hand through the thorny rose bushes until it bled. Seeing his other hand had escaped injury, he loudly announced, "Don't think you're going to get away from it either," and whipped the hand through the bushes until both hands were bleeding profusely.

Nelson didn't witness the rose bush incident but saw Stackhouse's temper firsthand while playing in the Odessa Pro-Am. The format was a two-man team, and Stackhouse's partner was already on the green in two shots, while Stackhouse was in the fairway in three. Knowing his partner was in excellent position for another birdie, Stackhouse picked up his ball, only to have the amateur three-putt the hole, costing the team a stroke. Stackhouse didn't say a word walking off the green, but going to the next tee box he reared back and punched himself in the jaw as hard as possible. Nelson, who was walking only a few feet away when the punch was thrown, was amazed. "Wow. I certainly wouldn't want him to hit me that hard," Nelson said. Stackhouse was also known to head-butt a tree if there was one available after a poor effort.

Stackhouse finally quit the Tour in the early 1950s and moved back to the family home in Seguin. Not surprisingly, his problems almost totally disappeared once he retired from professional competition. Stackhouse was recognized as the South Texas PGA Pro of the Year twice and became a noted teacher, helping launch the junior golf program at public Max Starcke Park. He dedicated his life to helping juniors and women learn the game of golf and volunteered hundreds of hours to help grow the game in South Texas. He died in 1979 of a heart attack while working at Starcke. Today, a plaque listing all of Stackhouse's golf accomplishments sits near the clubhouse. "I don't think pro golf ever fit his personality," Nelson said. But it provided the backdrop for many strange but true stories about Texas' loveable Lefty.

Golf's Texas Babe

To baseball fans anywhere, there was only one "Babe," the Sultan of Swat, Babe Ruth, but for golfers, especially those familiar with Texas golf history, the true long-driving Babe was Babe Didrikson Zaharias. Born in Port Arthur in 1911, Mildred Ella Didriksen, who changed the spelling to Didrikson at an early age, grew up playing baseball with the boys in the neighborhood of the Golden Triangle, earning her nickname after the number of long-distance home runs she would hit.

Zaharias was one of the greatest female athletes of all time. She was the best at everything she did, and she wanted to do everything. Plus, she wasn't shy about telling people how good she was or how impressively she would win before she would go out and back up every boast. "Babe loved playing with the men, and she loved beating them," said Aniela Goldthwaite.

Zaharias could at times be kind, funny, boastful, or quiet but always near the center of sports attention and usually at the top of the winners' list. "All my life, I've had the urge to do things better than anyone else," she wrote in her autobiography. That was certainly proven when she won the 1932 Amateur Athletic

Union team title by herself along with three Olympic medals, two gold and a silver, and three world records in the 1932 Summer Games in Los Angeles. Despite growing up near Tyrell Park in Beaumont, she didn't begin to take golf seriously until after the Olympics, taking some lessons from Dallas Country Club pro George Aulbauch while working at a local company.

She then won every major statewide and national amateur tournament around the country over the next 15 years, including the Texas Women's Open, the Texas Amateur, the U.S. Amateur in 1946, and the British Women's Amateur in 1947. Along the way, the rough-talking Zaharias overcame the stigma of genteel women's amateur golf, having one North Texas society player telling a newspaper, "We don't need any truck driver's daughters in our tournament." In the biggest tournaments, she turned in her best performances, winning the 1948 U.S. Open by eight shots, the 1950 Open by nine, and the 1954 Open by 12 shots, just 18 months after cancer surgery. "You see, Babe was simply the best," Fort Worth's Bertha Bowen said in an early 1990s interview. Babe won 17 straight amateur victories in the 1940s until defeated by Dallas' Bettye Mims in the 1948 Texas Women's Open at River Crest Country Club. Zaharias was named female athlete of the year six times and female athlete of the first half century by the Associated Press.

In 1949, Babe partnered with her husband, wrestler George Zaharias, PGA promoter Fred Corcoran, and several other Texans for her most long-lasting accomplishment, the formation of the Ladies Professional Golf Association (LPGA). The LPGA had 13 players originally, including Zaharias, Mims, San Antonio's Betty Jameson, and Richardson's Marilyn Smith, when

Port Arthur's Babe Didrikson Zaharias was golf's most dominant female player. (Photo courtesy of Institute of Texas Cultures/San Antonio Light Collection)

to watch," said longtime Texas resident and all-time LPGA winner Kathy Whitworth. "She always wanted to play from the back tees because she could hit it so far, but I'm not sure the rest of us did."

Zaharias suffered a recurring bout with cancer after winning the 1954 Open and died two years later, but before she passed away, she had one more tribute left to Texas golf. Staying at the home of her good friend Bowen over Christmas 1955, she asked to be taken to Colonial one more time. She could barely walk but made it to the second green at Colonial and rested her hand on the famous landscape. "I just want to see a golf course one more time," Bowen remembered Zaharias saying. She died at the age of 42, but the so-called freckled fireplug will never be forgotten, nor will her accomplishments on the golf course and in the sports field. Today, a museum exists in the Beaumont–Port Arthur area to showcase her unmatched life and career. "I only met her once, at age 12 and we played nine holes, but she was a kind, gentle soul and a great thrill and inspiration for me and for golf," Fort Worth's Sandra Haynie said.

The Arthritis Special

Dick Jackson was just an avid golfer with a serious arthritis problem that kept him off the links at his favorite places, Houston Country Club and River Oaks. Preston Moore Jr. was a young teenager just looking for another fast way to get home after his regular golf game. Together they made golf history, changing the game in America forever.

Moore's family held a membership at River Oaks and lived just off the 10th tee. Every day, he would

officially chartered in 1950. The first official winner of an LPGA event was another Texan, Fort Worth's Polly Riley, who captured the Tampa Open in 1950 as an amateur and kept her small trophy in her home near Colonial until her death, but Zaharias was the early star, winning 12 early LPGA tournaments and charming the galleries. "I loved her; she was really something

travel to the course and back home on his speedy Cushman scooter. One day in the mid-1940s, Jackson stopped Moore to inquire about the scooter and have a closer look. He explained how his medical condition was limiting his favorite sport and asked Moore where his dad had purchased the machine. That got Jackson to thinking of a possible new answer to his long-term problems. He purchased a scooter and had some modifications made at his automobile dealership. What evolved was the first motorized golf cart, which allowed Jackson to get around the links easily along with room for a caddy/driver and a few other friends. The cart was dubbed the Arthritis Special, and a dozen vehicles were made for Jackson and friends. The first golf cart was patented by Watson Cushman in 1948 and caused quite a stir at Houston Country Club and River Oaks because of its noise and tendency to kick up dust. Club minutes at Houston reported many complaints in the late 1940s about the buggies, which were initially restricted to players with a doctor's permission slip. In 1949, Jackson was denied unlimited permission to use the carts on Saturday, Sundays, and holidays, with the board saying that golfers using the buggies played too fast and interfered with walking golfers.

After Jackson died in 1951, Cushman began to make the carts on a larger scale. The king of Sweden was one of the first buyers, along with Ford Motor Company, which purchased them to conduct tours of its manufacturing plants. Today, carts have replaced caddies at almost every club in America, with cart rental adding a huge profit margin to a club's bottom line. "We could have never imagined it would take off like it did," Dick Forester, the head pro at Houston Country

Club at the time, once said. "It's enabled people to play much longer in life. There is no way we could go back." Today, one of Jackson's first carts sits in the pro shop of San Antonio Country Club. "It's an amazing bit of history," said club pro Chuck Westergard.

The PGA Tour Storms Texas

San Antonio had already proven to be a mainstay of the PGA Tour by the mid-1940s with its Texas Open and the U.S. Open staged at Marvin Leonard's Colonial in 1941, reconfirming a healthy appetite for professional golf in Texas. Several forward-thinking Texans envisioned having the pros play in Texas on a regular basis, leading to Texas being the home to more annual PGA Tour stops than almost anywhere.

As usual, Leonard was among the first to come up with the idea, almost as soon as the final putt dropped on his successful Open. But six months after the Open ended, the United States entered World War II after Pearl Harbor, and any talk about new golf tournaments was put on hold. In late 1945, with the end of the war in sight, Leonard's plan for an annual PGA Tour event took shape. He began to spread the word about the new event called the Colonial National Invitational. Like Leonard, the tournament itself would be unique. It would be 72 holes with just 36 players, and Leonard reserved the right to invite anyone he wished. "Nobody complained because it was his land, his money, and his tournament," said longtime Colonial tournament committee member Scott Corpening. "Sometimes I think we'd be better off with someone like that today."

Not only would Leonard offer a $15,000 total purse with $3,000 going to the winner but he would also add something else unique to the tournaments of the day. Unlike today's perk-filled events, pro tournaments in the 1940s sometimes didn't even allow the players in the clubhouse, forcing them to change their shoes in the parking lot, and offered almost nothing in the way of player services. But Leonard was determined to change that, using charm and good old-fashioned Southern hospitality to arrange lavish meals and other perks for coming to his event. "Everything you see on the PGA Tour in the way of player services originated at Colonial," Corpening said. The first tournament, held in the spring of 1946, attracted large crowds and a stellar field. The popular hometown champion, Hogan, won the first of his five victories at Colonial, leading many press members and fans to call the course "Hogan's Alley." Today, the Colonial is played at the same course and at the same time as it was in 1946, making it the second-oldest tournament on the PGA Tour to be played at the same course every year since it started, behind only the Masters—a linkage that would undoubtedly make Leonard smile.

In 1945, a group of Houston businessman also had similar thoughts about bringing the PGA Tour to Southeast Texas on a regular basis. There had been two previous Houston Opens, but neither lasted. To ensure that this version would be more long lasting, the early leaders formed the Houston Golf Association so that this Houston golf event would be a long-term success. After visiting the 1945 Texas Open in San Antonio, they were determined a similar tournament would flourish in Houston. The first Houston Open conducted by the Houston Golf Association was set for May 1946 at River Oaks Country Club. The event was called the Tournament of Champions and offered a total purse of $10,000. Fort Worth's Hogan and Dallas' Lloyd Mangrum shared the first-round lead at River Oaks with a pair of 67s before amateur sensation Frank Stranahan took the 36-hole lead. But on the third day, Nelson grabbed the lead with a 67 and cruised home with 68 for a two-shot win over Hogan in Sunday's final round. While enthusiasm had been high and a crowd of 10,000 had watched the first Houston Golf Association event, the excitement didn't cover the bills, and much like Jack O'Brien did with the first Texas Open, founders were forced to scramble at the last minute. They decided not to pass the hat like O'Brien, instead opting for a Houston bank loan to cover the prize money. Today, the Houston Golf Association still runs the Houston Open, no bank loans are needed, and the event raises millions of dollars for charity on the PGA Tour.

The first Dallas Open, the forerunner to today's Byron Nelson Championship, was held in 1944 at Lakewood Country Club. Known as the Texas Victory Open, the event was an easy win for Nelson by 10 shots over McSpaden. The total purse was $10,000 raised by local businesses, with Nelson taking home $2,000. Brook Hollow hosted the 1946 tournament won by Ben Hogan, but eventually the Dallas Open bounced around before being stopped entirely. It would wait until the late 1960s to become the Tour's tournament heavyweight.

Texas War Hero

World War II shut down much of professional golf in the mid-1940s, but of all the prominent PGA Tour players called into the service, few saw actual combat duties except for Lloyd Mangrum. Born in the tiny North Texas town of Trenton in 1914, Lloyd moved to Dallas to work for his brother Ray at the long-since-abandoned Cliff Dale Country Club. Lloyd spent hours working on his game and turned pro at age 15. "He hadn't played many amateur events, so he was a bit of an unknown quality to most people, but not to me," Nelson said. Mangrum won his first professional event in 1940 but was soon called into service and saw the worst of what World War II had to offer. He was wounded when his jeep turned over during the invasion of Normandy and later received shrapnel wounds during the Battle of the Bulge. He returned home in 1945 with four Bronze Stars and two Purple Hearts.

The battle-hardened Mangrum returned to the Tour a different man. He sported a thin mustache like Clark Gable and constantly chain-smoked, often hitting his shot with a cigarette in his mouth. He was called a cool customer and a tough competitor but said he saw golf in a new light. "I don't think any of the pro golfers who were combat soldiers will soon be able to think of a three-putt green as one of the really bad troubles in life."

His golfing highlight came in the first postwar U.S. Open in 1946, when he defeated Nelson in a 36-hole playoff at Canterbury Golf Club in Cleveland, Ohio. Mangrum was named to three Ryder Cup teams, was the captain of the 1951 squad, and won 36 PGA Tour events, a number that comes as a surprise to even the most avid golf fans, according to writer Charles Price, who once penned an article on Mangrum, "Lord, How This Man Could Play." Mangrum died at the age of 59 in 1973 after suffering his 12th heart attack, but the deeds of Texas' first professional golfing war hero should not be forgotten.

Hogan's Heroic Recovery

Ben Hogan had overcome childhood challenges and paid a decade of difficult golfing dues to gain his first PGA Tour victory. But his trials on February 2, 1949, and his incredible recovery showed everyone the amazing Hogan will to survive and thrive. Hogan and his wife Valerie were driving home from the Phoenix Open after he finished second to Demaret. Automobile travel was the most common way for players to get from tournament to tournament those days. Private jets or airplanes in general were out of the question. Trains were not much help to the professional golfer's geographically scattered schedule, leaving the long car ride as the main mode of transportation. Nelson said the one thing that always amazed him is that no Tour player was ever killed driving to or from an event, but Hogan came the closest of them all.

He had briefly stopped in the tiny West Texas town of Van Horn, the halfway point between Phoenix and Fort Worth, and had just restarted his trip when he had a head-on collision with a speeding Greyhound bus that was unable to see Hogan's car in the foggy and misty conditions. At the last second before impact, Hogan threw himself over his wife's lap to protect her, and this selfless act ultimately saved his own life as the driver's-side seat was impaled by the steering wheel with the impact of the wreck. Valerie Hogan was relatively unhurt, but the same could not be said for her husband. He suffered multiple broken bones, including his collarbone, ribs, pelvis, and ankle. He was in such deep shock from loss of blood and injury trauma that he was presumed dead by most people on the scene, and an ambulance was not even called until 45 minutes after the wreck. Hogan finally made it to a hospital in El Paso, but survival was very doubtful and golf not even a question.

Several golfers on their way to the Texas Open in San Antonio passed through the wreck scene and on recognizing his car journeyed to the hospital. "He was all strapped down," said Masters champion Herman Kaiser, one of the first to see Hogan. "It didn't look like he would make it," he was quoted in Hogan's biography. Four days after the wreck, Hogan began to make a remarkable recovery, and doctors said he might walk again one day and golf could at least be considered, but he soon took a turn for the worst, developing blood clots, and emergency surgery was needed. Hogan would not be deterred, and he left the hospital on April 1, 1949. His recovery continued at home, and unbelievably to even those who knew him best, Hogan was back on the Tour for the 1950 Los Angeles Open less than a year after the wreck, which would have killed those not as strong or determined.

When the news got out about Hogan shielding his wife at the last second, get-well messages poured in by the thousands. He managed to finish in a first-place tie with Sam Snead at the Los Angeles Open despite shuffling around in obvious pain on the hilly Riviera Country Club course, and won the respect of a sports-crazy nation with his playoff loss. It also caught the eye of Hollywood legend Glenn Ford, who made the Ben Hogan story come to life in a full-length film titled *Follow the Sun*, which debuted in March 1951 with the world premier in Fort Worth.

What Hogan had done awed the sports world, but what he did in the next decade would awe anybody who knew anything about golf and remarkable comebacks.

The 1950s
A Gambling Good Time

★

5 Highlights of the 1950s

★ The U.S. Open is held at the Northwood Club in Dallas in 1952.
★ Ben Hogan wins three majors in 1953 and is greeted by a ticker tape parade in New York City.
★ Charles Washington breaks the racial color barrier at Houston's Memorial Park in 1954.
★ Texas college golfing success includes a North Texas NCAA four-peat and the University of Houston golf dynasty.
★ Champions Golf Club in Houston is opened as Texas' premier host of championship events.

The Story of the Decade:
Texas High-Stakes Golf Gambling

Texas legend and myth has always been built on doing things bigger, bolder, and with more style and audacity than anyone else. Nowhere is that clearer than the high-stakes gambling game and pari-mutuel pools that came to symbolize Texas golf in the 1950s and early 1960s. To be sure, Texans didn't invent gambling on the golf course, but many golfers involved in that era think Lone Star golfers perfected it.

It came to be known as the Bar-B-Que circuit because of the preferred choice of after-golf meals. Texas golfers were some of the must colorful characters and best players in this extended period, with players and courses representing each region of the state. Golf was still a relatively minor, low-paying sport, a decade away from national television exposure, but Lone Star golfers invented their own fun and prize money. "You met a lot of colorful characters on the Bar-B-Que circuit in Texas and a lot of great players too," said Wichita Falls native Don Cherry, who qualified on both accounts. "I think Texas ruled the golf world for 25 to 30 years with top pro players, and the Bar-B-Que circuit was just an outgrowth of that. You could play anywhere for a lot of money and some great competition."

Cherry was the prime example of somebody who loved life on and especially off the course. He made his living as a nightclub singer, sometimes touring with Dean Martin, but was still good enough to excel on the golf course. He qualified for his first Masters tournament in 1953 when he had his first and only private meeting with club cofounder Clifford Roberts. The wisecracking, smooth-talking Cherry, who had grown up practicing in a vacant lot behind Wichita Falls Country Club, gambling for quarters because that was all the money he had, admitted he was a bit nervous when he got the summons. "He [Roberts] said, 'We've never had a lounge singer in the Masters before,' because he had seen my act advertised on a downtown billboard," Cherry recalled. "I didn't really know what

> ### TEXAS GOLF FACT
>
> Ben Hogan was the last professional golfer awarded a full ticker tape parade through New York's famed Canyon of Heroes.

to say so I blurted out, 'All the guys in the locker room wish they could sing.' I guess that was enough for him because he let me go."

The next morning, Cherry was playing a practice round when he saw Masters cofounder Bob Jones on the course. "That was a good answer you gave Mr. Roberts yesterday," Jones told Cherry. "Don't ever give that to him again." Cherry said all the players loved his carefree attitude and his ability to mix fun and golf. "I was in the nightclubs every night and the golf course every day."

Blessed with year-round weather to play golf and an endless string of small-town, mainly nine-hole, 18-tee golf courses, Texas players used the opportunity to get better every way they could. "Gambling is just part of the Texas culture," explained Texas golf pro Cameron Doan, who grew up in El Paso. "The golf courses are not that difficult in West Texas so you had to have something to keep your attention." Doug Sanders moved to Texas from his native Georgia and quickly saw a difference. "Texans are winners; they don't like to lose at anything."

The summertime was when competition and the stakes heated up. Seemingly every small town in Texas, especially in the oil-rich East and West Texas regions, would host annual tournaments, attempting to outdo the others for golf, fun, entertainment, and high-stakes action.

Jack Burke Jr., left, and Don Cherry were part of the 1950s Lone Star gambling good times. (Photo courtesy of Don Cherry)

The Abilene Invitational was usually on the Fourth of July, the Premier Oilman's was in Longview in August, and the Midland Invitational was near the end of the summer. The most lucrative and prestigious tournament of them all, the Odessa Pro-Am, was held just after the U.S. Open in June. "It's always easier to play for somebody else's money instead of your own, which is why so many of our guys did so well on the PGA Tour," said former national PGA president Joe Black. "The whole thing was an incubator for the pro tour." Doan agreed: "Playing for your own money hardens you."

With no pro sports to compete for Texas sports attention, golf, both professional and amateur, dominated the sports pages and the barbershop conversations statewide. Writer Dan Jenkins grew up in Fort Worth and witnessed the evolution in the state from amateur to college to pro sports. "In the 1950s, there was a tremendous amount of golf coverage in the newspaper. You had college football, Texas League baseball and golf, in that order, to talk about full time and those guys were our heroes."

While today's professional golf tournaments try to take care of players through free transportation, lavish meals, and entertainment for their families, the Texas tournaments of the 1950s aided players in another way, cutting them in for a piece of the lucrative pari-mutuel gambling action.

"I played in a tournament one time in Brady and found out there was no Calcutta pool and couldn't believe it," Cherry said. "So I got on the phone and started calling around and found out there was a tournament in Hobbs, New Mexico, with a big pool and I pulled out of the Brady tournament and drove all the way to Hobbs so I could participate in the action."

Former Champions Tour star Rives McBee grew up near Midland and said the amount of golf he played at an early age almost made golf seem like his vocation and the Bar-B-Que circuit tournaments like a summer job. "If you didn't bring cash, you'd better play well, and if you already had cash and played well, you could be rich," added Houston's Homero Blancas of the high-stakes gambling action. Dallas pro Dennis Ewing said the growth of the amateur circuit also brought in the full-time golf hustlers, always looking for another angle to make a quick buck on the golf course. Two of the best known were Alvin C. Thompson, better known as "Titanic," a nickname he picked up after sinking another opponent, and Dick Martin, a Dallas rental home landlord whose real job was hanging around Tenison Park Golf Course in East Dallas, cooking up another gambling game.

Tenison Park, which opened in the early 1930s, and Memorial Park, another 1930s design in Houston, were two places guaranteed to get up a money game at any time with an ever-changing cast of characters. The betting action became so famous or infamous at Tenison that one national columnist wrote a story titled "Where Pros Are Sent Home C.O.D." Ewing, who grew up playing Tenison in the 1950s, said the environment there could have come straight from a pulp fiction novel. "One of their favorite expressions there was, 'Never attack a lumber yard with a pile of toothpicks.' That meant the gamblers knew who they could beat and they would never send a kid to play a man."

Martin would typically arrive at Tenison in the mid-morning and hold court most of the day, talking with the younger players about the joys of becoming a bookmaker and working on setting up his next match. Martin was famous for loaning people money, only to ask for something in return. "Dick would always pay my entry fee for tournaments, then sell the clubs I had won to get his money back," Ewing said. Like a true hustler, Martin could play a good game along with talking one. "I personally saw him shoot a 76 using only a 7-iron and putter," Ewing added. Martin once sent Ewing to the Odessa Pro-Am with just seven dollars in his pocket, assuring him that would be enough for the weekend. "They had a lot of big meals for me to eat and the unairconditioned rooms were $2 a night. I came back with change."

Thompson, who was born in Arkansas, traveled more than Martin, showing up in dozens of Texas towns looking for his latest golfing mark. He also had a rougher background, reportedly killing several men and being involved in all kinds of cons. But he was good enough to play Byron Nelson in a Fort Worth match set up by his handlers and only lose by two strokes, 71 to 69, after getting a three-stroke handicap before the match started.

Thompson would travel the state with a number of partners, unknown to most future victims, including Masters champion Herman Kaiser, PGA Championship winner Bob Hamilton, and multi–PGA Tour winner Lee Elder, often pretending they were just caddies or people he had met off the street. "Honesty pays, but usually very little," he was famous for saying before his death in a North Texas nursing home in the early 1970s. Among the players Thompson befriended and ultimately tried to get to travel with him were Tenison regular Lee Trevino and Houston golfers Jack Burke Jr. and Jimmy Demaret. "I wasn't looking to travel that much," Demaret said.

At Houston's Memorial Park, longtime pro Jack Sellman, a teacher at Brae Burn Golf Club, was one of a long line of players who grew up playing under the guidance of former Memorial pro Robie Williams. Among the future pros who honed their skills at Memorial were Houston's Dave Marr, Jack Burke Jr. (who was Marr's cousin), Demaret, Tommy Bolt, and future Texas architect Jay Riviere, who ultimately did the renovation work at Memorial in the mid-1990s. Sellman said the daily money games and constant competition helped build up the players for future greatness. "We had a lot of gambling games around Memorial. You had to play good all the time or go to jail for not paying your debts," he said. At weather-beaten Memorial, the future pros learned a variety of shots. "It seemed like Memorial was never in good shape, so we had to hit a lot of different shots." Sellman said. "The circle of circumstances in Texas was not always easy," Burke added. "Texans had a survival type attitude."

Abilene native and pro Billy Maxwell became a legend in the 1950s with a string of 34 straight amateur victories stretching across Texas, but he said it was the state that made him famous, not the other way around. "Texas has done everything for me. They treat you great, but they don't spoil you."

The decade of high-stakes games and fun seemed to stretch on forever, but its high-water mark may have come in 1962, when Houston's Blancas and Baytown's Fred Marti teed it up in the Premier Oilman's tourna-ment in Longview. Marti shot a pair of 66s in the first two rounds to take a large lead over Blancas, who opened with rounds of 70 and 69. In the 36-hole final day at Premier, Blancas shot a 62 in the third round, while Marti shot 64 and still held a five-stroke lead. In the final round, Blancas started out with birdie, eagle, par, birdie, birdie, par, which led to a 27 on the front nine, eight under par. He didn't cool much on the back side with a seven-under 28 for an incredible total of 55, easily overshadowing Marti's final round 66 as East Texas oil money sailed through the air in record num-bers among opposing betting factions. "Things have changed now. Nobody tries to get together, nobody has a beer, nobody smokes and they all go to bed at 8 P.M.," Blancas said. "How much fun is that?"

The USGA, which had begun to warn about the evils of gambling pools at amateur tournaments in the mid-1950s, turned up the pressure by threatening to revoke the amateur status of any golfer caught up in a high-stakes Calcutta pool. "Maybe the betting did get a little out of hand at times," admitted Texas Golf Association executive director Rob Addington. The Odessa Pro-Am, "where you could easily bet a $1,000 a hole," Sanders remembers, was shut down in 1969 under pressure from the PGA Tour. "They were wor-ried we were taking their best players because they wanted to come here," Odessa Country Club general manager and former head pro Clay Kinnard said. "We always had the big entertainers like Dean Martin and Don Cherry, the biggest parties and the most fun."

The demise of the high-stakes tournaments was the end of a highly entertaining and for some a highly lucrative era for Texas golfers and another step in the process that would make them the most feared and fearless players in the golfing world.

The Open Returns to Texas

Slot machines and a pair of lifetime memberships hardly seem the basis of a North Texas private club powerhouse, but on those humble beginnings was built the Northwood Club in Dallas. A group of Dallas businessmen had decided there was a need for another private club in town in the late 1940s, so the Northwood Club was built in the fall of 1946 on land once home to a Methodist campground and once owned by Dallas businessman Buddy Fogelson. It suffered many of the growing pains of new clubs but survived on two lifetime memberships sold at the then unheard-of price of $5,000, along with the proceeds of clubhouse slot machines. Although the club was less than two years old, it birthed a visionary as bold and imaginative as Marvin Leonard had been a decade earlier. Jack Munger, whose father had bought the first lifetime membership, saving the Northwood Club from financial ruin, decided the Northwood Club needed a tournament—not just any tournament but the U.S. Open—to spotlight his beloved new course.

There was little doubt that the 1941 Open at Colonial had been a huge success by almost any measure. But another Open to another new course, one that had barely opened, in Texas was questionable to some both inside and outside the state. They just didn't grasp the determination and relentless political skills of Munger. Even at his home club, the mission of Munger to get the U.S. Open to come to Northwood was supported but not exactly universally embraced. "I

was amazed when he [Munger] made the first suggestion about the Open and even more amazed that the USGA actually might accept our suggestion," said original member Irion Worsham, the 1950 club president.

Munger was a man in a good position to make the club's case to the USGA. He was an outstanding amateur golfer and had competed in several national tournaments, including one quarterfinal appearance in the U.S. Amateur. Perhaps most important, Munger served on several USGA committees and knew personally many of the policy members who would make the ultimate site decision. Unlike most club decisions at Northwood, Munger, according to many original members, acted as a committee of one in pursuing the USGA and its prized event.

He made several trips to the USGA's national headquarters in Far Hills, New Jersey, sometimes at his own expense, to talk up the Northwood bid and invited committee members to Dallas to view the new club. "I can say with complete authority that it was a one-man deal to get the Open to Northwood," said original member Milton Threadgill. "Jack Munger was a great amateur and worked with the national committee to bring the Open."

Like Leonard before him, Munger was one determined Texan who would not take no for an answer. While he didn't have a $10,000 check or promise course renovations, he did have plenty of contacts in the golfing world and a desire to do whatever it took to get the Open back to Texas. Meeting at the USGA headquarters on April 21–22, 1950, the executive committee members heard Munger make his impassioned plea to bring the 1952 Open to Northwood. On August 21, 1950, members of the USGA executive committee filed into a conference room at the Minneapolis Golf Club in Minneapolis, Minnesota, for their quarterly meeting. "On motion it was resolved to accept the invitation of the Northwood Club, Dallas, Texas, to entertain the 1952 Open Championship, the terms having been agreed upon orally through Mr. Jack Munger."

Unlike Colonial, the USGA Open committee did not find any major changes needed for Northwood, but there was one huge tree on the sixth hole that the committee insisted had to come down. Many members were upset by this suggestion, but the USGA committee was unmoved by the club's dedication and stated that they would not hold the Open there if the tree remained. The members discussed whether that tree should be removed, but in a strange quirk of fate, the tree suddenly disappeared. According to club lore, Munger took a chainsaw out and cut the tree down one night around midnight. "I don't know if it's true or not, but I don't doubt Jack would have done something like that," Threadgill said.

As for the tournament itself, Ben Hogan was the clear favorite just as he had been at Colonial 11 years earlier. But this time, Hogan, who had made a remarkable car accident recovery, would be making a bid for his third straight Open title having previously won at Merion and Oakland Hills. "It paved the way for a lot of positive publicity, both locally and nationally, for the club," Threadgill said.

Crowds of 10,000 to 15,000 turned out for the championship on a typical hot summer week in Texas. The Open was broadcast on local television by WFAA-TV Channel 8, a first, which brought its massive mobile production truck to Northwood to produce the broadcast and beam it back to the few people who actually owned a television at the time. On radio, by far the more popular medium, the tournament was broadcast by WFAA radio 820-AM, with former baseball great Dizzy Dean doing the commentary.

When the first round opened under warm, clear skies, longtime pro Al Bosch seized the lead with a three-under total of 68, taking a one-shot lead over Hogan, five better than Julius Boros. In the second round, the expected favorite, Hogan, charged into the lead with a second straight 69 for a two-shot lead over George Fazio with Boros six shots back heading into the final 36 holes. In the third round, Boros turned in a 68 to move up the leaderboard, overtaking Hogan by a single shot headed to the fourth round, but most still expected a rally from the heroic Texan. A final-round bogey when Hogan hit his approach shot out of bounds on the infamous sixth hole opened the window of opportunity for Boros. He put on a short-game clinic on the back nine of the final round and emerged with a four-shot win over Ed (Porky) Oliver, five better than Hogan.

USGA executive secretary Joseph Dey praised Northwood for the ability to get such a young course in good shape. "Northwood was the youngest USGA course ever used for the Open Championship, but one of the finest." Colonial had been the second-youngest course used, and now Texas had seen golf's national championship twice in 11 years, furthering the spread of Lone Star golf greatness.

College-Bound Success

In the 1950s and 1960s, Texas colleges dominated NCAA golf championships as few have before or since. North Texas State, as it was known then, didn't even have a golf team until the mid-1940s, when a physical education teacher named Fred Cobb decided to try to form a competitive group. He did more than that; he formed one that came to dominate the NCAA landscape.

Longtime Texas golf pro Ross Collins, who grew up in West Texas putting on cotton-hull greens, was part of one of the first North Texas golf teams led by Cobb, a Texas native. "Fred Cobb was a good student of the game. I had never seen a green grass course until I came to North Texas, and never had a matched set of clubs until I was 26, but he knew how to handle each person individually," Collins said. Cobb, who always had binoculars around his neck, a walking stick in his hand, and a cigarette in his mouth, molded his North Texas team into a national powerhouse in a sport once the exclusive domain of East Coast Ivy League schools. From 1949 to 1952, North Texas State won four straight NCAA titles, losing only a single match in that time and becoming the first school in the modern era of college golf to win four straight.

He was one of the first coaches to understand the importance of recruiting good players and then getting out of their way and letting them play. At North Texas, Cobb had three of the state's best: Dallas native Don January, a future PGA Championship winner and star on the Champions Tour; San Antonio's Joe Conrad, who won the British Amateur title; and Abilene's Billy Maxwell, a former U.S. Amateur champion who became the NCAA title holder while also winning the National Association of Intercollegiate Athletes title. The threesome of Cherry, Maxwell, and January played on all three of North Texas' title teams and were joined by future pros Jacky Culpit and Babe Hiskey for a single season. "Fred was a quiet man, but a real inspiration," Conrad said. "He took us on a 1949 trip to Notre Dame, Michigan, and Ohio State when nobody did that."

January said Cobb wasn't a real inspirational mentor and wasn't necessarily a great teacher but knew how to connect with his teams. "He treated me very good," January said. "He was always smoking those Picuare cigarettes which were pretty strong because one day I made the mistake of borrowing one and it like to have killed me." North Texas won its last team title in 1952, and Cobb died of a heart attack in 1954. While the "Mean Green" never regained their lofty college footing, they had shown the way to college greatness.

Cobb was the first to showcase Texas college talent, yet nobody ever did it longer or better than University of Houston head coach Dave Williams. Starting with their first NCAA title in 1956, Williams's Cougars won a staggering 16 national titles over a 30-year period. Included in that stretch were five in a row from 1956 to 1960, four in a row from 1964 to 1967, and an amazing stretch of seven titles in nine years from 1963 to 1970. "Dave was a great coach and also a great recruiter," said Blancas. "He convinced us as players that nobody could beat us."

Cobb may have been the first to excel as a recruiter and a coach; Williams took that to a level never before seen. "Once there was only five good junior players in the country, and Dave would get four of them," said Marty Fleckman, who played on Houston's first national title team. Williams was famous for creating such a competitive environment that University of Houston practices were tougher than most college tournaments. "We were in constant competition all year long, and I knew that every day I wasn't practicing I was falling behind somebody who was," Fleckman added.

Typical was the scene faced by Beaumont's Bruce Lietzke and Waco's Bill Rogers, who arrived on the University of Houston campus with 21 other freshman golfers, many on full scholarships. "At the beginning of our sophomore year only me and Bill Rogers were left, and those were the two he wanted," Lietzke said. Rogers said Williams gave him an opportunity to succeed and made him a better player even if he didn't always understand or appreciate his methods. "He had a plan for every situation. You might not have always thought his plan was the fairest, but he was going to recruit and motivate and do things his way. Dave was famous for playing hunches, and his hunches usually turned out correctly."

George Hannon led the University of Texas to back-to-back national titles in 1971 and 1972 thanks to the talents of Ben Crenshaw and Tom Kite, but Williams was back with NCAA titles in 1977, 1982, 1984, and 1985, the last coming nearly 30 years after his first. Williams was also a promoter, turning his annual All-America Intercollegiate tournament into a huge moneymaker for the Cougars. "Dave thought golf was the single most important sport in America right up with football, and he was seeking to out-recruit the football team," said former Houston athletic director Harry Foulke.

Along with Cobb, Williams, and Hannon, other top college coaches in Texas included longtime Texas A&M mentor Harry Ransom, a former Ryder Cup member and part-time player on the PGA Tour; multiple PGA Tour winner Keith Fergus, who took over for Williams at Houston when he retired; and former Baylor coach

Tim Hobby, who won the U.S. Publinks Championship in 1989 and qualified to play in the Masters.

Hogan's Historic Triple

Despite his remarkable recovery from the near-fatal wreck in 1949, Ben Hogan never again lived a day without pain. The hours of uninterrupted practice he loved to do on a lonely range were now increasingly rare because of the hours it took to get himself ready. He took long, hot baths to soak his ailing legs, played in bandages, and took long massages before and after play, but no amount of pain could quell the fierce Hogan will to survive and thrive on the golf course.

In 1953, Hogan's injuries limited him to five PGA Tour tournaments, but he won four, including the three majors he played in: the Masters, the U.S. Open, and the only British Open he ever entered. The only thing that kept Hogan from attempting the Grand Slam was that the PGA Championship was held a week after the British Open, and 1950s travel arrangements, not to mention his fragile health, wouldn't allow him to make the trip.

This breathtaking accomplishment, even by Hogan's lofty standards, cast the Texan into an almost mythical figure. Golf writer Herbert Warren Wind called it the "Age of Hogan." Hogan's Fort Worth chronicler Dan Jenkins said it was the greatest single accomplishment in golf history. Longtime El Paso pro Bill Eschenbrenner had a simpler explanation: "Hogan was a god." While the wreck had robbed him of his strength and stamina, it had not diminished his legendary concentration. Byron Nelson saw that firsthand at the U.S. Open. Nelson attended alone but found

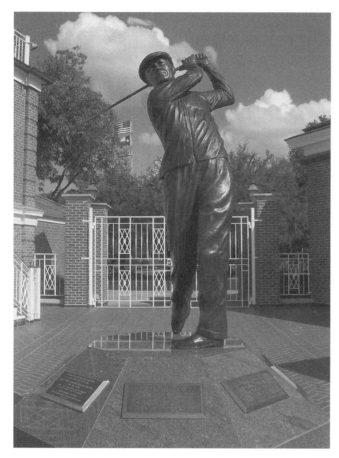

Ben Hogan at Colonial Country Club became a legendary figure with his three majors in 1953. (Photo courtesy of Colonial Country Club)

Hogan's best friend Marvin Leonard walking the fairways watching Hogan. "On one hole, he walked directly in front of Leonard, but never said a word," Nelson said. "Later in the locker room, I was standing directly behind Ben, and Marvin came up to congratulate him. Hogan looked up from his locker and said, 'Marvin, when did you get here?'"

Hogan won the 1953 Masters by five shots over Porky Oliver, who had defeated him at the 1952 Open at the Northwood Club. His 72-hole mark of 274 beat the Masters scoring record by five shots and led Gene Sarazen to call it "the four greatest scoring rounds ever." At the U.S. Open at famed Oakmont Country Club, Hogan won for the fourth time in five years. Despite having to go through a two-round qualifying, he defeated Sam Snead by six shots. The British Open, known as the Open Championship overseas, was perhaps the most impressive. Hogan had never seen the Carnoustie layout in Scotland (or any courses over there for that matter), but he arrived early via ship to practice in the cool Scottish conditions. The locals nicknamed him the "Wee Ice Mon" for his stoic demeanor and unflappable playing skills in the often-challenging conditions. Despite the unfamiliar landscape, the unpredictable weather, and the ever-present body aches, Hogan proved once and for all he would not be denied from his golfing goals. He won by four shots and had achieved the career professional grand slam, something no other Texan has ever achieved.

When he arrived on July 21, 1953, at the New York ship terminal, Hogan was greeted by thousands and bestowed an honor no other Texan and only one other golfer had ever achieved. Player agent and former PGA Tour head Fred Corcoran had arranged for a full New York ticker tape parade for Hogan. Down the famed New York Canyon of Heroes, Hogan and his wife Valerie rode to the cheers of an estimated crowd of 150,000 throwing millions of strips of confetti. "Amazing," Jenkins said. Only golfer Bob Jones, who received a New York parade to celebrate his Grand Slam of four majors in 1930, had been so honored. Not

Nelson's 11 straight, not Arnold Palmer or Jack Nicklaus, not Tiger Woods—only Hogan and Jones have received the singular honor. "I have a tough skin, but this kind of brings me to tears," Hogan said in his public remarks at New York City Hall. It had been a remarkable journey from the most tragic and humble of beginnings to his solo spot atop the golf world, but on that clear day in the summer of 1953, Ben Hogan had finally arrived on top.

Souchak's Record Texas Open

The Texas Open has been home to so much history, and the 1950s were no exception. Former Duke University fullback Mike Souchak arrived at the 1955 Texas Open in the midst of a rare cold spell in terms of both weather and his own golf career. He had won only a handful of events in his career, never a major, but when he left San Antonio four days later, he owned a record that would last 45 years. Souchak shot a 72-hole total of 257, a mark that would last until the 21st century in professional golf. He opened by tying the PGA Tour single round score of 60 at Brackenridge Park and never trailed in the tournament, ultimately winning by seven shots over Fred Haas.

But while Souchak was making history in a record-low way, he was also facing some record-low temperatures. The temperatures dropped steadily all week long and were below freezing for the final round, where Souchak shot a 65, leading him to quip afterward, "I shot 27 on the back nine, I'm 27 years old, and it feels like 27 degrees out here today." He said an unknown South Texas golf fan actually helped make his record tournament possible when he loaned him a pair of warm deerskin gloves for the final 18 holes. "It was so cold, I was afraid I couldn't grip the clubs properly, but this nice gentleman loaned me his gloves." Souchak never came close to equaling his record week again, but he will always be remembered for his record Texas Open win. Nearly a half century later, the 72-hole scoring record was returned to the Texas Open when Tommy Armour III shot a 254 in the 2003 Texas Open, shattering Souchak's mark by three shots at La Cantera Golf Club, just 15 miles northwest of Brackenridge Park.

Pan American Golf Olé

The Pan American Golf Association, the largest Hispanic golf association in the country, is another in the long line of golf organizations with roots in Texas. It was originally called the Fore Golf Association when it was formed by several regulars at Brackenridge Park in 1937, but the group disbanded during World War II and came back together in 1947 with the first San Antonio organizational group in a town with a large Hispanic population. "Before the Pan American Golf Association started, working people did not play golf," said organizational historian Jesse Garza. The group's San Antonio headquarters and national museum is at The Clubhouse, a small, white-framed building directly across the street from Brackenridge where the former Symons Golf Shop stood in the 1910s and 1920s. "When we started, we had nothing but blue collar workers, but now we have 35 percent of our members who own their own business," Garza added.

The first statewide meeting of the Pan American golf group was held in 1956 with seven chapters, and the first state championship was held in Dallas in 1958. Today, the national organization has more than 4,000 golfers and more than 50 chapters nationwide. The Clubhouse is still alive and well and hopping most weekends in San Antonio, with pictures lining the wall attesting to the group's Hispanic history.

A Texas Legacy Lost

Although Texas has been an ever-springing reservoir of great golfers and teachers, a generation in the 1950s was left to wonder what could have been with the stellar career of Austin's Morris Williams Jr. From the beginning of his junior career, Williams was clearly the top amateur in the Austin area. He was the youngest winner of the city junior and the Austin city championship. He had taken lessons from Harvey Penick at Austin Country Club almost since the start of his golfing career. "There is no doubt that Morris would have been as good as Ben and Tommy and some of the other boys," Penick said.

Williams stayed home to attend the University of Texas, where he led the Longhorns to three Southwest Conference titles. One person who saw Williams play in college said there was little doubt he was headed to professional stardom. "He could hit it long, and he could hit it straight," said Jenkins, who faced Williams when he played for Texas Christian University and actually defeated him in one of Williams's last college matches. "He had a great short game and a great smile."

After college, Williams enlisted in the Air Force with the Korean War still raging overseas and was sent to flight school. He continued to prove his golfing skills, winning the All Forces World Golf Championship

and playing exhibitions worldwide. But on a clear morning in 1959, all of that came to a jarring end as he was on a routine training run when he put his plane into a normal dive. For reasons never totally clear, he couldn't pull up, his plane crashed, and he was killed instantly. The sad news came to Austin from the U.S. Air Force public information office, but instead of going straight to Williams's parents, the call was placed to someone Morris Jr. loved almost as much: Penick. The officer asked the golf pro if he would relay the message about his star student, hoping it would cushion the shock to his father. So in the middle of the day, Penick left Austin Country Club and made the short journey to the *Austin American Statesman*. Walking into the newsroom, Williams Sr. looked up to see Penick and knew something was wrong. "What's happened to Morris?" he asked. Told the horrible news, he turned around and passed out, with Penick catching him before he hit the floor. "Saddest thing I ever had to do," Penick said.

There was a huge memorial service when Williams's body was returned to Austin with honors and speeches declaring his greatness as a person, a sportsman, and a golfer. The City of Austin named its newest course the Morris Williams municipal course and hung a picture of the smiling Williams in the lobby. But for some, the grief never lifted. "His parents never got over losing Morris," Penick said. Neither did Texas golf.

Country Clubs for the Masses

Robert Dedman grew up in poverty in rural Arkansas but moved to Dallas when he attended college and became a lawyer, eventually working for legendary oilman H. L. Hunt. While separated by a few decades from golf dreamers like John Bredemus or Marvin Leonard, he still shared their same vision. He wanted to expand golf in his adopted home state by any means necessary, but Dedman's method to achieve this dream was and still remains unique. He wanted to build country clubs that would cater not to the elite few but to the growing middle class. "Bob was a true visionary and had a great concept," said Joe Black, who served as Dedman's first director of golf and ultimately vice president of golf for all the courses that Dedman's new company, ClubCorp, would own. "He offered Cadillac memberships at Chevrolet prices."

To achieve his low-priced goal, Dedman used what he called an economy of scale. His first course, Brookhaven Country Club, was in a sparsely populated section of northwest Dallas on land once used as a hunting ground by local businessman C. F. Hawn. Construction began in November 1957 with three 18-hole golf courses, a huge tennis complex, and an Olympic-size swimming pool—a Texas-size complex considered revolutionary for that time. But Dedman correctly figured that with the ability to attract three times as many members as a single private club with one clubhouse, he would have three times the income. At the start-up prices he was offering, a $200 initiation fee in 1957, he could attract a much wider group of potential members than the elite private clubs.

Dedman wrote that the top private clubs in Dallas at the time—Dallas Country Club, Brook Hollow, and the Northwood Club—were aimed at the top 1 percent of the local society. He said he was going for the top 10 percent and more who had worked hard for their money and were looking for some recreation but wouldn't mortgage the family future to gain it. To design Brookhaven's three courses, he called on Press Maxwell, whose father, Perry, had been one of the three architects at Colonial. The first course opened in 1959 with large number of members enlisted at the reduced fees. Dedman's ideas revolutionized the private club industry. ClubCorp has grown to manage or run 220 courses worldwide using Dedman's economy of scale and Robert's three rules of order: "a warm welcome, memorable moments, and a fond farewell."

A Home for Champions

As a veteran of the PGA Tour, Jack Burke Jr. had long been considered a champion. He won four straight PGA tournaments in 1952 and captured a Masters title, adding to the legacy of a Texas golf legend who grew up in Houston, where his dad was head pro at River Oaks Country Club.

But in the late 1950s, he teamed with longtime friend and fellow Houstonian Demaret for a project that would stamp them as champions for all times. Burke and Demaret, the latter a three-time Masters champion, were coming to the end of their playing careers and wanted to build a golf course they could call their own—just a peaceful place to have their many friends in and to encourage the top-flight golf they had been associated with. The duo began to scout land, but even in the 1950s economy, the land in Houston was very expensive. Discouraged by their lack of progress, Burke mentioned his quest to a regular golfing partner, Horace Norman, who was a land broker in the area. He suggested they take a drive "way out in the country." When they completed their journey

Bob Dedman's idea of building private country clubs affordable for the upper-middle class revolutionized the golf industry. (Photo courtesy of ClubCorp.)

mined it would be the spot of their new course. They commissioned architect Ralph Plummer to design the first 18-hole championship layout. A lavish press conference announced the plan to the world in February 1957, and the name chosen was Champions Golf Club, which reflected the type of golf they hoped would be played there.

Houston already had plenty of top-notch private clubs, all closer to the central city and the business establishment, but Burke and Demaret succeeded in selling memberships to a place many people didn't know existed. One biographer of the club's early history wrote, "Only men the stature of Burke and Demaret could have pulled off that plan."

Plummer finished construction on July 15, 1958, and the course opened to its eager members three months later. Today, it's one of the heaviest populated areas of Houston. Land that went for $600 an acre in the late 1950s has been known to sell for as high as $200,000. Burke and Demaret worked with Plummer to fashion a championship course that is consistently ranked as one of the top in the state. More important, the two founders used the club to promote golf on both the amateur and the professional levels. Since its opening, Champions has hosted more major tournaments than any other single venue in Texas, including a U.S. Open, a Ryder Cup, a Tour Championship, and the first U.S. Amateur held in Texas in 100 years.

Asked if he was surprised that his course, in what was once considered an uninhabitable part of the city, has become a big success, Burke replied with his trademark bluntness: "I thought if I stayed anywhere 47 years I could be successful. I never wanted to run off and go somewhere else and have to start all over again." For

north of what is today Highway 1960, they found a 500-acre tract of dense forest land known as Jackrabbit for its primary animal resident. The land was just $600 an acre, and the twosome along with some friends purchased the acreage for their newest course, then only a dream.

While most Houstonians considered the area too remote for anything useful, Burke and Demaret deter-

that, Texas golf fans will be forever grateful that a true Texas golf champion stayed and built a home for Champions.

Only the Balls Were White

Although the decade of the 1950s was one of gambling good times and great promise for many Texas golfers, it marked a period of exclusion and frustration for many of the state's minorities, who were routinely denied access to many of the state's public golf courses. Lone Star State Golf Association founder Charles Washington was determined to change all that. A golf dreamer with no less of a cause than his Texas golfing forefathers, Washington helped found Houston-based Lone Star in 1945, primarily to promote the interests of the state's African American golfers. They had succeeded in getting the City of Houston to open its courses to them on one day, Juneteenth, but were excluded the rest of the year.

In the early 1950s, Washington and several black city business leaders filed suit against the City of Houston alleging the city golf courses should be open to all. The case eventually made it to the U.S. Supreme Court, which turned down Houston's bid to keep its courses segregated, and on June 3, 1954, Washington had the honor of hitting the first tee shot at Memorial Park as a fully integrated course. Other big-city municipal courses soon followed suit, making the game more accessible to all.

The opening of the Houston courses also spotlighted two of the greatest African American golfers with Texas ties. Lee Elder, who broke the color barrier with his initial appearance at the Masters in 1971, was born in Dallas. Charlie Sifford, the first black man to win a PGA Tour event and a 2004 World Golf Hall of Fame inductee, lived a portion of his career in Kingwood outside of Houston. "There is no game in the world as great as golf, but it's a tough sport for a black man to play," Sifford wrote in his autobiography, *Just Let Me Play*. In Texas, the golf dreams for people of all color had just gotten easier to achieve.

In the following decade, Texas' greatest golfing star would be a player who came from its poorest and most disadvantaged background.

The 1960s
Unlikely Dreamers and Golf's Major Winners

5 Highlights of the 1960s

★ *Shell's Wonderful World of Golf* debuts in 1962.

★ PGA Championship returns to Texas with the 1963 tournament in Dallas and 1968 in San Antonio.

★ First and only Ryder Cup held in Texas at Champions Golf Club in Houston in 1967.

★ Kathy Whitworth, golf's all-time professional winner with 88 titles, is named Golfer of the Decade by *Golf Magazine*.

★ Byron Nelson Classic is begun at Preston Trail in Dallas in 1968 and becomes the Tour's leading charity money raiser.

The Story of the Decade: Lee Trevino's Incredible Golfing Rise to Greatness

The movie on the life of Lee Trevino has never been made. It's not now in production, and there are no current plans to film his story. The reason is simple. Trevino's tale from his birth in a ramshackle Dallas house, which has long since bulldozed and paved over to build a freeway, to learning the game of golf on a broken-down driving range is too incredible to be believed.

Who would believe a story line of a young minority golfer building par 3s, moving carts, and shining shoes en route to another golf victory? The tales of playing with a taped-up soft drink bottle, winning outrageous bets, and roaming the municipal courses of Dallas with a patchwork set of clubs would be considered pure fiction all the way.

Trevino's Texas life story would be an unforgettable movie if only people would accept his unbelievable tale of rising from rags to riches to become one of golf's all-time champions. "You can say I made it as a poor man in a rich man's game. I broke the mold when I won because nobody with my background had ever won this much in any sport," Trevino said.

Perhaps no one in Texas golf history had bigger, more improbable dreams yet achieved more by starting with less than Lee Buck Trevino. He was born on December 8, 1939, in Dallas to circumstances that could be considered anything but a laboratory for a future golf superstar. There was no golf background in his family, no country club membership, not even any golf clubs.

TEXAS GOLF FACT

The fabled Lee Trevino–Raymond Floyd high-stakes match at Horizon Hills Golf Course in El Paso in 1966 helped launch both men's careers. Floyd went on to be a consistent PGA Tour winner for three decades, while previously unknown Trevino finished fifth in the U.S. Open less than a year later.

But Trevino not only overcame his humble surroundings but transcended them. He arrived at the 1967 U.S. Open, staying in the cheapest motel he could find, eating at the same diner every night, and walking to the course because he had no other means of transportation, but finished fifth en route to PGA Tour Rookie of the Year honors. He came back the next year to win the Open and went on to capture the British Open and the PGA Championship twice. In 1971, he captured the U.S., Canadian, and British Opens in a span of 21 days, becoming the first player to hold three national professional golf titles at one time.

Longtime El Paso golf professional Bill Eschenbrenner grew up in Fort Worth watching Ben Hogan play and practice before moving to West Texas. He says he never saw anybody accomplish what Trevino did. "I don't know anybody who ever did more starting from a background like that." Trevino began as a caddy at the age of eight at Dallas Athletic Club near his home and began to play the local municipal course perfecting his fast-talking style. "When I was growing up, me and my buddies could only scrape together one set of golf clubs, so when we were walking down the fairways

Lee Trevino overcame incredible odds for Texas golf stardom. (Photo courtesy of Lee Trevino)

favorite and perhaps most accurate sayings. He joined the Marines at age 17 and played golf all over Southeast Asia, meeting fellow Texan Orville Moody, whom he would later play on the PGA Tour. After four years in the Marines, Trevino returned to Dallas, where he went to work for local pro Hardy Greenwood at Hardy's Par 3 in the Old Town section of Dallas.

The Trevino work ethic and desire to improve was on daily display at Hardy's. "One thing about Lee, he was never lazy," said longtime Dallas golf professional Dennis Ewing, who saw Trevino in action. "He worked cheap and hard, from 11 A.M. to midnight every day at Hardy's, picking up balls, mowing the greens, building the par 3. There was nothing about Lee just showing up to hit balls."

None of that hard work bothered Trevino when he got his chance to play. He would always spend the early morning hours at Tenison Park at East Dallas, looking for the next match he could take part in. While at Tenison, Trevino became legendary for playing entire matches with a taped-up 32-ounce glass soft-drink bottle or playing with a single club or driving a ball underneath a distant railroad trestle all for the right wager.

Yet mention the word "hustler" to Trevino, and he takes deep offense. "I never hustled anyone in my life. You have to understand what hustling is. It's lying about your handicap to con somebody else out of money. I always told people I was a scratch handicap, and I would give them six shots and still beat them. Maybe I didn't tell them I was a plus-six, but I never hustled them." While at Tenison, he met legendary gambler Alvin "Titanic" Thompson who knew the art of a con job and tried to convince Trevino to join him in his journeys statewide. "At Tenison, Lee would

together, we would always have to shout out, 'Hey Billy, throw me the 5-iron, hey Whitey, I need the putter,' and that's how I got started."

He dropped out of school in the eighth grade, spending time caddying, gambling, and playing golf with anyone he could find. "Real pressure is playing for $5 with only $2 in your pocket," was one of Trevino's

always want to tee off early and play from the back tees in all that early morning dew," Ewing said. "Lee could do it all."

Trevino's early morning routine was as much about his work schedule as his chosen tee time. He was expected to report on time every day at Hardy's, and the morning was the only time he had to play golf. "Tiger Woods has the desire to be the best; I had that same desire," Trevino said. After a falling out with Greenwood, Trevino moved on to El Paso in 1965, going to work at Horizon Hills Golf Club and meeting Eschenbrenner, and he soon fell into the regular pattern of work, golf, gambling, and good times. "You could always count on Lee to be there at 7:30 A.M. every morning to play or practice. Not many guys are like that, but there was never a day when he wasn't there," Eschenbrenner said. Trevino admitted no matter what the previous night had brought on either side of the U.S.–Mexico border, he was determined to get better. "With my swing I needed a lot of work and I never broke stride on the practice tee. I wasn't always feeling good out there, but I was always there working on my game."

His experiences in the Marines had shown him he could compete successfully with players from around the country in unfamiliar situations. His constant gambling and hustling games at Tenison Park and El Paso had hardened him as a player and competitor, but three days at Horizon Hills in late 1966 showed Trevino he was ready to take on the PGA Tour. Some of Trevino's gambling buddies from Dallas contacted him about setting up a match with Raymond Floyd, already a multiple winner on the PGA Tour.

Floyd agreed to come to El Paso to play the unknown cart boy/clubhouse attendant/assistant pro Trevino. Sure enough, when Floyd showed up in the West Texas desert, he was greeted by Trevino, who carried his bags to his room and cleaned and shined his shoes. "Who do I play?" Floyd asked. "You're playing me," was the answer, earning Trevino a funny look from the young golf star. When some of Floyd's financial backers asked if he would like to see the golf course, he declined, saying, "I'm playing this boy here; I don't need to see any golf course."

The action-addicted El Paso golf crowd turned out the next afternoon to see Trevino and Floyd tee off. Trevino said the local farmers were throwing down $100 bills on the match like most people throw down singles, and Floyd, who was single at the time and up for any challenge, had plenty riding on the match himself. In the first day, the unknown cart boy bested the young pro 65 to 67. The second day was similar, as Trevino won by a stroke, 65 to 66, and when Floyd asked for nine additional holes, Trevino said his golf course work chores prevented any additional golf. "I can't believe it," Floyd said. "Here I am playing the bag storage man, and I can't beat him."

The third day brought a wary and determined Floyd, eager to avoid total financial humiliation in his trip to West Texas. He shot 31 on the front nine at Horizon Hills to finally defeat Trevino for nine holes, and when Trevino missed a short eagle putt on 18, Floyd earned a close victory and a slim financial salvation, departing El Paso as quickly as he could with a little pride and money intact. "There are a lot easier ways to earn a living than this," were his parting words, but nearly 40 years after the match, Floyd still has a vivid memory. "Lee wrote about it in his book; I wrote about it in mine. It's all there and all true." The two men would go on to dominate the pro golf tours, winning 10 major championships and more than 50 Tour events, but neither would forget their three fateful days at Horizon Hills.

After making the 1968 U.S. Open his first Tour victory, Trevino quipped his only goal was to make enough money to buy the Alamo and return it to the Mexicans. "Two things that never last, dogs that chase cars and pros that putt for pars," was another favorite line. "I'll work with a golf teacher when I can find one who can beat me," was a third. His cheery, joking demeanor, which included throwing a rubber snake at Jack Nicklaus before the start of another playoff, earned him the nickname the "Merry Mex" and his lively gallery "Lee Fleas." "I was the kid from the other side of the tracks. The one from the poor neighborhood, who had made it to the top and that showed anything was possible," he said. "We had a bunch of fans out here. They may have not known a lot about golf, but we had a good time."

Trevino survived an on-course lightning strike, the breakup of his first two marriages, and enough career comebacks to be recognized as one of golf's all-time champions and one of the best ball strikers ever. "Ben Hogan used to say I was the only one who could hit his clubs. Of course, Mr. Hogan never called me by my name; he just said 'that Mexican boy in Dallas.'"

That boy achieved more than he or anyone else thought possible when he started and carved out a unique niche as perhaps the ultimate Texas golf dreamer who reached for the stars and hung on for a wild and mostly successful ride. "This is America; you can do anything you want to, if you work hard enough and practice hard enough. That's what I did," Trevino said. That's what he did, indeed.

Shell's Wonderful Journey

In the early 1960s, golf's major championships were televised to an eager audience, but for the most part, golf was a rarely seen sport on television. Weekly tournaments were shown on a hit-or-miss basis, with only the final two rounds shown if at all. If fans wanted to see a great golf destination, their only option was to visit it in person or hope the promotional brochures were very vivid.

A Texas-based company and an outgoing Texas host were getting ready to change all of that. Beginning in 1962, Houston-based Shell Oil Company served as the major sponsor for *Shell's Wonderful World of Golf*, a groundbreaking golf travel program that would introduce the game to millions of golfers and spotlight its most scenic and historic locations.

Another factor in its early success was the visionary thinking and planning of a fairly new convert to golf, Boston native Fred Raphael. The producer came up with the idea of showing top current and former players at historic locations. Because the matches were taped and aired in a one-hour time slot, the most dramatic action could be shown along with some interviews and instruction. The first match was aired on January 21, 1962, from the Old Course at St. Andrews, Scotland, between legends Gene Sarazen and Henry

Cotton. The chance to see famous golfers in historic locations proved to be a big hit in the monthly format. An estimated audience of 10 million to 12 million tuned in for each show, with ultimately 92 matches in 50 different countries.

After the first couple of seasons, Raphael asked Houston's Jimmy Demaret to serve as a host, working with Sarazen to set up the matches, provide commentary, and interview the players. It proved to be another wise move as well, as the easygoing Demaret brought a spark and a charm to the program. He traveled approximately 80,000 miles a year to dozens of different countries to spotlight the matches. "Sarazen didn't miss playing a single course we visited," Demaret said in his biography. "I always walked around the course to become acquainted with the layout, but I spent most of my time sightseeing."

The golf travelogue opened the game for fans to view several different countries and see many of their former heroes, many who hadn't played for years. It was a nostalgic concept Raphael would return to in a big way a decade later in Texas. In the late 1990s, Midland's Terry Jastrow, who ran a California production company, helped return the show to the air, and to date it has aired more than 150 matches to a new generation.

Hometown Pro, Hometown Win

After spending a brief two years on the PGA Tour, Earl Stewart decided his family and a permanent home base were more important than whatever success he might earn on the pro golf tour, so in 1953 Stewart took the head pro job at Oak Cliff Country Club. It wasn't the most thrilling of jobs, but it was good steady work.

It allowed him to stay in golf and more important stay with his family and help raise his kids.

So when the PGA Tour's Dallas Open announced it would be coming to the Oak Cliff Country Club in 1961, the Tour found Stewart instead of the other way around. As was custom, then and now, many PGA Tour events will give the host course's head pro an exemption to play in the tournament. It's usually no more than a harmless thank you for his weeks of work preparing for the tournament and allowing the world's greatest players to use the course for a week.

Many head professionals are way too busy to even accept the free invitation, and those who do make it a strictly last-minute deal with the majority of their time getting ready for the golf tournament and hardly enough time to find their clubs or shoes, much less practice or hit balls. Stewart certainly fell into the case of the latter.

Yet no one counted on Stewart's competitiveness and golf competition background. "My dad was unique in two senses," said Chip Stewart, a longtime Dallas top amateur competitor. "He was a great golfer, and a man who favored family and a stable home life over the quest for fame and fortune." While playing at Sunset High School in Dallas, Earl Stewart had won two high school state titles and then attended Louisiana State University, where he led the Tigers to the NCAA title in 1940 and 1942 and captured the individual title in 1941.

After turning pro, he won the Greater Greensboro Open and the Ardmore (Oklahoma) Open in 1953 and finished seventh on the official money list. So club pro and tournament host or not, Stewart determined he wasn't in the 1961 Dallas Open field just to take up space; he was there to compete and, if possible, win. That is exactly what happened, as Stewart shot a final-round 71 to defeat Arnold Palmer, Doug Sanders, and Gay Brewer by one stroke with a four-day total of 278. He remains the last club professional ever to win a PGA Tour event and the last to win on his home course. "He was not surprised that his feat was never equaled," Chip Stewart said. "Most professional golfers with enough ability to win a PGA event and gain the prize money would be highly unlikely to forsake a lucrative tour career for a club position."

That's what happened to Dallas' stay-at-home professional who forsook the Tour to spend more time with his family but whipped them all when they showed up at his home course. "I asked to caddy for Earl because I figured he knew the course so well and I knew I wouldn't have to shag practice balls the way the other kids did because Earl didn't have time to practice during the tournament," said his 1961 Dallas Open caddy Randall Meeks during public remarks at Stewart's funeral services. "Then he won."

While the 1961 victory marked him as the answer to one of golf's great trivia questions, he wasn't finished with his contribution to golf by a long shot. He came up with the idea of the original PGA Tour qualifying school in 1967 and saw it adopted by the Tour a year later. He served as the head coach for both women's and men's golf teams at Southern Methodist University, leading the Lady Mustangs to an NCAA title in 1979 and recruiting future two-time U.S. Open winner Payne Stewart to play for the men.

He never left his home of Dallas for an extended time, staying close to golf but staying close to family as well. One of the most famous Stewart stories at Oak Cliff Country Club came in 1965, when he aced two holes on the front nine of the course but declined to play the back nine because he had already committed to coaching one of his son's baseball games that day. To the end, he was a top-notch golfer and family man, earning championship medals and legendary status for both.

The PGA returns to Dallas

After John Bredemus and Sol Dreyfuss had helped kick-start golf in the North Texas area by bringing the 1927 PGA Championship to Cedar Crest in Dallas, the season's fourth major championship took a nearly 35-year break from returning to Texas, but Graham Ross was determined to change all that. The longtime Dallas head pro began his career at Bob O Link golf course, where Ralph Guldahl got his start, then moved over to Glen Lakes Golf Club, where the downtown Dallas Athletic Club staged its golf matches.

When the Dallas Athletic Club decided to build its own course in far northeast Dallas near the Garland–Mesquite border, Ralph Plummer was the architect to build first the Blue Course, then the Gold Course. Ross was the choice as the first head pro at Dallas Athletic Club. With his nearly three decades of work, Ross had built an impressive list of contacts and friends, all of whom he used in attempting to persuade the PGA of America to return the PGA Championship back to Dallas for the 1963 event at the still fairly new Dallas Athletic Club.

Ross, along with prestigious and influential local real estate developer Herschel Brown and businessman Ralph Harris, helped persuade the business-oriented

Graham Ross, second from left, helped bring the 1963 PGA Championship to the Dallas Athletic Club. (Photo courtesy of Dallas Athletic Club)

Salesmanship Club to serve as volunteers and financial muscle to help sell sponsorships. "The PGA Championship really helped put DAC on the map," said current club head professional Dennis Ewing. "Back then it was really in the boondocks." So much so that when Salesmanship Club executive Don Houseman went to the club for meetings, he kept getting lost in the country.

Ross's stint as president of the Texas PGA and later national vice president of the PGA of America served him well, as the PGA awarded its championship for 1963 to the Dallas club in late 1961. The terms were the first $40,000 in income plus $50,000 in receipts to the PGA along with $80,000 of the television revenues, still a fairly new notion in the early 1960s. W. L. Todd, who had filled a similar role at Northwood for the 1952 U.S. Open, was brought in as general tournament chairman, with Ross's team and the Salesmanship Club handling the sales duties with a goal of $350,000.

Just as Walter Hagen had entered the 1927 tournament as the dominant golfer of his era when he won at Cedar Crest, the newest dominant golfer, Jack Nicklaus, was one of the first to arrive in Dallas, fresh off his wins at the Masters and U.S. Open earlier in the

Jack Nicklaus, meeting the press, made the 1963 PGA Championship in Dallas his first PGA championship title. (Photo courtesy of PGA of America)

year. Nicklaus showed his power and promise early by winning the long-driving contest with a smash of 341 yards and proved he might be the only golfer hotter than the blazing August temperatures, which reached 103 degrees by Sunday's final round.

Club professional Dick Hart made an ace in the opening round en route to a 66 and a three-shot lead and followed that with a 72, which kept his lead at three shots going into the weekend over local golfer Shelly Mayfield, England's Tony Lima, and Julius Boros. In the third round, Australian and one-time Texas resident Bruce Crampton charged into the lead with a 65, one shot ahead of Dow Finsterwald Sr. and four better than Nicklaus. But when final-day temperatures hit triple figures, Nicklaus hit a low gear and cruised home for his first PGA championship victory by two shots over club pro Dave Ragan, three better than Crampton and Finsterwald.

The huge PGA Championship trophy had been sitting in the sun all day long and was too hot for Nicklaus to pick up except with two large white towels. The photo of him still hangs in the Dallas Athletic Club clubhouse. "He was in a tremendous frame of mind, the course set up well, and the people have treated us tremendously here," said Charlie Nicklaus, Jack's dad, after walking with his son to victory. As a memory of his first PGA Championship win, Nicklaus carried his PGA money clip for more than 40 years. The club had one more bit of Texas hospitality to perform for the new winner, as Brown personally flew Nicklaus from the Dallas-Garland Airport to Dallas' Love Field to catch his flight home, just part of another memorable championship exhibition for Texas golf.

Texas' All-Time Winner

The flat, ever-blowing terrain that makes up the tiny West Texas town of Monahans hardly seems like fertile ground for golf's all-time professional winner, but that was the setting that helped produce Kathy Whitworth, a professional golf champion 88 times over in her career. She was born there in 1939 and eventually moved to equally small and nondescript Jal, New Mexico, at age 12, where she had the good fortune to have her career shaped by one future and one current Texan.

Whitworth's good fortune started with her work ethic and determination instilled by her blue-collar parents, Morris and Dama, and continued when she found out that the head pro at the nine-hole Jal Country Club was Hardy Loudermilk, who would spend nearly two decades as head pro at Oak Hills Country Club in San Antonio and was a disciple of Texas teaching legend Harvey Penick. Loudermilk was the first to impart his teaching wisdom to go along with the talent and determination of Whitworth. "I was very fortunate to have Hardy Loudermilk as my pro at Jal. You didn't have to be rich to play when I was growing up because goodness knows we didn't have a lot of money, but we had opportunity and access."

Perhaps the most important thing that Loudermilk did for Whitworth was pick up the phone in the pro shop and call his teaching mentor, Penick. "He told me he had taught me everything he knew and was turning me over to Harvey," Whitworth said. It was a 420-mile one-way trip from Jal to Austin, where Penick was performing his teaching wonders for Whitworth and her parents, "a pretty long haul," she said, but worth every mile and minute. "I started going to see Harvey at age

16 and I came back and played every day, I mean every single day and the rest was just a Cinderella story."

After winning the New Mexico Amateur Championship twice, she returned to Texas for a stint at Odessa College, but her real calling was the LPGA Tour. Her first wins came in 1962 at the Kelly Girl Open and Phoenix Thunderbird Open, but that only tapped a dependable source of victories that followed for more than two decades. In 1963, she won eight times, including the San Antonio Civitan, and defended her Civitan title with a repeat win in 1964. When she recorded her last professional win in 1985, she had captured 88 victories, six more than the 82 achieved by Sam Snead on the PGA Tour

Whitworth was named *Golf Magazine*'s Golfer of the Decade in the 1960s and was named Associated Press Athlete of the Year twice. She was inducted into the Texas and New Mexico Golf and Sports Hall of Fame along with the World Golf Hall of Fame. Since retiring from active competition in the mid-1980s, she has represented the LPGA in a variety of different ways as its greatest living legend and has turned to teaching. "I'm trying to give back to others what Harvey and Hardy gave to me," she said. "I want to try and help them enjoy the game." Perhaps no Texan enjoyed it and was more successful with the game of golf than Kathy Whitworth.

Marvelous Dave Marr

Dave Marr was one of the many who grew up playing his golf at Houston's Memorial Park golf course, but one of the few who wound up with the title of PGA champion after his name. The son of a Baytown golf pro, Marr was raised on the golf course with Memorial pro Robie Williams hiring him to work and providing career guidance. Second-cousin Jack Burke Jr. provided inspiration, as did legendary golf pro Claude Harmon, who hired Marr for his first pro job at famed Winged Foot Golf Club in New York. After seven years with Harmon, the pro told his young assistant he had enough talent make it on the PGA Tour and possibly make as much as $15,000 a year. "To a guy who was making $150 a week as a club pro that sounded like winning the lottery," Marr once said.

He turned pro in the early 1960s and won four times on the PGA Tour, but one tournament turned out to be a career changer. Marr held off Jack Nicklaus and Billy Casper to capture the 1965 PGA Championship and propel him onto the victorious Ryder Cup team that year. When he began to cut back on professional golf in the early 1970s, he was hired by ABC-TV as its analyst for golf broadcasts, sometimes pairing with Texas legend Byron Nelson. He held that position for nearly two decades, using his wit and wisdom and his low-key Texas mannerisms to educate Americans about golf.

Marr was named captain of the 1981 Ryder Cup team, another U.S. win, a position he called the greatest honor of his life. He teamed with fellow Memorial Park alumni Jay Riviere to design courses later in life before dying of stomach cancer in 1997 in his hometown. From municipal golf course assistant to PGA champion, TV commentator, Ryder Cup captain, and golf architect, his was one Marr-velous life.

A Costly Ryder Cup

Jackie Burke always said he wanted his new course, Champions Golf Club, to be the host of high-quality professional and amateur golf tournaments. While golf's Ryder Cup in the 1960s was a mere blip of the giant figure it cuts in the golf world today, Champions hosted the only Cup matches ever held in Texas, with Burke showing his ability to sacrifice for the good of the game.

The 1967 matches were an artistic success. Burke and the Houston Golf Association went all out to make sure the visitors from overseas had a good time. There was a lavish pretournament dinner at the Houston Club, "one of the nicest I've ever seen," Burke said, and the University of Houston band marched through the fog before the opening matches to play the respective national anthems.

The club had been negotiating with various golf bodies to attract prestigious tournaments to Champions since it opened in the late 1950s and was awarded the Ryder Cup by the PGA of America, thanks to the help of longtime Houston pro Dick Forrester, who was on the PGA board at the time. Forrester told Burke and cofounder Jimmy Demaret he had all the votes if they wanted the Ryder Cup for Houston. They did, and the 1967 matches headed to the Lone Star State for the first and only time.

Although Burke said the club and the city of Houston were proud to have the matches in town, there were a few basic problems. Very few Texans knew or even cared about the Ryder Cup because of the Americans' biannual blowout. "It was a much bigger deal when we played in England," Burke said. The Houston Open had been played in the spring of the year, drawing large crowds, and the Ryder Cup was held in the middle of fall football season, specifically the all-important Texas–Arkansas game held the same weekend. The result was a financial and crowd disaster. "There weren't many people; we basically left the gates open on Saturday," Burke said. Longtime Houston Golf Association Burt Darden said the event cost the Houston Golf Association "tens of thousands of dollars to put on and really put us in a bind."

Burke typically took the view of the Texas golf dreamer and promoter he had inherited from his father and Lone Star golf idols. "It was something that needed to be done for golf in Texas." Great Britain went home a record loser (23½ to 8⅓) and Champions and the Houston Golf Association suffered a financial loss, but golf in Texas took another step forward as Burke's new course was showcased on an international level.

South Texas Major

E. J. Burke achieved most of his fame as a South Texas home builder, being inducted into the National Home Builders Hall of Fame and being recognized nationwide by his peers. But his one and only entry into golf also brought Texas golf a first, the only major championship ever held in South Texas. Burke was the driving force behind the construction and opening of Pecan Valley Golf Course just south of downtown San Antonio. During grand-opening ceremonies in 1963 on the formerly brush-covered 210-acre tract of land crafted into a championship course by Press Maxwell, Burke announced, "One of these days we want to bring a big, national golf championship to San Antonio."

Thanks to his hard work, vision, and contacts with the PGA of America, that's exactly what happened when the 1968 PGA Championship was awarded to Burke's Pecan Valley course. PGA of America president Warren Cantrell served in 1964–1965 and was head professional of a private course in Lubbock. Burke made sure Cantrell knew of his interest in hosting a major championship and invited him to Pecan Valley on several occasions to see the Maxwell design, which had been officially opened on October 11, 1963, by Texas governor John Connally.

Maxwell, whose father Perry had helped design Colonial Country Club in Fort Worth, said the new San Antonio course could be equally good. "The brush and the area was so thick, I had to design three holes without ever stepping on the ground," Press Maxwell said.

The PGA Championship was held the same summer as the international Hemisfair, which attracted three million visitors to San Antonio to see the huge Hemisfair Tower in downtown, only a few miles from Pecan Valley. Burke helped raise a $1 million budget for what he saw as his mission to promote golf in San Antonio. "Without E. J. Burke, this championship PGA event would have never been scheduled in San Antonio at this time," said PGA Tour official J. Edwin Carter. "He expended large sums in assuring its success and aiding its plans."

Among the most honored players at the 50th PGA Championship, held in high heat in mid-July, was Lee Trevino. He had come from the driving ranges of Dallas to become U.S. Open champion in 1968, and to San Antonio and its huge Hispanic population, Trevino was the golfing hero they had long been looking for. The City of San Antonio declared July 15, 1968, Lee Trevino Day, and the Merry Mex was seen everywhere to support the tournament and delight his many fans.

Play finally got under way at the par-72, 7,138-yard course in temperatures in the high 90s, "typical Texas summer, hot, hot and hot," said the defending champion, Dallas' Don January. Houston's Marty Fleckman took the first-round lead with an opening 66, just one off of Sherman's Miller Barber's course record. Trevino shot an opening 69 but faded as Fleckman led after every round but the last, when it came down to the oldest man in the field and golf's king needing this final major championship jewel to complete his crown.

Julius Boros, 48, who had won the U.S. Open at the Northwood Club in Dallas 16 years earlier, was tied with Arnold Palmer, who needed only the PGA Championship to complete his career grand slam. They were two shots behind Fleckman going to the final round. The former Houston Cougar Fleckman faded, and Palmer appeared to have captured his elusive major when his 3-wood approach on the par-5 18th hole finished 12 feet from the cup. Palmer missed the putt and watched Boros get up and down for a par and one-shot win. Boros's 281 total was the highest winning score in PGA Championship history, in a week that saw Jack Nicklaus miss the cut at the PGA for only the second time in 20 years. Afterward, pros praised Burke's prized facility and quest to bring championship golf to the Alamo City. "This is a great course; I wish we played one like this every week," Chi Chi Rodriguez said.

A Moody Open

While Champions' hosting of the Ryder Cup turned out to be a beating on the course and at the cash register, the 1969 U.S. Open, which the USGA awarded to the club, turned out to be a much larger success in many ways, even crowning a home state winner. The Open was awarded to Champions during committee meetings on January 25–26, 1967, roughly a year after the PGA had announced the Ryder Cup would be played there. Respect for Burke and Demaret was huge in the golf world, and what they wanted with their prized new course usually came to pass.

One change that greatly aided the success of the Open was the cancellation of the 1969 Houston Open, then known as the Houston Champions Invitational, which meant Houston golf fans would have only one chance to see pro golf that year. The chance to see golf's best players led by Arnold Palmer, Jack Nicklaus, and defending champion Lee Trevino was always a powerful lure to draw fans in record numbers to Champions, which averaged 15,000 to 20,000 fans daily to watch the action.

Burke had now moved into the realm of Marvin Leonard and Jack Munger as single-minded men determined to bring the best of championship golf to their home state of Texas. The Ryder Cup and U.S. Open within a three-year span was proof of that, and there would be much more to come. "It wasn't a surprise we had the Open here; that's what we wanted and planned for when we opened the course," Burke said.

The Open was unique in many respects, as it was the first U.S. Open to use female scorers after winning special permission from the USGA to use them even though the national organization asked future Open sites to "make a concerted effort to dissuade the host clubs from using lady scorers." The players also complained the rough was too short, but Burke said they would make up in thickness what they lacked in length.

Teeing off in 90-degree temperatures and high humidity, Bob Murphy grabbed the first-round lead with an opening 66, one shot better than Sherman's Miller Barber. Future PGA Tour commissioner Deane Beman led after the second round by one shot over Barber and Murphy. Barber surged to a three-shot lead going into the final round with a third-round 68. "The hotter it is the better I like it," he said, but the final-round winner was the most unlikely of PGA Tour pros.

Orville Moody was a career military officer who met Lee Trevino during his stint with the Marines. After seeing Moody's game up close and personal and losing a little of his military pay to his fellow Texan, Trevino encouraged him to leave the military and go pro. He encountered Moody again when he was working at Horizon Hills in El Paso and Moody was the pinsetter for the military bowling alley at Fort Bliss. "One of the best ball strikers I ever saw," Trevino said. "Putting was the only thing that ever held him back."

On this magical Sunday at Champions, Moody, who had finally left the military a year before, was hitting the ball as well as ever and making every key putt he needed. When Barber bogeyed five of the first eight holes at Champions, Moody found himself in the lead. While the so-called good putters and veteran players faded on the back nine, Moody remained solid with several clutch par putts. When he arrived at the 18th hole, he had two putts to win the Open, his only victory on the PGA Tour. Afterward, the awards ceremony was held up for 15 minutes as Moody fielded a phone call from his former commander in chief, Richard Nixon. "I was in such a daze I don't remember everything," he told the local media. "Nixon said the victory was a great thing, not for the elite, but for the middle class." Not to mention suspect putters having a super Sunday.

Lord Byron's Tournament

The large, late-model 1960s luxury car stirred up clouds of thick dust as it sped along the North Texas countryside en route to the large Roanoke ranch. Inside the car were two of Dallas' most prominent businessmen on a golf-minded mission. Longtime newspaper executive Felix McKnight and Northwood Club cofounder W. L. Todd were going to see golf legend Byron Nelson. He and McKnight had been friends for years, and when McKnight suggested the meeting in the fall of 1967, Nelson told him he would be happy to meet in Dallas in the coming days. McKnight said that the meeting was urgent and that the men would be at Nelson's residence in 45 minutes.

Members of the Salesmanship Club, the men had come to see Nelson about affixing his highly respected name to a new tournament the club would sponsor and run. The old Dallas Open golf tournament had had a nomadic and inconsistent existence for several decades, moving to five different places in six years. Now the local leaders were sponsoring a new PGA Tour tournament at a new course, Preston Trail, and needed only the Nelson name to complete the ambitious golfing project.

The tournament would grow from those humble, dusty beginnings to one of the most successful PGA Tour events of all time, one that would raise more than 10 percent of all the charity dollars raised by Tour events nationwide the previous year, averaging $6 million to charity. The combination of the hard work and business contacts of the Dallas-based Salesmanship Club and the revered Nelson name proved marketing magic beyond anything anyone on the pro golf circuit had ever seen.

The Salesmanship Club, which raises money for youths who have gotten in trouble with the law or their parents and need a new start, had more experience with the boxing matches they had sponsored since World War II or exhibition Dallas Cowboys football games. But their part in the successful 1963 PGA Championship had made them think about using a professional golf tournament to raise money, and in Nelson they figured they had found a perfect spokesman. Typically modest, Nelson was surprised with the mid-morning visit and that they would even consider him as their namesake. "I was shocked they wanted to use my name," he said.

Nelson agreed to the name change, and the Dallas Open had been transformed into the Byron Nelson Classic. It would grow from its first tournament in 1968 at the brand-new, men-only Preston Trail Golf Club to an annual May event on the Dallas sports calendar that draws stellar fields, record crowds, and millions of dollars for charity. "You never really thought about those things back then, how long it would go or how much money we would raise," Nelson said.

To get the first Byron Nelson PGA Tour event off to a good start, Salesmanship Club officials staged a lavish kickoff party the likes of which Dallas had never seen. Former Texas governor John Connally was the master of ceremonies; a host of entertainment stars were on hand to kick off the exciting week of golf. "That was the only pretournament party my mother ever came to in all my years on the Tour. It was quite an event," Nelson said.

The first Nelson winner was Texas native Miller Barber, who caddied for Nelson at age 14 and had retained a close friendship since. The total purse was $100,000, and the amount raised for charity was almost the same. The third Nelson tournament was one of the most memorable, as Jack Nicklaus captured the first of his back-to-back wins with a dramatic playoff victory over Arnold Palmer. "Without a doubt it's the best thing that's happened to me along with my wife Peggy," Nelson said of his tournament. "There is no doubt it's kept me alive and kept my name active in the game of golf." Not to mention establishing a PGA Tour tournament heavyweight for all time.

The 1970s produced a pair of Texas golf heavyweights who combined for as long and successful an era as any duo since Nelson and fellow Texan Ben Hogan.

The 1970s
Twin Texas Towers

5 Highlights of the 1970s

★ Ben Crenshaw and Tom Kite lead Texas to back-to-back NCAA titles and tie for the 1972 individual championship.

★ Ben Hogan plays his last competitive round at the 1971 Houston Open, designs Trophy Club in 1974, and continues with the Ben Hogan club company.

★ Horseshoe Bay opens in 1974, kicking off the ongoing Hill Country golf boom.

★ The Woodlands community opens outside of Houston in 1974, attracting the Houston Open and eventually every major golf tournament in Houston.

★ The Legends of Golf begins in 1978 at Onion Creek Country Club, paving the way for the Senior Tour to start officially two years later.

The Story of the Decade: A Texas Twosome for the Ages

Greatness in Texas golf has always seemed to come in pairs, as if each individual golf dreamer needed a companion in his respective era to challenge and compete against. Hogan and Nelson, the two Fort Worth caddies, took different paths to golf stardom but were forever linked in their careers. Texas natives Burke and

Demaret partnered in golf and in building a great course, Champions, which would serve as Texas' shrine for championship golf.

Nowhere have two individual golfers been linked more directly and for a longer period of time than Austin's Ben Crenshaw and Tom Kite. Since the time Kite moved with his family from McKinney to Austin at age 12 and began to play and practice at Austin Country Club, where Crenshaw was already established, the two have been connected in one form or another. "We started playing together in junior high and high school, and it didn't take us long to get linked together," Crenshaw said. "Tom was just an outstanding player, and we always had good competition, which had to help all of us."

Same town, same teacher, same university, same NCAA titles, same success on the golf course and in off-course activities. While some have called their relationship a rivalry, the two men have never seen it that way. "A deep mutual respect," is the way Crenshaw describes it. Kite called the two friendly, not social, but with a deep respect for each other and what they have accomplished separately and together. "Ben and I had breakfast at a [PGA] tournament one morning and just talked about how much fun the course is to play and all the things we've done together," Kite said.

When Kite captured his first major title, the 1992 U.S. Open at Pebble Beach Golf Links, Crenshaw sent his friend a handwritten letter of congratulations. When Crenshaw captured his second Masters title in 1995, the same week their teacher Harvey Penick died, Kite wrote him how special his win was and how proud Penick would be of him. It was Crenshaw who introduced Kite for his induction as part of the 2004 class for the World Golf Hall of Fame.

TEXAS GOLF FACT

During the 1970s, the University of Texas and University of Houston combined to win four NCAA golf titles, two for each school. They combined for three straight from 1970 to 1972 along with two runner-up finishes by Houston and three straight NCAA individual titles by Texas' Ben Crenshaw.

Crenshaw, whose father Charlie was a three-sport athlete at Baylor University, settled in the Tarrytown section of Austin, where Ben attended Austin High School, and spent his time at the club, hanging out with his older brother Charlie and meeting Penick for the first time. Crenshaw, unlike Kite, was a feel player and a natural for the game. He said he vaguely remembers the first time his dad cut down a club and took him to Penick for his first lesson. The longtime pro at Austin Country Club put his hands on Crenshaw's grip and gently showed him the correct way to cradle the club. Naturally, Crenshaw picked it up immediately, and the often-repeated story has Penick showing his young student a shot from 75 yards out and then telling him to go putt the ball into the cup. "If you wanted it in the hole, why didn't you tell me that the first time," Crenshaw said.

He won the Texas State Junior Championship twice; captured various club, city, and state championships; and was awarded a college golf scholarship to the University of Texas. There he won three NCAA titles for coach George Hannon, who had taken over for Penick as head coach, and helped the Longhorns win a pair of national championships. "Ben was the

Tom Kite, left, Ben Crenshaw, center, and Northwood Club head pro Bob Elliott grew up together in Austin. (Photo courtesy of Bob Elliott)

poster child for people growing up with all the success they had and still keeping a level head and enjoying it," said Tinsley Penick, who succeeded his dad as head pro at Austin Country Club.

Kite, whose family moved to Austin so his dad could work at the state headquarters for the Internal Revenue Service, was far from a natural player like Crenshaw but was no less successful. Crenshaw always mixed his golf with swimming or running around with his brother and meeting girls, wearing jeans and a T-shirt and sporting wavy blond hair and a ready smile. Kite mixed his golf in with more practice, more golf, then more practice, complete with long dress pants and coke-bottle glasses. He was, according to a headline in the 100-year Austin Country Club history, "The Boy Who Made Fun Out of Work."

Both methods proved to be amazingly successful, but one thing Penick always made sure of is that neither of his star students learned from the other. For more than 40 years, Kite and Crenshaw never practiced together, and Penick never gave lessons to one while the other was present. "What applies to one of them does not apply to the other," Penick said. In fact, when the three men participated in the film version of Penick's *Little Red Book* in the early 1990s, it was the first time they had ever been together for a practice session. "Harvey will always link us together, along with our parents and Austin Country Club," Crenshaw said.

Kite, who is two years older than Crenshaw, was the first to attend the hometown University of Texas, playing for Hannon while still taking lessons from Penick. He was joined by Crenshaw a few years later, and

Harvey Penick, left, and Tom Kite are forever remembered at Austin Country Club. (Photo courtesy of Austin Country Club)

together they led Texas to 13 tournament titles, including back-to-back national team titles, the first in school history. "You don't find many like those two," Hannon said, "much less on the same team." The climax came in 1972, when Kite, the senior, and Crenshaw, the sophomore, tied for the NCAA individual title and, because there was no provision for a playoff between teammates, shared the championship. "I was happy for Tommy when he tied for the NCAA title as a senior and doubly happy because the boy he tied with was Ben Crenshaw," Penick said.

Crenshaw stayed for one more season in 1973, when he captured his third NCAA individual title, and then departed to the PGA Tour. He didn't have to wait long

to continue the success he had enjoyed as an amateur as he won his first tournament as a professional, capturing the 1973 Texas Open at Woodlake Country Club in San Antonio. He defeated Texan Orville Moody by two shots and George Archer by three with a 270 total for his historic first pro win, which is still commemorated by a plaque near the first tee at Woodlake.

Therein lies a pattern that has repeated itself for their entire careers. Whatever Kite could do, Crenshaw could do just a little bit better. Kite was named PGA Tour Rookie of the Year, but Crenshaw won his first tournament, in his home state no less, something Kite never accomplished in his entire PGA Tour career in more than 100 tries despite winning more than two dozen times and $9 million in prize money. Crenshaw won his second Masters title the week that Penick died; Kite missed the cut. Crenshaw led the biggest comeback in U.S. Ryder Cup history as captain; Kite lost as captain in one of the United States' biggest upsets. Kite was inducted into the World Golf Hall of Fame in 2004, naturally a couple of years after Crenshaw.

Kite said he accepted comparisons as people's natural measuring gauge and never let it deter him from his ultimate goal of golfing success. "There were comparisons when we were 12 and 14, and there still are today. We have a great relationship, and it has made us better. It gave us competition with each other and other players," he said. Kite achieved the ultimate on a windy Sunday afternoon at Pebble Beach in 1992 when he withstood brutal conditions and the world's best players to capture the U.S. Open title in front of his wife Christy and his dad, Tom Sr., who had flown in for the final round. "I said it never bothered me not winning a major championship, but it bugged the heck out of me," he said after his win. "It was a mixture of shock and relief to win."

After the victory, Kite was off to another corporate outing, but he had Christy deliver one special package. On Monday morning after returning from the Open, she drove to Austin Country Club, where she delivered the U.S. Open trophy to a startled Penick in the middle of a lesson, literally putting it down in his lap. It brought tears of joy from the teacher, and today the club has a huge bronze statue behind the ninth green with Penick forever giving a lesson to Kite, pointing the way to another victory.

Crenshaw's professional highlights came in waves. After the hot start, his career leveled off, in part because of health and marital problems. He rebounded for his first Masters victory in 1984, sinking a 60-foot putt on the 10th hole with his trademark "Little Ben" putter en route to his first major victory. His second Masters title 11 years later was one that Masters fans and followers will still be talking about for decades to come. Shaken by the death of his longtime teacher, who had given Crenshaw one final lesson from his deathbed a week earlier, Crenshaw was an emotional wreck. He had flown back to Austin with Kite to bury his mentor and then returned for the first round without even thinking of practicing or playing. Without a victory for more than a year, little was expected of Crenshaw, but working with his longtime Augusta caddy Carl Jackson and what he called a 15th club in his bag, Harvey Penick, he more than lived up to his headline in the Austin Country Club's 100th anniversary book, "The Boy Who Made Magic."

Somehow Crenshaw summoned the strength to win his second Masters title in 1995, collapsing in tears on the 18th green as the final putt went in the hole. "I can't explain it; it was just fate and Harvey," he said after his win. And then there was his historic Ryder Cup rally two years later, when Crenshaw issued the epic Saturday night quote with his team facing a record deficit: "I'm a big believer in fate and I've got a good feeling about this," his finger waggling to the assembled press corps. Crenshaw remains one of golf's most loved and inspirational figures.

Kite and Crenshaw currently pursue the Champions Tour schedule for the over-50 set, and both have been successful off the course as well. Crenshaw and his design associate Bill Coore have designed some of the best and most acclaimed courses in the country, including Barton

Creek Cliffside and Austin Golf Club in Austin; Talking Stick in Scottsdale, Arizona; Sand Hills in Nebraska; Kapalua Plantation in Hawaii; and the newest course at Bandon Dunes in Oregon. Kite has designed some top courses as well, such as Comanche Trace in Kerrville.

Both still live in Austin, and both are active in the community, their church, and their university. Both still credit their families and Penick for guiding their career to greatness, and both still embrace each other and their twin billing, which has made them a Texas twosome for the ages. "Harvey taught us to learn from every player, but not be awestruck," Kite said. "I think we've done a pretty good job." Any watchers of Texas golf twosome would certainly agree.

Out-of-This-World Texas Golf

With Texas golf and golfers impacting almost every state in the country and several more countries overseas, the only remaining frontier was outer space, and naturally Lone Star golf dreamers paved the way in a heavenly fashion. Astronaut Alan Shepard was doing his final training for an Apollo mission to the moon, which blasted into space in February 1971. Training at the NASA headquarters in Houston one day, Shepard was introduced to entertainer Bob Hope, who was taking a tour of the facility and wanted to do a simulated space walk in the zero-gravity chamber. While getting suited up for his space walk, Hope grabbed his trademark golf club and began swinging it as he floated in the outer-space chamber.

That was all the inspiration Shepard, a golfer himself, needed for his upcoming space mission. He had a NASA employee call River Oaks head pro Jack Hardin

and ask if fashioning a golf club for Shepard to hit a shot while he was on the moon would be feasible. Shepard had played at River Oaks during his training and figured that if anybody could pull off the feat, it would be Hardin and his staff. When he measured the club, Hardin found that his 6-iron was approximately the same length as the lunar utility tool used to grab rock samples and promptly turned his Wilson Dyna-Power 6-iron into one of the most famous clubs of all time.

Because of the bulky suit needed to walk on the moon, Shepard found he could swing with only one arm to hit the ball. During his practice sessions in Houston, he hit the ball only 60 to 75 yards. With Hardin's encouragement and club, along with three Surlyn golf balls with Jack Hardin's name stamped on the side, Shepard blasted off and waited for the right moment to try out the Texas golf experiment.

That moment came at 4 A.M., Texas time, February 6, 1971, when Shepard ambled down the steps of the lunar module and calmly announced he was going to "try a sand shot." With little hesitation, he dropped Hardin's three balls to the dusty surface and promptly took a mighty one-handed swing. Amazingly, an earthbound chili-dip shot that would have gone only 30 yards in gravity-bound Texas soared majestically into the weightless outer-space atmosphere. His first shot traveled 180 yards, with the next going nearly 600 yards before sinking back to the moon's surface. "Looks like a slice to me" was the report from Houston's Mission Control. "It goes for miles and miles" was Shepard's reply. With the out-of-this-world conditions, the ball stayed aloft for nearly 20 seconds, almost six times as lengthy as Shepard's longest drives in Houston.

When the miles-high golfer finally landed back on earth a few days later, the first and so far only golf shot ever hit on the moon was the talk of the world's press and the River Oaks 19th hole. Hardin's club was promptly whisked to the United States Golf Association Museum in Far Hills, New Jersey, where it sits today in honor with his three golf balls still resting somewhere on the moon's surface. Hardin left River Oaks a year later, but not before helping take Texas golf to a place no golfer had ever gone before.

West Texas Master

Charlie Coody was one of the many talented players who grew up in a small West Texas town, excelling in the Bar-B-Que circuit and looking for his next opportunity to play against his friends, maybe earning a little extra spending money or living out another great golf adventure. But his career path from casual golfer to future golf master was first turned around in 1952, when Ben Hogan came to his tiny hometown of Samford for an exhibition. "I knew of Ben Hogan to an extent, because of reading in the newspaper and hearing some on the radio, but we didn't have a TV back then so I had never seen him. It was very impressive," he said.

The next bend in Coody's championship golfing road came when his uncle took him to Fort Worth to see the 1952 Colonial tournament, also won by Hogan. "That really whetted my appetite for golf," Coody said. He wound up at Texas Christian University, playing both football and golf but launching his pro golf career when he graduated from the university with a degree in business in 1963. He captured his first tournament a year later at the Dallas Invitational,

edging Jerry Edwards by a single shot at Oak Cliff Country Club.

Coody's final and most dramatic career changer came just seven years later at the 1971 Masters, when the stocky West Texas farm boy who had been influenced by Hogan birdied two of the last three holes at Augusta National to defeat Jack Nicklaus and Johnny Miller by a single stroke for the Masters title. "I was in a state of shock when I won, I still couldn't believe it," Coody said. He was the first Texan since Jack Burke Jr. to capture the coveted green jacket. He also won the World Series of Golf that same year, capturing a career best of $94,000 in prize money. He never left his humble, small-town West Texas roots, ordering up thick Texas T-bone steaks for the Masters Champions Dinner when he returned to defend his title in 1972.

After turning 50, Coody won five times on the Champions Tour along with the three Legends of Golf titles. He now owns and operates the Diamondback Golf Club in Abilene, just 40 miles from where he grew up. "When I grew up it was head-to-head combat, in the wind, the cold, and the heat. It turned out to be a good proving ground." Indeed it did for the West Texas master who let his small-town Texas roots take him all the way to Augusta National and a Masters title.

Hogan's Final Stand and New Venture

After all the heroic times Ben Hogan had enjoyed in his native state, the end for him in competitive golf also came in Texas at the 1971 Houston Open. Then the tournament was being held at Champions Golf Club, one of Hogan's favorite courses, where he was good friends with co-owners Jack Burke Jr. and Jimmy

Demaret. They made sure to take special care of Hogan, renting a house for him across the street from the club, reserving him a special table for dinner each night, and attending to any personal needs.

At age 58 and recovering from another surgery on his shoulder, a continuing result of his bus accident, even the indomitable Hogan had begun to wear down. There were whispers about when he would retire. Some said it would be after the 1967 Ryder Cup at Champions, where Hogan served as the U.S. team captain; others thought it would be the 1967 Masters after he fired a 30 on the back nine at Augusta National, but he continued on.

One of the reasons Hogan continued to play was that, unlike Nelson and his other golfing equals, Hogan had no passionate outside interests, so intense had been his gaze on championship golf competition. It was already a sad time for Hogan, as his great friend and Texas golf visionary Marvin Leonard had passed in 1970 after crafting two additional North Texas courses, Starr Hollow and Shady Oaks, where Hogan still played and practiced when he could.

So there Hogan was on the front nine at Champions on another typically hot and humid Houston May afternoon. After three consecutive pars to begin his round, Hogan made a nine on the rugged par-3 fourth hole when he sent three tee shots into the brushy ravine that guarded the green. He further injured his gimpy knee climbing down to look for his ball and walked with a pronounced limp, making the turn at eight-over-par 44.

After another bogey, Hogan knew the end for his competitive career had finally arrived. He stumbled so badly coming off the 11th tee that he nearly fell and,

unable to continue on foot, bid farewell to his playing partners, Texans Charles Coody and Dick Lotz. A cart carried him into the clubhouse. "As long as I've been playing golf, I know anything can happen," he told the news media after his round, but for Hogan he would never tee up in competition again.

Eventually, he found other ways to fill his time. He engaged in his one and only golf course design in 1972, not far from his Fort Worth home at the Trophy Club in Roanoke between Dallas and Fort Worth. Hogan teamed with veteran Florida golf course architect Joe Lee to fashion the largely nondescript piece of land into a championship test of golf. Not surprisingly, Hogan was involved in every aspect of the design of the Trophy Club layout, and not surprisingly the original 18-hole tract matched his golfing personality. "It's pretty much what you'd expect a Hogan course to be," Byron Nelson said in a *Private Clubs* magazine review: "Long and hard." From the back tees, the Hogan–Lee design measured 6,953 yards at par 72.

Lee, who recently passed away, once said Hogan took personal delight in walking every proposed hole and personally marking each tree slated for removal. His aching knees, which had ultimately contributed to his retirement, never slowed him down on his daily rounds with Lee. "Ben showed a flexibility in his mind about golf," Lee once said. "We looked at it from the viewpoint of a cross-section of golfers."

Hogan's work ethic, mind, and golf ability were still sharp, as he personally tested every hole, dropping balls in the dirt, and teeing off in khaki pants and snakeskin boots to see how the shots would react from different lies. "He walked every hole and climbed every fence. His legs had to be hurting like mad, but he never complained," Lee said. One time, Lee said Hogan's legs were so cramped up after a visit that he had to lift them over a steering wheel to get him back in the car.

When the course finally opened in 1974, the results were not at all what the championship-minded Hogan was used to seeing. It attracted little publicity nationwide, and one *Golf Today* survey had it ranked 94th out of the top 100 Texas courses, results that cut the perfectionist Hogan to the core. "With Hogan it had to be a certain way or he wasn't going to do it," said all-time LPGA winner Kathy Whitworth, who represented the Trophy Club in the 1970s. "He was real disappointed it wasn't more highly regarded, and that's why I heard he tried to take his name off the course."

Hogan's name is still associated with the Trophy Club course, but he was never involved in another design project. He turned his attention to a much more successful venture, the Ben Hogan club company with headquarters in Fort Worth. It gained a reputation for a traditional club made for low-handicap golfers. The company has endured for the past 50 years, and Hogan spent the last years of his life there. He still made his daily trips to Shady Oaks, where he shot a 64 on his 64th birthday and still had lunch at the same window-side table every day, watching over the sport he had dominated for so long.

Hill Country Heaven

Harvey Penick and John Bredemus had helped make Austin and San Antonio South Texas golf capitals, but in the early 1970s Norman and Wayne Hurd had a dream for thousands of rolling, tree-covered acres just west of Austin as the site of the next great Texas golf boom. They scouted land around scenic Lake LBJ as the site of the first golf resort in Texas' Hill Country region.

The cousins not only dreamed the project would make sense and bring golf to a new area but also put their money where their mouths were by plunking down $55,000 to purchase 2,100 acres of land, a former cattle ranch near Marble Falls, 50 miles west of Austin. Befitting the Texas-sized vision of the Hurds, they imagined a huge resort hotel complete with multiple golf courses; boating, swimming, tennis, and conference facilities; and even a 6,000-foot landing strip on property for their guests to fly in their own private planes. In the early 1970s, this was all fairly revolutionary stuff, but the naysayers who said nobody was interested in heading off to the Hill Country to play golf would not deter the Hurds.

To design their first course, they called in legendary architect Robert Trent Jones Sr., who had never been to this part of Texas but landed on their private airstrip and immediately pronounced himself impressed with the scenic surroundings. His first course opened in 1974 and was called Slickrock because of the massive waterfall that bisected one of the fairways. The huge Horseshoe Bay Resort was an immediate success because of the beautiful views, rugged terrain, and inviting waters, not to mention Jones's spectacular course complete with bent-grass greens.

All pronounced themselves pleased with the first course and resort except for one loudmouth Horseshoe Bay member who boasted after the first member tournament at Slickrock that the Jones course really wasn't that tough and that he didn't consider himself very challenged. Wayne Hurd overheard the conversation and was determined to call Jones back for a second course and ordered him to hold nothing back in the design toolbox.

The result was the Ramrock course, a 6,956-yard, par-71 beast, where Jones used nearly every trick and treat of the architectural trade to toughen his layout, including his signature railroad ties, narrow fairways, small greens, hidden shots, and water and sand snaking its way across the property. Ramrock is usually ranked among the toughest courses in the state—and for good reason, as attested by anyone who has ever attempted to play there with less than their best game.

The third course at Horseshoe Bay, also designed by Jones, was Applerock, taken from some of the highest and most scenic land on the property and opened in 1986. Since then, the resort just keeps getting better with an 18-hole grass putting course, indoor and outdoor tennis courts, a new luxury hotel, and plans for a fourth golf course on the property. "The courses have many beautiful vistas and views of Lake LBJ," said former director of golf Byron Cook. "It has remained a picturesque course since it opened."

Like many other Texas golf dreamers before them, the Hurds' grand vision was validated, as the Horseshoe Bay/Hill Country area is now home to several golf resorts, all featuring great golf, great views, and great enjoyment. But none of them has yet surpassed the birthplace of the boom.

Texas' Golfsmith

All Carl Paul wanted to do was make his own set of clubs from golf club parts without going to what he called "The Big 3": Wilson, Spalding, and MacGregor. Starting in the basement of his New Jersey home in

1967, Paul began to assemble clubs from components and quickly discovered there was a market for his services. First neighbors and friends begged him to help them with a custom set of clubs, then a small ad in a local newspaper brought in a flood of business.

By the 1970s, Paul's literally homegrown golf club component business, Golfsmith, was bursting at the seams, and an expansion was desperately needed. Blessed with a background as an engineer, Paul did most of the work himself but in 1972 brought in his brother Frank to help with some of the marketing and expansion duties. The first decision was relocation and the place the Paul families chose was Austin, fairly close to their original hometown of Bishop. "Austin was a good distribution point for the Sunbelt," Carl Paul said.

In the few short years since they began, the Pauls had managed to invent a niche in the golf club business that did not exist a decade earlier. Before Golfsmith came along, average golfers did not have the opportunity, resources, or materials to assemble their own set of custom clubs. The choice was either buy from the Big Three or hope to find a talented club maker somewhere with the time and talent to build a set of new clubs, more often than not a futile search. "We were able to get all the parts together and get people in the club-making business," Carl Paul said. "A lot of people saw they could make their own clubs and not have something mass produced."

Having let the regular golfer in on the golf club-making science, the Pauls, who operated Golfsmith from a small windowless building on Interstate 35 in Austin, were determined to tell as many people as possible. They began to host the Annual Golf Clubmakers

Association Conference in Austin, drawing as many as 500 people from around the world to learn how to build their own clubs.

Paul estimated there are 100,000 golf club makers around the world, thousands of whom have been trained personally by the Golfsmith staff. "Through marketing they create value," Paul said of the mass-produced competitors. "We've cut out the middleman and are selling directly to the golfer." Golfsmith published a huge catalog, shipping worldwide and listing the club components for sale and how they could be obtained for in-home work along with detailed instructions on how to construct the clubs.

One national golf magazine once proclaimed, "The golf club component industry is reshaping the golf club industry," and the sales off the initial $300 investment from the Pauls' New Jersey basement were astounding. By the early 1990s, Golfsmith was shipping two million golf clubheads each year, and by the end of the decade they had moved into a lavish 330,000-square-foot headquarters less than a mile from their original building. Sales were reaching $100 million annually, and a new 30,000-square-foot superstore was opened in Austin.

Along the way, the Pauls opened the Harvey Penick Golf Academy, featuring the golf legend himself coming in for weekly talks along with a golf store that carried all types of finished and component golf clubs and other golf-related items. In 1995, the decision was made to expand the superstore concept nationwide with 24 stores in 12 states, along with the United Kingdom and Canada.

Not bad for somebody who just wanted to assemble his own clubs and run his own small business. "I was in the business 10 years before I had my first competitor; now there must be 100 people doing the same thing," Paul said. Just another way a Texas visionary, temporarily detoured in New Jersey, was able to give power to the people in a whole new area.

The Woodlands Is Born

George Mitchell had already created a successful home-building business in Houston before he set his eyes on Montgomery County, but his success in this now booming minicity, The Woodlands, surpassed anything Mitchell had conceived before or since. He initially set up his own government structure and announced lavish plans that would include golf, resort lodging, and houses for ultimately 100,000 people. Yet when he began the project in 1974, all he had was a two-lane gravel road into a massive wooden forest.

Like Leonard and Burke before him, Mitchell proved to be a true visionary who was able to see the future when nothing existed. "I remember the two-lane gravel road running all the way down where Woodlands Parkway exists now," said longtime Woodlands golf teacher and professional Mark Steinbauer. The Mitchell vision was for every part of The Woodlands to be built around a separate village. Each village would have its own shopping center, houses, and, most important, golf course.

Grogan's Village opened in 1974 and included the first 36 holes of golf in The Woodlands, then known as the Woodlands Country Club, made up of the North and South Course. The Houston Golf Association was impressed enough with Mitchell's first village and overall vision that they signed a 10-year contract to move

The vision of Houston's George Mitchell helped build The Woodlands golf community. (Photo courtesy of The Woodlands Resort)

the Houston Open to The Woodlands. The annual PGA Tour event had had a nomadic existence since beginning in 1946, and this was its longest site contract. Of course, there was no course at the time the contact was signed, but such was the faith in Mitchell's vision and track record.

The Woodlands Resort and Conference Center opened in October 1974 as the first commercial building in the area and served as the perfect headquarters for the Houston Open. Another factor important to early success was Mitchell's hiring of the colorful Doug Sanders as the first director of golf and Mancil Davis, better known as the King of Aces, as his assistant. "What we needed was instant recognition," Sanders said of The Woodlands. "We needed a major tourna-

ment, like the Houston Open." With the PGA Tour's best players coming to new territory, showing them a good time was up to people like Mitchell, Sanders, and Davis, and the mission was accomplished.

Sanders's network of contacts both in and out of the golf world attracted plenty of early attention for the Houston Open and The Woodlands. "Sanders had the flash to attract celebrities and was the perfect mix to promote the facility," said Steinbauer. "They got the Houston Open, the *Golf Digest* intercollegiate, the section office; one by one every major golf event came to The Woodlands. The Woodlands meant golf." The stadium course was opened in 1985 and proved to be the dramatic background for two decades of Houston Opens. Villages opened all over The Woodlands, now boasting more than 100 holes of golf with courses by Arnold Palmer, Gary Player, Jack Nicklaus, and Tom Fazio—all from a visionary and a two-lane gravel road that led to the golf capital of Houston.

Designated Colonial

With a highly successful U.S. Open to its credit along with a very popular annual PGA Tour event, the classic Colonial course in Fort Worth had always proved to be an inviting venue to PGA Tour players and officials. So in the mid-1970s, the PGA Tour executive committee came to the club membership with a proposal. They were attempting to get a designated tournament off the ground, a highly prestigious event that all top PGA Tour players would be required to attend and that would receive extra attention because of its increased purse and prestige. Today, the event is known as the Players Championship, but its birthplace was in Texas.

While Colonial had been known for its small, select fields chosen by the local tournament committee, PGA Tour officials presented Colonial with the idea they could promote all the name players who would be making the trip to Fort Worth for the prestigious designated tournament. CBS-TV made its first appearance in 1974 to broadcast the event in a relationship that continues to this day. The assurance of players like Jack Nicklaus, Arnold Palmer, Johnny Miller, and Lee Trevino in Fort Worth generated record crowds for Colonial and new highs in sponsorship sales.

In 1975, the designated tournament was changed to the Tournament Players Championship, and once again the PGA turned to Colonial to host the event. The new name also necessitated a new date, if only for one year, in mid-August, but the play at Colonial was hotter than the weather, and huge crowds came out to see Al Geiberger set new tournament records for his three-shot win over Dave Stockton.

After one more year on the road, the Tournament Players Championship moved to its new home at the TPC-Sawgrass course with the famous Pete Dye-designed island green, but a plaque on Colonial's Wall of Champions signifies Colonial's role in birthing the Players Championship.

The King of Aces

For most people, making a hole in one, an ace, is a lifelong if mostly fruitless dream. The odds are better of getting struck by lightning on the course than making an ace, but Houston's Mancil Davis has made a career out of it—not lightning but aces. Known as the King of Aces, Davis has collected 50 aces on the golf course. Starting at age 11, Davis has proven a unique knack for getting the ball in the hole with one swing of the club. "Two things I'm always doing: I'm aiming at the hole and never use a tee," he said. "I may be having a bad day, but when I get to a par 3, I'm thinking about a hole in one."

With more than four dozen to Davis's credit, that's a lot of thinking. Among his most amazing statistics are at least one hole in one every year from 1967 to 1987. He made three within five days in 1967, aced the same hole five times at Odessa Country Club, and aced all four par 3s at the Trophy Club. His longest ace was 379 yards on a par 4, and his shortest was 124 yards. He has made a hole in one with every club in his bag except a putter, sand wedge, or pitching wedge and has a career total of 8,519 in yards covered for his aces.

Not only is he an expert with aces, but he's made the even rarer double eagle 10 times, another world record. Davis says he doesn't consider himself especially lucky, just somebody who thinks like a King and is ready to record another "1" when he steps to the tee.

East Texas Crown

Arthur Temple was a highly successful timber tycoon, harvesting much of the rich East Texas forest to provide jobs and income for himself and thousands of people in the area. Being a proud Texan, he got tired of coming home from another business meeting on the East Coast where he played a customer's great golf course with nothing to offer in return.

Temple's lumber companies are located around Lufkin in East Texas, about an hour north of Houston, in the middle of dense forests with few people. That didn't stop Temple from wanting a spotlight golf course that he could show off to his friends and customers when they came into town.

Thankfully, he had plenty of land, which was virgin territory for East Texas golf, and he engaged Houston architect Robert von Hagge and partner Bruce Devlin to do their first joint design on his property he titled Crown Colony. "Mr. Temple wanted a place for himself and his friends, and he found the perfect piece of land to work with," longtime pro Bob Diamond said. "It

was acreage dedicated to golf because it was all Mr. Temple's land to start with."

Construction began in 1977, with nine holes done by 1978 and a full 18 finished by 1979. "The cost was between $800,000 and $1 million to build it, which is less than a sprinkler system is now," Diamond said. The results were universally praised for their beautiful location and top condition. Crown Colony has been ranked as high as number one among all the courses in the state. "We're in a pretty remote area, but people in Dallas and Houston still seek us out to play," Diamond said.

In its two-decade history, Crown Colony has hosted two Texas State Amateur tournaments, two Southern Amateurs, and one Trans-Mississippi national amateur event, all a testament to people going off the beaten golf path to find Temple's genius for a course he could call his own.

The Texas Legends

Sometimes an idea is so good, so on the cutting edge, and so right with the times that it only has to be set in motion; step away, and let it pick up momentum on its own. In the most simple of terms, that's exactly what happened with the Legends of Golf and the Senior PGA Tour. Launched in 1978 at Demaret's new Onion Creek Country Club in Austin, the tournament matched golfers 50 and over in a two-man competition, providing the basis for the Senior, now Champions, Tour, and a second lease on golfing life. "I'm still amazed by how well it's worked out," said original Senior Tour star Don January. "When we started, a lot of the guys just wanted an excuse to get out of the house, and now we're playing for millions."

The Onion Creek course, located in far South Austin, was a Demaret design, relatively short but tricky, with tight fairways and the Onion Creek coming into play on nearly half the holes. Demaret had originally started piecing together the land in the late 1960s but didn't actually have the grand opening until June 1974. He used a mixture of his show-biz and sports connections for a lavish opening tournament that included Jack Burke, Mickey Mantle, University of Texas coach Darrell Royal, and singers Tennessee Ernie Ford and Willie Nelson in one fivesome. Burke stole the show with an ace on the par-3 second hole. That got Demaret to return to an idea he had mulled over for years. Could former golf stars like Burke and many others still compete in a format that would be of interest to the public?

He found a willing ally in former *Shell's Wonderful World of Golf* producer Fred Raphael. Having filmed former legends all over the world for the golf travelogue, Raphael was convinced they still had plenty of skill and charisma for the golfing public. He was able to sell the idea to NBC-TV for the first two-man Legends tournament held at Onion Creek in the spring of 1978.

The 11 50-and-over two-man teams played for a $100,000 first-place purse, the largest prize at the time of any golfing tour. The first-year winners were Sam Snead and Gardner Dickinson. The all-time leading winner on the PGA Tour, Snead, made three birdies on the final three holes to lift his team to victory. The crowds were large at Onion Creek, and the television ratings were decent, but like the Texas Open down the road in San Antonio, the second tournament ensured the Legends' future.

The 1979 tournament spilled into sudden death with Julius Boros and Roberto de Vicenzo defeating Tommy Bolt and Art Wall on the sixth extra hole after a display of brilliant golf by both teams. The extended playoff pushed the golf into prime time, and the ratings were huge, almost as large as professional baseball and football in some markets. "When Jimmy and Fred came up with the idea for the senior reunion, they had the perfect place, the course Jimmy built at Onion Creek," said former Onion Creek pro Brent Buckman. "It was a natural."

So was the PGA Tour's interest in a full-time Senior Tour, which they formalized in 1980. The first year started with two tournaments, then five the next, and now the Champions Tour has more than 30 events with players competing for millions in prize money, more than most players ever made playing the regular Tour. "In the early days, we went to the pro-am parties and mingled with the amateur partners, because that's what was keeping us afloat and out of the house," January said.

Arnold Palmer turned 50 in 1980, and his tremendous popularity helped spur the growth of the Senior Tour in Austin, in San Antonio, beginning in 1984, and nationwide. The Legends stayed at Onion Creek until 1990 before moving over to Barton Creek in Austin, but Demaret's quaint and challenging design will live on as the birthplace of the Senior Tour.

The 1980s brought a pair of Texas-born Senior Tour superstars who dominated in the early years of the Tour and one Texas golfer who dominated for a single season as few ever have.

The 1980s
Brilliant Years and Lasting Memories

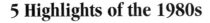

5 Highlights of the 1980s

★ Dallas' Don January and Sherman's Miller Barber dominate the early days of the Senior PGA Tour, 1980 to 1984.

★ LPGA moves its headquarters from New York to Sugar Land, 1982 to 1989.

★ Carrollton's Scott Verplank wins the 1984 Western Open as an amateur, the first amateur to win a PGA Tour event in 29 years.

★ Billy Ray Brown wins the NCAA title as a freshman and helps lead the Houston Cougars to their 14th, 15th, and 16th and final NCAA golf championship in 1982, 1984, and 1985.

★ The Dominion opens in San Antonio in 1984 with the state's most elaborate clubhouse, and Barton Creek opens in Austin in 1986 as the state's newest premier golf resort.

Story of the Decade:
One Singularly Brilliant Year

Long ago, Ralph Guldahl set the Texas standard for a brief but brilliant career that inexplicably quickly faded away. For a single year of Lone Star brilliance seldom seen before or since, few could top the 1981 season of Bill Rogers. For one solitary, magical 12-month period, nobody in the world played better professional golf than William Charles Rogers. Then gradually, often painfully, he sank from the golf spotlight before voluntarily exiling himself for more than a decade before emerging stronger and happier in the game he still loves.

The Waco native who moved to Texarkana at an early age earned all-America honors at the University of Houston before turning pro for the 1975 season, steadily improving until he won the 1978 Bob Hope Desert Classic. Rogers, known as "Panther" for his quiet but intense manner and flashing eyes on the course, had given some indication of his impending burst onto the world golfing stage for those paying attention. In April, he captured the Hilton Head Sea Pines PGA Tour event; then, as the summer heated up, so did Rogers. "Back then, I used to think I could shrink the course with my irons," Rogers said. "He was a better putter than given credit for, and could hit his irons very, very straight," said fellow competitor Lanny Wadkins.

That summer, he broke through to capture the British Open at Royal St. George's in England, defeating Bernhard Langer by four strokes for his first major championship, and three weeks later won the World Series of Golf at Firestone Country Club and its 10-year exemption. He followed that with a home-state win at

the Texas Open in San Antonio at Oak Hills Country Club the following month. But Rogers was still not finished, adding international victories in Australia, New Zealand, and Japan before the year was out.

Not since Byron Nelson captured 11 straight wins in 1945 and 18 total in the season had a Texan been as dominant in a single season. Rogers won slightly more than $365,000 in his incredible year, a multimillion-dollar haul if figured in today's dollars.

His home course, Northridge Country Club in Texarkana, flew the Union Jack from the top of its flagpole when Rogers was in town, much like the Queen being in residence. There were Hall of Honor tributes, Bill Rogers Day celebrations, and parties galore. The problem for the lanky, likable Texan was that after the 1981 season, there was not a year even remotely similar and, after a win in the 1983 USF&G Classic in New Orleans, very few good times at all.

College roommate Bruce Lietzke, Rogers's closest friend on the PGA Tour, was a firsthand witness to the bitter aftermath of his friend's singular season. "If you're going to do it right, after you win seven times in one year, then you have to defend seven times," he said. "I don't know if he ever thought of himself as a world class player after 1981. He didn't have time to

Left: After his brilliant 1981 season, there were few happy on-course times for Bill Rogers, behind the steering wheel, shown with good friends Bruce Lietzke, left, and Ben Crenshaw, second from left. (Photo courtesy of Bruce Lietzke)
Right: Bill Rogers. (Photo courtesy of Beth Rogers)

rest in the off-season, got tired and burned out, and his confidence was shot."

Rogers continued to play, seeking to fulfill his seeming destiny as Texas' next great pro player. "After 1981, they were writing I was the 'Next' player. I loved reading that, but that's not what happened." The longer he played, the worse it got for Rogers, who was increasingly pulled toward home by the birth of his two kids in 1983 and 1986. "My career was always going up just like this," Rogers motions with his hand

on a steadily upward plane. "And then after 1983, it went just like this," he continues with a steady downward motion.

Then, the self-described perfectionist who beat himself up mentally on the golf course and admittedly could bring his sour moods home, discovered something even worse than not having success on the golf course: loathing the very sport he had played since age nine. "The low point for me came in 1986 to 1988 where my most vivid thought was I would rather be anywhere else but on the golf course. I'd be walking down the fairways, and the demons would come, and I'd think I'd rather be tarring roofs or flipping hamburgers or anything than doing this."

The end for Texas' next great star came early in the second round of the 1988 Texas Open as Rogers walked off the third green in disgust heading for the clubhouse and leaving professional golf as far behind as possible. It was another dissatisfying hole in another dissatisfying season in what had become a very dissatisfying professional golf career, and Rogers was finally finished. "I just threw my hands up and said I had had enough," Rogers recounts. "Boy, that was a low point."

His brother Rick, the pro at Northridge Country Club, was caddying for him that awful day and said the memory is still vivid. "Anybody who knows Bill knows quitting in the middle of the round was so out of character for him," Rick Rogers said. "He's never brought it up, and I haven't either, but I think he was just so embarrassed by the way he was playing out there and he felt he was cheating the people who had paid money to come see him compete."

More than a decade later, Rogers made a brief return to the Champions Tour for the 2003 season, and he currently plays a handful of tournaments a year while serving as part owner and director of golf at Briggs Ranch Golf Club in San Antonio. Few who witnessed Rogers's play in the early 1980s would ever have thought his career would be anything but a steady upward path.

Growing up at Northridge Country Club under the watchful eye of longtime pro Jerry Robinson, Rogers was always near the top of junior golfers in Northeast Texas, winning several amateur events and

playing in the Texas State Junior Championship at Brackenridge Park. One day, he received a call from legendary golf coach Dave Williams at the University of Houston asking him to come play for the Cougars. "He gave me a chance to achieve my goals. You might not have thought his plan was the fairest, but he had a plan for everything," Rogers said.

He met up with Lietzke, a Beaumont native, at Houston, where they became roommates and friends. Both excelled on the college scene. Rogers won the 1972 Southern Amateur and played in the 1973 Walker Cup matches against Great Britain while earning two-time all-America honors at the University of Houston. Back home, a group of local businessmen began taking up a collection to help fund what promised to be another can't-miss PGA Tour career.

Rogers appeared to validate their faith by making steady progress after turning pro in 1974 and capturing his first Tour victory in Palm Springs at the Hope tournament in 1978 by two shots over Jerry McGee. "My career is not one season," Rogers said. "I started as a first-team all-American at Houston and won and won. I think 1979 was probably my best year; then in 1981, I won seven times around the world." He had 11 top-10 finishes in 1979, nine in 1980, and 10 more in 1981, when he was named to the Ryder Cup team and was PGA Tour Player of the Year.

His breakout season seemed to prove what Rogers's fans, fellow competitors, and golf writers had long been saying. He truly was the next great Texas golfer, ready to join the ranks of the many Lone Stars who had come before him.

Rogers started his record season on fire with back-to-back top-seven finishes at Tucson and the Bob Hope, losing to his good friend Lietzke. Strangely for the steady Rogers, he then missed the 36-hole cut in five of the next six weeks. But his win at Hilton Head snapped him back into early season form, and he followed with a tie for seventh at Greensboro and a fourth-place finish at the Mony Tournament of Champions. "I had as much talent as the next guy in my generation playing, and I achieved more than I ever thought possible so it's very gratifying," Rogers said. "Sometimes I think I used to do this as well as anybody out here."

He finished tied for second with George Burns at the 1981 U.S. Open at Merion, three shots behind Dallas resident David Graham, and used that momentum as he headed overseas to the British Open at Royal St. George's, a player clearly at the top of his game. Rounds of 71, 67, and 69 at the Open Championship left Rogers with a five-shot lead headed into the final day, and, despite some early fourth-round struggles, he cruised to an easy win. "I remember there was a train crossing to get to the course, and I had a dream one night I was stuck behind this long train, never able to get to the course," he said. But that would have been about the only thing that could have kept him from his Open victory. "Bursting through the crowds onto the 18th fairway is still the most vivid memory for me," he recalled years later.

Rogers defeated Tom Kite by a shot to win the World Series of Golf and its then-record $100,000 first prize, then fired a final-round 63 at the Texas Open and birdied the first playoff hole to defeat Ben Crenshaw for the victory. He went overseas and picked up three more wins, seeming to accept another winner's check or trophy every time he teed up. "It was an incredible season," Rogers stated the obvious.

The reasons he never came close to repeating that magical year have been, like the sudden Guldahl career fade, studied, discussed, and written about for years. Rogers said the bottom line came down to poor post-season planning and ultimate lack of desire. "I loved reading I was the 'Next' but I was a bad time manager, and I chased every opportunity. There wasn't a deal I didn't jump on."

After the brief blip following the New Orleans win in 1983, each succeeding season seemed to get sadder and lonelier. "I don't think it's unfair being labeled a burnout victim; that's what I was," Rogers admits. "I burned it at both ends; that was part of the equation, my family and the loss of desire was the other part." His wife Beth was an eyewitness to the good and bad of Rogers's career and agreed with her husband's assessment. "Of course, Bill burned out. It broke my heart to see it."

He ended his full-time career following the 1988 season. "It was easy, really. After it quit hurting to play bad, it was time to go home." Rogers then did something he said no self-respecting PGA Tour pro, much less a major championship winner, would ever do. He applied for a job as a club professional, dusting off his college typewriter to type out his résumé for the head pro's job at San Antonio Country Club in his newly adopted hometown.

The decade-plus that Rogers spent folding shirts in the San Antonio Country Club pro shop, arranging member–guest tournaments, and giving lessons to juniors proved to be hugely therapeutic. "I think that's well put, that it helped me in my healing and helped overcome some scarring," Rogers said. "It came along at exactly the right time, and it was a good thing for me.

I know while I was on Tour the one thing you never wanted was to be a golf pro, but the scarring was pretty deep, and I wanted to get as far away from competitive golf as possible." He scattered his pro golf trophies so far apart that even his family has a hard time remembering where they are today, but he found peace, freedom, and a new golfing life as an anonymous club pro.

In 1999, U.S. captain Crenshaw asked Rogers and Lietzke to serve as his assistants for the Ryder Cup team, and the thrilling American comeback win helped reignite Rogers's passion for competitive golf. Qualifying as a past Tour champion, he gained a full exemption for the first year of the Champions Tour after turning 50. He met with decidedly mixed results, never winning or coming especially close, but the new Rogers had learned to handle the highs and the lows better than the younger Panther ever could. "I've certainly got one of the most unique stories," Rogers said. "Some people never get started; some people never get to the top. I've been at the very top, been to the very bottom and every station in-between."

Not to mention one unforgettable year to start the 1980s that ranks with the best in Texas golf history.

LPGA Moves to Texas

Texans have made up a good portion of the early stars of the LPGA, and for a majority of the 1980s, the LPGA headquarters was located in the Houston suburb of Sugar Land. The organization, which had evolved from a female barnstorming tour to a premier professional league, was looking for ways to save money for its newly established pension fund. Original LPGA commissioner Ray Volpe calculated the organization could save $2 million by moving from New York City to a more central location.

Also part of the equation was a chance to build a golf course dedicated to the LPGA's needs and future tournaments along with a permanent Hall of Fame and a place to conduct a teaching school, a qualifying tournament, and executive leadership meetings. Clearly, the LPGA was moving away from its freewheeling beginnings to a more stable business model. "We had a lot of good times and a lot of good stories when we started," said LPGA founder and Texas resident Marilyn Smith. "It was some fun times."

Volpe entertained bids from cities nationwide for the LPGA headquarters, but it was Texas developer/dreamer Gerald Hines, who headed Sugar Land Properties in 1982, who came up with the best deal for the female golfers' organization. John Laupheimer had succeeded Volpe as commissioner, but he authorized the move to Texas, and Hines's development at Sweetwater Country Club in Sugar Land wowed the LPGA executives. "This is the culmination of a long-range dream," Laupheimer said at the opening. "It's an opportunity to make a contribution to the Houston sports scene."

A quartet of LPGA superstars with strong Texas ties—Betsy Rawls, Carol Mann, Judy Rankin, and Debbie Massey—came together to advise longtime golf architect Roger Packard on the 36-hole complex at Sweetwater in a booming suburb west of Houston. He moved 900,000 cubic yards of Texas flatlands, formerly sugar and rice fields, to route the nines through stately pecan groves and hardwoods draped with Spanish moss, all with the championship female golfer in mind. A massive clubhouse designed by Californian Charles Moore was equally elaborate and included indoor and outdoor tennis courses, racquetball courts, and a health club along with large dining and banquet facilities. "When I moved to Houston in 1983, I saw a great golf situation," Mann said. "Golf in Houston had to expand to meet the pent-up demand."

The grand opening of the course and clubhouse took place on October 27, 1983, in a gala celebration that attracted hundreds of fans and some of the LPGA's greatest legends. "Never in my wildest dreams or ambitious hopes could I have envisioned all of this as a home for the LPGA 35 years ago when we started," LPGA legend Patty Berg said during her public remarks at the grand-opening ceremony.

The first LPGA National Qualifying Tournament was held at Sweetwater Country Club at the end of the 1984 season, and the Mazda Hall of Fame Championship won by Nancy Lopez was held at Sweetwater, July 4–7, 1985. The first permanent LPGA Hall of Fame was dedicated at the same time next to the course. This multimillion-dollar facility was designed by Jack Elby and finally gave the LPGA a showcase facility for its rich history. The female game's greatest player, Babe Didrikson Zaharias, was included in the Hall of Fame exhibits, although she had her own museum less than 50 miles away in the Beaumont–Port Arthur area.

Despite the huge buildup and work done to give the LPGA a proper home in Texas, its stay was a brief one. After the 1986 tournament won by Amy Alcott, the event ceased to exist because of financial woes, and a year later the LPGA announced it would be moving headquarters again to Daytona Beach, Florida, ending the brief but memorable stay in Texas.

Texas Senior Superstars

After Texas and Texans had helped launch the Senior, now Champions, Tour with two groundbreaking Legends of Golf Tournaments in 1978–1979, they would also supply its original superstars, Don January and Miller Barber, when the Tour officially got under way in 1980. "When we started, the people at the Tour office said you're kidding yourself, but then they got behind us," Sherman's Barber said. The Senior Tour was officially incorporated in the spring of 1980.

The first official tournament was held June 20–22 at Atlantic City Country Club in Atlantic City, New Jersey. Dallas' January won the first official event by two shots over Mike Souchak. "A casino owner, Leo Frazier, put up a lot of money for us to play for that first time, and they treated us like kings," January said. With his son Richard caddying for him, January helped kick off the now familiar routine of two pro-ams during the week, lavish sponsor dinners, plenty of good times, and war stories from golf's former legends.

January was the leading money winner of the four-tournament first year, adding a second-place finish at the SunTree Classic in Florida to capture $44,100. It began a trend of either January or Barber, who joined the Tour in 1981, as the dominant players for the first five years of Senior Tour play. Barber was the leading money winner in 1981 and 1982, while January came back to capture the money title in 1983 and 1984. Barber won the most tournaments in 1981, 1982, and

1984, while January led all players with six victories in 1983. "It got to be one of those things. If he wasn't going to win, then I probably would, and it got to be pretty competitive," Barber said.

Another trend established by the two North Texas golfers was players excelling on the Senior Tour after being in the shadows during their PGA Tour careers. Between them, they had won just one major PGA Tour championship: January had captured the PGA Championship in 1967 over fellow Texan Don Massengale, but Barber, a former caddy for Byron Nelson, had won the first Byron Nelson Classic in 1968 at Preston Trail and had been disappointed several times on the regular Tour. Both players excelled after turning 50. "I won all the big ones," Barber said. "I certainly had my day and enjoyed every moment of it." He won the U.S. Senior Open in 1982 and captured back-to-back U.S. Senior Opens in 1984 and 1985.

Both players said they realized that the first years of the Senior Tour were like the early days of the PGA or LPGA Tour, where the players were basically staging traveling exhibitions but with large checks awarded at the end. "It seemed like it was pretty well run, but we were barnstorming those first couple of years," January said. After his five-figure tournament winnings in 1980, the purses quickly jumped to the six-figure range. January won $328,000 in 1984, more than either he or Barber ever made during their PGA Tour career. "It was like finding it on a tree. We never thought we'd play for that kind of money," January said. "We got the idea for the old Legends of Golf tournament. It proved people wanted to come out to see us."

Barber, who finished with 24 Senior Tour wins, set a record that still stands for wins in consecutive seasons from 1981 to 1989 along with a record for most Tour starts, 604, and most combined starts between the PGA and Senior Tours. January won 22 times on the Senior Tour and still holds the record for most Super Senior, 60-and-older titles at 35.

Both players realized that without the 50-or-older circuit, they would be at their Texas homes, working a "real" job or existing on their past tournament memories. But the Senior Tour gave them opportunities for new victories and new memories and golf fans nationwide an opportunity to see former greats from Texas and beyond who still had plenty of skill and golfing charisma to contribute. Today, the renamed Champions Tour is alive and healthy, with a new generation playing for millions thanks to the legacy handed down by two Texas pros with a dream for golf on the back nine of life.

Hats Off to Texace

Texas players and Texas companies have always been famous for big talk and the ability to back it up, but one Lone Star company ruled its part of the golfing world in the 1980s without making a sound. The Texace Corporation had been in San Antonio since the early 1940s, and the headwear company was known primarily for making military helmets, fishing hats, baseball caps, and a few golf hats.

Oklahoma native and longtime San Antonio resident Bob Coleman purchased Texace in the early 1980s and turned the company's focus toward becoming the world's leading provider of golf hats. Coleman was playing in a Texas Open pro-am in 1984 with Corpus Christi native Tommy Aycock. "He [Aycock] said it was a good company, but the quality had really gone down," Coleman recalled from their pro-am conversation. While not an expert in the golf hat business, Coleman was a shrewd businessman and South Texas civic leader and found he could turn Texace toward its true mission. "We looked at what Texace could do best, selling golf headwear."

The main reason that San Antonio's Texace company remained unknown in its home state and nationwide while gaining the industry leadership position was that it manufactured only hats with other company's names on them, such as Ben Hogan and Titleist, or elite golf clubs, such as Kiawah Island and Cherry Hills in Denver. Only the smallest of Texace symbols identified the hats as Texas' own golf industry leader. "Texace is the number one manufacturer of quality golf headwear in the entire world," Coleman said in a 1980s interview. "Eighty five percent of PGA Tour pros wear Texace product."

The numbers from the early 1980s until the end of the decade bear out Coleman's statement. When he took over Texace, its annual sales were just $2.5 million, barely any of that devoted to golf. By 1993, sales had zoomed up to $16 million with 400 employees straining to keep up with golf headwear demand at their downtown San Antonio headquarters. Coleman supplied the official hats for the U.S. Ryder Cup team along with several other major golf events. He used some of the proceeds of his company to purchase the National Basketball Association's San Antonio Spurs and also led the drive to bring the U.S. Olympic Festival to the Alamo City—thanks to a golf headwear company few people had ever heard of, one that conquered the golfing world one hat at a time.

Austin Teaching Greats

The capital city of Austin has always produced its fair share of golfing greats in the teaching world. Austin Country Club head pro Harvey Penick had been a teacher ahead of his time since taking over as head pro in the early half of the 20th century and was later joined by teaching legends Jackson Bradley and George Hannon. But the 1980s brought a new crop of top teachers to Austin, enough to guide the state into a new century.

Chuck Cook was a young beginning golf pro when he got the call to move down to the new Jack Nicklaus property and teaching center at The Hills of Lakeway in 1980. Dave Pelz was just another former NASA engineer living in Abilene when he got the call to move to Austin in the mid-1980s. They were later joined by teachers like Bill Moretti and Joe Beck to make Austin the golf teaching mecca of Texas and nationwide.

Cook served at Lakeway from 1980 to 1986 at what is now known as the Academy of Golf Dynamics run by Moretti. Cook then served at Barton Creek for a while before going off on his own and recently returned to Barton Creek as director of the Chuck Cook School of Golf. "Texas has always been a great golf state, and Austin is the best place to live," Cook said. "The golf teachers have a chance for interaction with each other, and of course, some of us got to study with Harvey."

Perhaps more than anyone, Nicklaus the designer and Cook the young teacher blazed the modern teaching trail. Along with the original Hills of Lakeway design by Nicklaus, his first in South Texas, with its signature par-3 waterfall, the Nicklaus design team put together an impressive teaching center with three full-size teaching holes, a video replay room, a practice green, and a double-ended range. The facility was off the charts for golf practice centers nationwide in the early 1980s and served as the standard and the attraction for top golf teachers to head to the Austin area.

Cook also used his Texas facilities and impressive personal résumé to attract some of the leading Tour players of his day to Austin. Among the players he taught in the 1980s were future U.S. Open champions Payne Stewart, who was schooled at Southern Methodist University in Dallas, and Austin's Tom Kite. "I was very fortunate to teach some of the top players in the country, and Austin, especially with them, was one of the finest and prettiest places to do it," Cook said.

Pelz, a true rocket scientist in his NASA days, was working in Abilene at a club-manufacturing company until he came to Austin in 1986 to work at the Hills facility about the same time Moretti and Mike Adams arrived as lead instructors. "I was able to do my short game research at the University of Texas. I had known Ben [Crenshaw] and Tom [Kite] for many years and there can't be any better place to live than Austin," Pelz said. "I just love the greens in Austin. The grass is so much better than you'll find up north, plus you can play on them almost all year. Since I'm a short game guy, having good greens was very important to me."

He first started his short game school at The Hills of Lakeway and has since branched out to some of the top resorts across America. He has also started his very popular one-, two-, and three-day schools at locations all over America, drawing a wide range of amateurs, including former Dallas Cowboys quarterback Troy Aikman, looking to improve his game. Pelz has been named one of the most influential teachers of the 20th century but still keeps his world headquarters in Lakeway, not far from the course where he first started his teaching empire. "There are a lot of opportunities here. I've done a lot of short game areas at Barton Creek, the Hills, and many other places in the Austin area."

A Touch of Color in Dallas

Southern Methodist University golfer Payne Stewart graduated from the Dallas university in the spring of 1979, but he made plenty of trips back to Dallas in the 1980s enjoying many high and low times in the North Texas city before finally capping his Texas career with a milestone victory. The easygoing Stewart hadn't yet donned his trademark knickers or plus-four pants, complete with the Scottish floppy hat, while playing for the Mustangs, but he brought style and a flare all his own while competing in college with the likes of future PGA Tour winners Fred Couples at the University of Houston and David Ogrin at Texas A&M.

Stewart graduated from Southern Methodist with a degree in business but failed to earn his PGA Tour card in his first couple of tries. He headed off to the Asian Tour to find his game and ultimately his future wife. He returned to his college home in the mid-1980s with his full PGA Tour exemption and a chance to play in the Byron Nelson Classic. Stewart had played in the Colonial as the Southwest Conference Champion in 1979, defeating Couples for the honor, but had never played in the Nelson until 1982–1983, missing the cut both times. He returned in 1984, finishing tied for ninth, and was back the following year full of confidence.

Southern Methodist University golfer Payne Stewart brought needed personality and color to the world of professional golf. (Photo courtesy of the Salesmanship Club Dallas)

He opened with a three-under 67 in 1985 to put him among the leaders before grabbing the solo lead with a third-round 66. He cruised into the final round and appeared ready to cement a popular hometown win, taking a two-shot lead into the final hole. But a double bogey at 18 caused by an approach shot in the greenside bunker and a poor recovery shot sent Stewart into a playoff and sent the pro-Stewart crowd into

stunned silence. On the first playoff hole with Bob Eastwood, Stewart three-putted the par-5 16th to cost him the PGA Tour title in his college hometown. A crushed Stewart and his wife walked alone off the 16th green and more than a mile back to the TPC-Four Seasons clubhouse.

Just five years later, Stewart was back in Dallas for the Byron Nelson and this time would not be denied. He fired rounds of 67, 68, and 67 to grab the lead, then waited until a daylong rainstorm washed out the final round to claim a victory by two shots over Dallas' Lanny Wadkins, a victory Stewart called one of the most meaningful of his career. "He was always the life of the party at SMU or the Tour or anywhere else he went," said Texas golf writer Eddie Sefko, who attended Southern Methodist with Stewart and later covered his career while writing for the *Houston Chronicle*.

Texas was the final destination for Stewart in the tragic plane crash that took his life in 1999. He was scheduled to fly to Dallas to look over some northern Collin County property and meet with some former Southern Methodist classmates, then continue on to Houston for the Tour Championship. His chartered plane developed trouble soon after takeoff, causing it to fly widely off course and ultimately crash in South Dakota. The golf course was never built, but Southern Methodist still honors its former golf star by holding a benefit golf tournament in his honor every spring, raising $100,000 annually for the program he helped put on the map. The Salesmanship Club, operators of the Byron Nelson tournament, planted a tree in his honor on the 16th hole, remembering the two decades of contributions the colorful Stewart made to Texas golf in the 1970s and 1980s.

Ol' Four-Eyes Wins for Houston

Growing up in the Houston suburb of Sugar Land, all Billy Ray Brown wanted to do was play golf for the University of Houston and its legendary coach Dave Williams. The son of former National Football League player Charlie Brown, Billy Ray had been an active member of the Houston junior golf scene since he was a young kid, playing in several Houston Golf Association tournaments and competing on the Sugar Land Dulles golf team.

He turned down several full scholarships to colleges such as Texas, Texas A&M, Oklahoma, and Oklahoma State to play for his beloved Cougars and Williams. But Brown was fighting an inconsistent game when he arrived at the Houston campus and didn't even qualify for the school's team the fall of his freshman year, serving as a ball boy for the football team. That spring, motivated by Williams's stinging criticism and a desire to improve, he finally made the golf team but wasn't a major factor in the team's season, individually finishing ninth on the team's home course as they placed second during the Southwest Conference golf tournament held in Houston.

Qualifying for the National Collegiate Athletic Association (NCAA) Championship in Pinehurst, North Carolina, in 1982, he arrived wearing glasses for one of the first times in his career. The change had been suggested by his dad and approved by Williams, and the results were immediate and nothing short of astounding. Brown became one of the first freshmen to win the NCAA individual title and helped lead the Cougars to their 14th national title, the most for a single school in the NCAA modern era. "I still can't believe it happened," a jubilant Brown said after the NCAA tournament. "It's truly like a dream come true."

Two years later at Houston's Bear Creek Golf World, the Cougars were considered a heavy favorite to win and wrap up another NCAA title in the first college national championship held in Houston. But the Cougars were just in 19th place after a poor first day. They climbed to fifth place after the second day but still trailed by five shots midway through the final round before staging an improbable rally on the back nine. It was capped by Houston's Steve Elkington, who managed a two-putt par on the final hole at Bear Creek to capture the team title by one shot over Oklahoma State. "It was incredible," Elkington told the *Houston Post* after the match. "I was just trying to keep my composure." A year later, Houston won its 16th NCAA title by four shots over Oklahoma State, and Williams soon retired, ending a college golf dynasty never before seen and never since repeated.

Amateur Hour at the Western Open

Among the long line of great Texas amateur golfers, Carrollton's Scott Verplank certainly earned his way onto the list. He scored a U.S. Amateur victory in 1984, a pair of Western Amateur victories, and multiple all-America honors while playing for Oklahoma State, helping lead the Cowboys to an NCAA title in 1983 and a pair of runner-up titles. Few would have guessed that Verplank would do something in 1985 that no Texas amateur golfer, before or since, would ever achieve.

On a cloudy Dallas Sunday afternoon with his parents nervously sitting on the edge of their couch, alternating holding their breath and biting their fingernails, Verplank entered the final round of the PGA Tour's Western Open with the lead. Four hours and one playoff later, Verplank emerged with a victory over Jim Thorpe, becoming the first amateur in 29 years, since Doug Sanders in the Canadian Open, to win a PGA Tour event. "Nervous? No, I was ahead going to the last round, and I felt great with a lead," Verplank said in *Texas Golf Legends*. "I said to myself, 'why the hell wouldn't I win now that I have the lead?'"

Verplank, who grew up playing at Brookhaven Country Club in Carrollton, among other local courses, and served as a walking sign boy for the Byron Nelson Classic, passed up a chance to turn pro after the tournament and left the $75,000 first-place prize money to Thorpe. He won the NCAA individual title in 1986 for Oklahoma State, as they finished second to Wake Forest, and turned pro shortly afterward with the most precareer fanfare for any Texas golfer since Ben Crenshaw.

Crenshaw won his first pro event, but Verplank, with already a PGA Tour win to his credit, struggled at the beginning of his professional career. He finished 177th and 173rd on the Tour money list in his first two years before rallying to capture his second Tour win in 1988 at the Buick Open by two shots over Doug Tewell with a final-round 66. While his career has been up and down because of elbow injuries and a continuing battle with diabetes, Verplank has never lost his Texas-tough attitude, winning the Comeback Player of the Year award from his fellow Tour players in 1998. He

was named to the U.S. Ryder Cup team in 2002 after Tour victories in 2000 and 2001 at the Reno-Tahoe Open and the Canadian Open. Although Phil Mickelson became the second amateur in the decade to win a PGA Tour event, Verplank remains the only Texan to exhibit professional winning talent as an amateur. "It's still the thing people will always remember me for, because it is so rare," he said.

Firewheel Starts a Public Golf Blaze

Long before upscale municipal golf became a hot topic with urban planners as a real, live, city moneymaker, the forward-thinking folks of Garland, a Dallas suburb, were way ahead in the municipal golf game. They decided this fast-growing city next to Dallas would be the home to top-rated public golf, open to all. The first 18 holes at Firewheel, named for the course-side wildflowers, opened in 1983 and sparked a public golfing boom in the Dallas area and across the state.

The original 18 holes, dubbed the Old Course, like all 63 holes at Firewheel, were designed by architect Dick Phelps. They took advantage of the gently rolling terrain, once cow pastureland, and the dozens of huge oak trees sprinkled throughout the course. "I think the City of Garland has made a real commitment to golf over a number of years and can certainly be shown as a catalyst to growth," said longtime director of golf Don Kennedy, who served as an assistant to original head pro Jerry Andrews when the course first opened.

Firewheel has more than stood the test of architectural time, having hosted the PGA Tour First Stage

Qualifying twice since it opened and the Texas State Open three times. The Old Course was rated the number one public course in Texas several times in the 1980s by a statewide survey. "It's a premier facility that would make any country club member feel at home," Kennedy added. After the initial 18 opened in 1983, Phelps came back to add 18 more in 1987 and an additional 27 holes called the Lakes Course in 2001. Nearby Carrollton added a premier public facility, Indian Creek, in the late 1980s, and the race was on for Texas cities to promote golf through upscale municipal facilities.

LPGA superstar Carol Mann saw the public golf potential when she moved from the East Coast to Houston in 1983. She was a big part of getting the LPGA to move its headquarters to Houston and was a trustee for the Women's Sports Foundation. She saw the Houston public golf growth firsthand with 54-hole facilities going up at both Bear Creek in West Houston and Cypresswood closer to the international airport in the 1980s. "That was really the way to spur growth," Mann said. "Success breeds success, and that's what we did with golf courses in the Houston area." Combined with the highly rated 27-hole Old Orchard, public golf in Southeast Texas was off to a roaring start in the 1980s.

Barton Creek and Dominion Open

The opening of Barton Creek Golf Club in Austin had all the intrigue of a political thriller, with some of the top political and business names in the state coming together to form one of the finest golf and resort combinations in Texas. The opening of The Dominion in San Antonio set the standard for luxury on a scale never seen before in Texas. Together they ushered in a wave of high-priced, high-quality golf layouts that symbolized the early to mid-1980s.

Barton Creek was originally part of the massive Robert Spelling Ranch in West Austin in some of the most scenic and dramatic land in the capital city. Former Texas lieutenant governor Ben Barnes, a golden name in Texas politics, and former governor John Connally, who was wounded in the Kennedy assassination and later ran for president in 1980, were the driving forces behind the establishment of Barton Creek.

They scouted the land and found the most dramatic site for golf, housing, a conference center, and a hotel. Barnes hired architect Tom Fazio to do his first Texas course and help burnish his legend as golf's greatest living architect. "Ben scouted all the top architects: Arthur Hills, Robert Trent Jones, etc., but fell in love with Tom Fazio," said original head pro Brent Buckman, who left Onion Creek to open Barton Creek in 1985. "Barnes was willing to pay the freight for a first-class job. He was one of the great visionaries of our time. His vision was 10 years ahead."

When Fazio first stepped onto the rocky, hilly Central Texas landscape in 1984, he couldn't believe he was standing in supposedly flat, arid Texas. "People ask me all the time if I can see a hole or a course when I'm out for the first time," he said. "I didn't envision this layout, but I knew it was a dramatic site." With Fazio handling the architecture and Barnes seeing to all the day-to-day duties, the stage was set for success on a huge scale. "Barton Creek

Austin's Barton Creek help kick start the Hill Country golf boom. (Photo courtesy of Barton Creek Resort & Spa)

covers all the bases," said former pro Paul Earnest. "Great shot values, awesome beauty, kept in great condition and fun to play."

The public/private resort officially opened in 1986 as a 6,956-yard, par-72 masterpiece. The par-4 10th hole dropped 100 feet from tee to green, as did the par-4 11th. The par-4 16th had a huge waterfall in front of the green, and the par-5 18th had an authentic bat cave in front of the green with another greenside waterfall. When Barnes and Connally ran into financial problems

in the late 1980s, former University of Texas football player turned businessman Jim Bob Moffitt stepped in to ensure that Barton Creek's first-class tradition continued. "When he took over, Jim Bob wanted it to be the best there was, and Jim Bob didn't spare one cent," Buckman said. Barton Creek soon elbowed alongside Colonial and Champions Golf Club vying for the title of best course in the state.

Today, Barton Creek has four highly rated layouts, including one by Arnold Palmer, one by Ben Crenshaw, and a second from Fazio. There is a huge hotel, a conference center, a nature trail, and a spa, all with the imagination and vision of true Texas legends.

In San Antonio, The Dominion, a private facility on the city's far northwest side, opened in 1984 with the simple philosophy of building the best regardless of the cost. The course was designed by Utah architect/player Bill Johnston, who did only seven in his career, but the massive clubhouse gave new meaning to the words "huge," "grandiose," and "Texas-sized."

Architect Ralph Bender spent $17 million on a luxury creation unmatched in the state if not the country: Start with 2,000 tons of imported, hand-carved stone for the facility. A hand-painted golden dome sits on top of the building. Glittering chandeliers are spread throughout along with a private library with a constantly updated stock ticker and an extensive downstairs wine facility. "If this isn't the Taj Mahal of Golf, it'll do until somebody builds it," Chi Chi Rodriguez said the first time he saw The Dominion facility. The club hosted a Senior PGA Tour event for nearly 20 years and is still ranked atop the list of best clubhouses anywhere in Texas.

Both facilities came from Texans with a dream and a vision for the best there ever was. The dream would expand in the next decade to an undersized Texan who made up for lack of height and bulk with a burning desire to compete and practice and win.

The 1990s
Long Drives to Major Titles

5 Highlights of the 1990s

★ Colonial Country Club in Fort Worth hosts the 1991 Women's U.S. Open, the first national female professional tournament ever held at the historic course.

★ Tour 18 opens in Houston in 1992 as the first full-scale replica course with 18 of the most famous holes in America. It survives a protracted lawsuit and opens a Dallas-area location.

★ The 1993 U.S. Amateur comes to Champions Golf Club in Houston, the first national amateur championship held in Texas in 100 years.

★ Dallas' Justin Leonard wins the 1997 British Open at Royal Troon in Scotland, the first major for the Texas native and resident.

★ Tiger Woods makes the 1997 Byron Nelson Classic his first appearance after his historic Masters victory, giving the tournament its first sellout and setting the trend for annual Tiger appearances at the Nelson.

Story of the Decade:
One Determined Golf Dreamer

Whack by determined whack, hit by intentioned hit, the oak trees shading the practice range at Royal Oaks Country Club in Dallas became a little less dense almost every day. After weeks, months, of this consistent effort, there were clearly defined holes to let in the North Texas sunshine or rain. When Royal Oaks junior Justin Leonard came out to practice, which was nearly every day, there was always a method to his seeming golf madness, and one method was to knock out the acorns in the trees above the Royal Oaks range with his trusty 5-iron. "Tree trimming" is what Leonard called it.

Most Royal Oaks members knew Leonard, as his dad played often and would sometimes invite the undersized Leonard to play with the adults. The elder Leonard liked to showcase his son and created situations to toughen him for future golfing trials by throwing tees or rattling keys during his backswing. Other times, the younger Leonard would just spend hours on the range with veteran Royal Oaks pro Randy Smith. In this tree-lined northeast Dallas golf laboratory, Leonard learned his golfing lessons, which would one day make him the equal of the professional golfing world.

Although Leonard's golf maturation took place as a junior player at Royal Oaks, then as a high school and amateur hero in the 1970s and 1980s, he truly burst onto the U.S., then world, golf stage in the decade of the 1990s. He became the first player to capture four consecutive Southwest Conference titles and the 1992 U.S. Amateur trophy while playing for the University of Texas, the same year his Longhorn predecessor

> ### TEXAS GOLF FACT
>
> Texas golf pro Art Sellinger helped found one of the hottest trends in the last decade of the 20th century, the national long-driving tour. Sellinger formed the Long Drivers of America based in North Texas and staged a nationally televised world championship outside Las Vegas with qualifying events in dozens of cities.

Tom Kite won the U.S. Open. Leonard turned professional in 1994 and won four times in his first decade as a pro, including a Players Championship victory in 1998, plus Buick Open and Kemper Open titles in 1996 and 1997.

But nothing in the decade of the 1990s showcased his transformation from determined, undersized, hard-working grinder to world-class champion than his 1997 British Open victory at historic Royal Troon, rallying from a five-stroke final-round deficit behind Jespar Parnevik to win his first major at age 25. He became one of the youngest winners of the 20th century at the Open Championship and did it with the largest final-round rally of the century. "I feel like my game was always improving with my skill level." Leonard said. "I'm always learning, and that's another great thing about this game."

He capped his victorious decade by proving that one of golf's smaller players, at a thin five feet, nine inches, could stand big in the brightest of world golfing stages. With the United States staging the most improbable of rallies on the final day of the 1999 Ryder Cup, Leonard staged his own incredible comeback against Jose Maria Olazabal, winning four straight

Dallas native Justin Leonard used willpower, talent, and practice to rise to the top of the pro golf world. (Photo courtesy of Colonial Country Club)

back-nine holes before rolling in a 45-foot birdie putt on the 17th at The Country Club to earn the decisive half point in the largest Sunday comeback in U.S. Ryder Cup history. *Sports Illustrated* titled it "The Putt Heard around the World," but to Leonard it was proof positive that hard work can overcome almost any golfing obstacles placed in his path. "I know a lot of people come up to me and say they didn't know I was this size, but that's the greatest thing about golf is your score doesn't know how big or small you are. I'd love to be 6-1, but that's probably not going to happen, so I have to keep working with what I have."

While a junior player at Royal Oaks, Leonard's main concern was getting his tee shot over the large ditch that bisected the ninth fairway. He made steady progress under first Royal Oaks pro Buddy Cook, who gave Leonard his initial lesson, then after Cook departed he switched over to Smith and formed nearly a 20-year partnership with the low-key Royal Oaks pro. "It made me work harder to learn what to teach him, because he soaked up everything I gave him," Smith said. "The first turning point was when he won an AJGA junior tournament, and you could see the wheels turning. I finally had met somebody who wanted to learn more than I had to teach."

Leonard starred at nearby Lake Highlands High School, again one of the smaller members on the team but leading the Wildcats to the Division 5A state title. Leonard earned a scholarship to the University of Texas, where he followed in the footsteps of alumni

Ben Crenshaw and Kite, with Leonard attracting almost as much success.

After his four conference titles, the 1994 NCAA title (like Kite and Crenshaw), and the U.S. Amateur crown, Leonard earned the Dave Williams Award as the top college golfer in America in 1994. Because of his early PGA Tour success, he then became one of only three golfers in history to go straight from college to the PGA Tour without any time in Qualifying School.

Since turning pro in 1994 as a slight player with limited driving distance, Leonard has achieved a remarkable career with ten PGA Tour titles by getting the most out of his natural ability and by hard work. "I don't think about it much since turning pro, but I've learned what I can do and feel like I've done a good job. I've worked hard and feel I've gotten a lot out of my game. It's been a good career so far. I've done a pretty good job of getting the most from what I had."

The meticulous and focused Leonard, who was known to pick lint off of Smith's shirt and once faithfully faxed his daily practice lessons to his sports psychologist, showcased the incredible work ethic of another undersized Texan with an unstoppable will to win, Ben Hogan. "I'm very much a feel player and when I'm on the course, I have to feel it for myself. If I'm always relying on somebody else, I can't do that," Leonard said.

Leonard, as much as anybody, showcased the new generation of Texas pros who were drawn to the game by Lone Star players they watched as a kid. He attended several Byron Nelson and Colonial tournaments as a junior, getting autographs from players like Crenshaw, Raymond Floyd, and Tom Watson. He said he often thinks about that when giving out autographs of his own during the Texas tournaments he has made a regular point of attending as a PGA Tour player.

As a professional, Leonard has played every Byron Nelson and Colonial tournament, missing only one tournament he was eligible for at the Houston Open and the Texas Open. "I always thought Texas players should support Texas events," he said. "It's a good feeling to play well in front of supportive crowds." He won twice at the Texas Open in 2000 and 2001, flashing the University of Texas, "Hook'em Horns" sign at the 18th-hole crowds, less than 70 miles from where he went to school.

Another advantage to being a homegrown Texas star is keeping his base of operations and his personal and inner circle all within the North Texas area. He recently moved into a new home in Westlake and has memberships at Brook Hollow Golf Club in Dallas and Vaquero in Westlake.

Several of Leonard's favorite dining hangouts are nearby, and Leonard is close enough to Austin to slip down and watch his beloved Longhorns play on occasion. His close friend and sometimes fishing buddy Smith is close by at Royal Oaks whenever Leonard is able to get away from the pressures of the PGA Tour lifestyle. He also moved his agent and media team to Dallas, bringing almost all members of his inner circle within an hour's drive of his home.

Leonard has continued his world-class PGA Tour player pace, making the season-ending Tour Championship for eight straight years. He made a playoff in another British Open and has three top-five finishes in the PGA Championship. Through the first decade of his career, Leonard has won $17 million in prize money and enough career highlights to last a lifetime.

Not bad for a small North Texas kid who specialized in tree trimming as a junior and has chopped down worldwide golfing goals ever since.

President Golfer

Georgia native turned Texas legend Doug Sanders always said golf was magic, "bringing presidents, diplomats, celebrities from all walks of life together." Never did that prove more true than on a sunny May 1992 afternoon in the Houston suburb of Kingwood when George Bush, the 41st president of the United States, set down in his Marine One helicopter on the driving range of Kingwood Country Club.

Bush was in town at the express invitation of his good friend Sanders to play in the Doug Sanders Kingwood Celebrity Classic, becoming the first sitting president to play in a Champions Tour event and the first U.S. president to travel to Texas for golf since William Howard Taft's disputed trip to Austin Country Club nearly 70 years earlier.

The event was the 300th tournament staged on the Champions Tour schedule and was eventually won by Mike Hill by two shots over Larry Mowry and Gibby Gilbert. The focus was squarely on the Leader of the Free World and part-time Houston resident who popped out of the U.S. helicopter in golf clothes to the hearty handshake of the white-haired Sanders. "I've been friends with the Bushes for a long time and George Bush is the nicest man I've ever met in my life," Sanders said.

The friendship began in the late 1980s after Bush had been elected president, and Sanders, a friendly and flamboyant personality, wanted to congratulate him. He decided to send him a full box of dress socks with the simple note, "For the man who has everything." Having grown up in poverty, often walking barefooted, Sanders knew the gift would be appreciated. "Nobody ever has enough dress socks especially for a man in his position and I enclosed all colors so it's a gift nobody can turn down." Bush responded with a nice note thanking Sanders, and the friendship was on.

Over the years of the Bush presidency, Sanders was invited to the White House on several occasions and even spent time with Bush at the presidential retreat Camp David. More than 200 notes from Bush are framed at the Sanders' Galleria-area home. "Celebrities just adopted me," Sanders said. "Vice President Quayle came to play in the tournament the year after President Bush."

Sanders, who helped bring the Houston Open to The Woodlands for the first time in the mid-1970s, parlayed his close relationship with celebrities into his own Champions Tour event. The event was naturally named after the host and started in 1981 as a pro-am celebrity event much like the old Pebble Beach Crosby Clambake, with 36 well-known friends of Sanders showing up for the first year. The tournament grew to be the second-longest-running event on the Champions Tour at the time, drawing people like Chicago Bears football coach Mike Ditka and singer Phil Harris to mix with players like Jack Nicklaus and Arnold Palmer. "When all the guys came to the tournament here, it was a boost to the entire city of Houston," Sanders proudly said. "They saw what golf was all about here."

The arrival of Bush as his top amateur for 1992 remains one of his shining moments. Sanders had been after him for several years to play in his pro-am event, and Bush finally agreed at the beginning of a tough reelection campaign against Bill Clinton. His arrival triggered unprecedented security arrangements for a pro golf event in Texas or elsewhere, including emptying the media center to sniff for bombs, but the unflappable Sanders and the mild-mannered Bush took it all in stride. Houston businessman Scott Talley was a marshal for the historic event and had a brief encounter with Bush. "There were security men everywhere in the woods, and I was standing next to the lake where nobody had hit it all day. President Bush hit one way over me and when he came over to look for the ball, he asked me why I didn't stop it." "A little too tall, sir," was Talley's reply. "He was a very nice man."

Sanders continued his tournament for most of the decade, having Bush and Quayle back several times to his event after they left office. Sanders liked to call his tournament "Golf's Great Happening." Nobody ever mixed the famous on the course with the famous off it better than longtime Houstonian Doug Sanders.

Houston's Tour Championship

After an absence of nearly two decades, Jack Burke's Champions Golf Club got back into the professional golf picture in a big way. He was asked by the PGA Tour to host their first season-ending Tour Championship in 1990 at Burke's beloved Champions course. The tournament had begun only a few years earlier at Oak Hills Country Club in San Antonio and had begun to move around to the top golf courses in America to host that year's leading money winners. "We want this to be a championship course for championship players" was Burke's reasoning for hosting the event.

Despite lackluster fall crowds because of competition from the football season and a lack of promotion from the sponsor, similar problems the Ryder Cup at Champions had run into, the final result was a success. Jodie Mudd, who has won the U.S. Public Links title at Houston's Bear Creek in 1981, won an exciting playoff victory over Billy Mayfair to capture the $450,000 first-place prize, a Tour record at the time.

The tournament was also a success in the eyes of the PGA Tour, which returned the Tour Championship to the classic Champions layout two more times in the 1990s, won by David Duval in 1997 and Tiger Woods in 1999, and brought the event back to Houston five times over a 13-year span. It became a true PGA Tour Championship for Texas' home of championship golf events.

Colonial's Female Open

Colonial members and golf tournament committee members desperately wanted to host the 1991 U.S. Open to celebrate the 50th anniversary of the first Open in Texas, the first national exposure for Texas golf at the design of Lone Star visionary Marvin Leonard. But with the 1991 Open going to Hazeltine National in Minnesota, Colonial was awarded the Women's Open instead, and what followed was a hot time on and off the course.

The early June temperatures soared into the mid-90s, and groundskeepers hosed down the crowds to keep them cool on the weekend, but nothing could cool down the LPGA's hottest golfer, Meg Mallon. The 28-year-old Mallon had recently been voted the most popular golfer on the LPGA Tour, but in 1991 she was also one of the best. Mallon captured the LPGA Championship in late May and came to Fort Worth on a hot streak, literally and figuratively.

Mallon opened with a one-under 70 to stand one shot behind first-round leader Pat Bradley, who was attempting to win her 30th ladies professional tournament and automatic entry into the LPGA Hall of Fame. At the midway point, Mallon fell three shots back of Bradley and was two back going into the final day, but she rallied with a final-round 67 for a two-shot victory over Bradley, three better than Amy Alcott. "No one is more surprised than I am right now," Mallon said during the awards ceremony on Colonial's historic 18th green. "Once you get that winning feeling, you never want it to stop."

The Women's Open was historic for other reasons as well. Little-known Open competitor Susan Stone did something no tournament professional had ever accomplished at Colonial, acing the par-3 fourth hole, the second member of the Horrible Horseshoe. She used a 4-iron from 195 yards for the historic hole-in-one on one of Colonial's toughest holes.

Golf legend Ben Hogan, for whom the course was named "Hogan's Alley," came out to the tournament on Sunday afternoon to watch protégé and good friend Kris Tschetter, who shot a women's course-record 67 on Saturday to tie for fifth going into the final day. "I remember I got a call on the radio that somebody had seen Mr. Hogan walking in the crowd following Kris," said longtime Colonial golf committee member Scott Corpening. "I had somebody race out there with a cart so he wouldn't get mobbed by the crowds once they figured out who he was, but Mr. Hogan said he was fine and had just come to see the tournament and see Kris. That shows you he was a supporter of all golf, especially the great golf played at the Women's Open."

The 1991 Open remains the only female professional event ever played at Colonial and only the fourth Open Championship played in Texas. Despite some griping about the heat and the tough pin placements, the large and appreciative crowds showed championship golfers that players of all levels and genders would be supported in Texas.

Amateur Week at Champions

If fans ever needed proof that Jack Burke was Texas' most active living proponent of championship golf in the Lone Star State, they need look no further than the 1993 U.S. Amateur Championship held at Champions Golf Club. The son of a golf pro who grew up learning the game in the caddy yards of Houston, Burke had often said he owes any success in golf to amateur golfers. "You have to support amateurs," Burke said. "My dad made $3 an hour when he started teaching amateurs. I learn from the amateur players because amateur players are looking for help."

As a result, Burke and Champions hosted the first U.S. Amateur championship held in Texas in 100 years. "If amateurs don't come back and give back to the game, you can say adios to golf," Burke said. "I want to give back to amateurs. Can you believe there hasn't been a U.S. Amateur here in Texas in 100 years?" He cured all of that by getting the 1993 U.S. Amateur for Champions and commissioning a special statue dubbed "Tomorrow's Champions" for the club grounds as a reminder of the historic event.

Texas' Justin Leonard was the defending champion for the Amateur Championship, but his bid for a rare repeat was shot down with an early round loss, and when Leonard faded, so did the crowds. Minnesota insurance executive John Harris, at age 41, became one of the oldest U.S. Amateur champions of all time by defeating Danny Ellis, 5 and 3, in the finals in front of a sparse crowd of witnesses. "Of course I lost money on the event, that's not a money maker for the club, but I did it to promote golf. To promote Texas golf, that's what you have to do in this game."

Texas Tour 18

One day, Texas golf partners Dennis Wilkerson and Barron Jacobson had just finished a weekend round of golf and were watching the final holes of a televised professional tournament that was taking place on a famous course. The two partners, along with several friends, started talking about how cool it would be to actually play on a course like the one being showcased on television. Thanks to the innovative duo, Texas golfers and visitors soon got to experience world-class courses in an imaginative way. "Inherent in what people think about Texans are big dreams and big plans and that's what we accomplished here," Jacobson said.

The idea was beautifully simple but complex in its execution. Jacobson and his partners would fashion exacting replicas of 18 of the most famous golf holes in America, call it Tour 18 Golf Course, and place it all on a 200-acre suburban Houston site in Humble. Thanks to new computer mapping technology and aerial photography, the Texas twosome could prove that journey from far-out golf dream to instant golf reality was closer than most people would think.

They initially came out with 300 famous holes and whittled it down to America's most famous 18 holes for the first Tour 18 course, which opened in the fall of 1992. Included in the initial 18 replica holes were designs from Pinehurst, Harbour Town, Pebble Beach, and the three most famous holes, making up Augusta National's "Amen Corner." The cost for this golfing Fantasy Island was $5.5 million for the first Tour 18, with a slightly higher figure for a 1995 version that opened outside of Dallas in the town of Flower Mound.

When the first Tour 18 course opened, there was only one other replica course in America, and it captured only a few famous holes, not a complete 18. With the 1990s golf boom just beginning to take shape in Houston, Tour 18 was an instant success with long lines of golfers willing to play a premium to play the famous copies of historic holes. "We hit the market at just the right time," Wilkerson said. "It had to be as close as possible to be believable and with the computer animation available, we were able to get very, very close."

It was an idea that almost died before it could get started. On December 7, 1993, Tour 18 was sued by Pebble Beach Golf Links and ultimately joined by Harbour Town in Hilton Head, South Carolina, for illegal copies of holes that could cause harm to their original courses. Despite rumors to the contrary, Augusta National declined to join the suit; Masters Chairman Jack Stephens announced, "Imitation is the sincerest form of flattery."

The trial was held in the courtroom of Houston-based U.S. District Court Judge David Hitner. The two sides and their combined attorneys argued back and forth with multiple appeals for nearly five years. "What this person has done is take a famous course with a famous name and tried to make money off of it," the Pebble Beach attorney said. While Wilkerson opened the Dallas-area Tour 18 while waiting on the verdict, the most basic of arguments came down to whether one golf course could copy another and whether there are any truly original golf course designs in existence in America or elsewhere.

At stake was the future of the Tour 18 concept and other replica courses nationwide. After all the legal dust settled, Hitner finally issued a legal victory for the Texas twosome and Tour 18. "They fought us in the courts for five years, but we finally prevailed," Wilkerson said. What the judge decided was that golf courses' design concepts were free to be copied as they had been for hundreds of years, while specific course landmarks could be protected. The legal victory ensured the continuation of the still highly successful Tour 18 idea and provided validation for two Texas golf dreamers who made available the most famous of golf holes to the average golfer in exacting replica format.

Homemade Homesteads

Texas has always been home to courses designed by the most famous names in golf architecture. Legendary names like Tillinghast and Ross and Nicklaus and Fazio grace the names of the Lone Star State's most famous courses. But in the 1990s, one new trend was the build-it-yourself course. Not satisfied or able to pay millions to a big-name designer for a golf course of their dreams, some Texas golf dreamers simply did it themselves.

A prime case in point was Dick Murphy, a retired American Airlines pilot who designed and built the public Turtle Hill Golf Course in Muenster, Texas, just south of the Texas–Oklahoma border. Murphy and his wife first bought the 242-acre cattle ranch in the 1980s and planned to graze livestock on it in their retirement years, but he decided on something a little more exotic. Already investing in an emu farm and investigating the possibility of wind power, building his own golf course wasn't much of a stretch for the forward-thinking Murphy. "I went to the library and found every book I could find on golf course architecture and building," he said. "I started writing to the Unites States Golf Association and asking questions about their green section committees and how to find the right grass for the area. I started talking to farmers and ranchers and getting their advice."

Murphy formally broke ground on his 18-hole pet project in late 1989, but because he was a one-man crew and still working at American Airlines, work progressed slowly. He spent 15,000 man-hours and $1.2 million to build Turtle Hill, but when the first nine holes opened in 1993, it was hailed as having some of the best greens in the area if not the state. "One good thing about building your own course, is you can do it exactly like you want it," Murphy said. "One day I was sitting on my tractor having lunch and I got to looking at this green, and I just didn't like the way it was sitting. So I jumped down, fired up the tractor and spent all afternoon totally changing it."

The masterpiece of the public daily-fee facility that opened a second nine in 1995 is the par-3 11th hole, which drops 120 feet from tee to green. On a clear day, you can see into Oklahoma. "It was a lot of work but something I'm very proud of," Murphy said. "I want to be able to leave something for my family to enjoy."

Other examples of do-it-yourself builders included Stanley Marsh's Cadillac Ranch outside Amarillo with cars stuck nose first into the ground and a little room for golf in the back. McAlister's 2-Hole Ranch in Yantis, outside of Sulphur Springs, is actually a nine-hole course with multiple greens and tees and is a well-conditioned public layout, as is the fairly new Pine Dunes course in East Texas.

Perhaps the most famous golf course owner is country music legend and golf addict Willie Nelson. Nelson has own course on the banks of Pedernales River just west of Austin. The rustic clubhouse contains mementos of Nelson's matchless career and a gold record or two, and the property boasts a lounging stray dog and some drop-dead gorgeous views of the Texas Hill Country. If players can't play well at Willie's course, then at least follow the owner's lead and play fast. He roams the property in his golf cart with a large wire bucket containing balls that he promptly hurls to the ground if his ball search ever exceeds five seconds. "I thought I played fast until I met Willie," said regular visitor and Texas coaching legend Darrell Royal. Nevertheless, Nelson remains as proud of his course as anything Tillinghast, Bredemus, or Marvin Leonard ever did. "See that hole over there on the hill," Nelson once told a visitor about the opening layout at the nine-hole Pedernales Country Club. "I made it a par 12 and I almost birdied that sucker the other day."

Hogan's Final Mystery

After a brief illness at his home near Texas Christian University, Ben Hogan passed away in 1995 at the age of 83. His funeral was held on a blazing-hot day at University Christian Church and attended by almost all the leading lights of Hogan's generation, including Sam Snead, Jimmy Demaret, and Jack Burke Jr.

The one person missing was Hogan's childhood contemporary, the fellow he grew up caddying with, Byron Nelson. He was missing among the honorary pallbearers, missing among the golfers who carried Hogan's casket from the church, and missing from any public notice or mention. After the services started, Nelson slipped in the back door with wife Peggy and sat quietly while Hogan's pastor talked about his many good deeds. Nelson declined to comment about his absence from the official service but just shrugged his shoulders when asked about his friend and said simply, "That's the way he was."

Even in his later years, Hogan's life was shrouded in mystery. In one famous meeting with world number-one player Nick Faldo in the early 1990s, Hogan was cold and distant with the player who had made the long trip to gain some of Hogan's wisdom, especially about winning the U.S. Open. "What's the secret?" Faldo was reported to have asked. "Shoot the lowest score for four days," Hogan said. "How did you do it?" Faldo continued. "Nick, you're a good player, you can figure it out for yourself," Hogan replied. Finally after the brief lunch, Faldo begged Hogan to watch him hit balls on the Shady Oaks range and offer a few pointers. "Does he play our clubs?" Hogan asked an associate. Told that

Faldo played Dunlop clubs, Hogan declined. "I don't think so," he said. "Ask him if Mr. Dunlop will go watch him hit balls," he said according to one popular story.

Tigermania in Texas

To be sure, Tiger Woods wasn't born or raised in Texas, but he visited early and often, and his first visits as a professional were some of his most memorable anywhere. He first arrived at age 14 to visit the fabulous Four Seasons Resort and Club in Las Colinas just outside of Dallas to play in an American Junior Golf Association tournament at the same course that hosted the PGA Tour's Byron Nelson Classic. There he met the tournament namesake for the first time. The living legend and the new wunderkind formed a fast friendship that has lasted for years. "I always told everybody Tiger was the best 14-year-old player I ever saw, the best 15-year-old, the best 16-year-old," Nelson said.

Woods made a visit to San Antonio at age 16, winning the American Junior Golf Association's Texace San Antonio Shootout at San Antonio Country Club while being heavily chaperoned by his father Earl, who wouldn't let media members talk to his son until they promised a positive story. He also played in Houston at the *Golf Digest* college tournament at The Woodlands, with his father again deflecting members of the Texas media from any nonworshipful stories.

Woods's first visit to San Antonio as a professional occurred at the 1996 Texas Open at La Cantera Golf Club and caused plenty of stir in the normally laid-back Alamo City. He had booked a series of seven tournaments in a row while attempting to earn enough money for the PGA Tour card after his dramatic pro entrance in the summer of 1996 in Milwaukee. Woods had already pulled out of one tournament citing fatigue, and after winning at Las Vegas the week before San Antonio, his Tour status was guaranteed, but the lure and the history of the Texas Open were too much to pass up. "The Tiger has landed," tournament director Tony Piazzi said when Woods arrived. He was in contention until the final holes, where he drove the green on the par-4 16th hole, then three-putted for par to derail his chances. Hometown hero David Ogrin captured the 1996 Texas Open title, while Woods was third in his only Texas Open appearance.

Woods's next visit to Texas will be remembered as one of the most spectacular trips to the Lone Star State since Santa Anna marched on the Alamo, and it attracted almost as many media members as the Alamo attracted Mexican soldiers. The site was the 1997 Byron Nelson Classic in May, exactly one month after Woods's record-shattering 15-shot victory at the Masters. Already, Woods's mere presence had proven to be marketing gold for any tournament that had him in the field, and he had turned down twice as many invitations as he accepted, including a personal phone call from Bob Hope to play in his namesake event.

After his historic Masters win, Woods went into almost total seclusion for a month, turning down all offers for golf or anything else. Among the calls that went unheeded during the time was one from President Bill Clinton to appear at a ceremony honoring Jackie Robinson's number at Shea Stadium in New York City, along with those from desperate tournament directors nationwide begging him to play in their events.

Tiger Woods made the 1996 Texas Open in San Antonio is first Lone Star appearance as a professional. (Photo courtesy of Gary Perkins Photography)

time in a month at an almost Elvis-like Tuesday press conference that was carried live by five television networks and three radio stations, not to mention being attended by 800 members of the press corps. The 45-minute session covered a wide variety of topics from what he'd been doing on his prolonged vacation to what it was like to turn down a presidential request and discussing his future golfing goals. Woods spoke glowingly of his respect for Nelson and his long ties to Texas.

Once the tournament began, Woods did not disappoint, jumping near the top of the leaderboard in the early stages and staying there for all four rounds. Daily crowds topping 100,000 jammed the TPC-Las Colinas course, raising money for the sponsoring Salesmanship Club and its charities to new record levels. "We literally could not fit any more people on the course because of the facilities needed to handle such a crowd," said Salesmanship Club executive Frank Houseman. Indeed, when Woods played his one round at neighboring Cottonwood Valley, the backup at the tunnel that led to the course was 45 minutes. Woods was tied with little-known pro Lee Rinker going to the final day but emerged with a two-shot victory, his first in Texas as a pro. At the 18th-hole awards ceremony, Woods thanked Nelson and his hosts and said he looked forward to returning the following year. It became a recurring theme, as Woods has rarely missed a trip to the Nelson tournament in his stellar pro career.

His longtime friendship with Nelson and reverence for his golfing deeds proved to be the magic touch to get Woods back on the fairways. The news that he was playing in the 1997 Byron Nelson tournament made the annual event an instant sellout for the first time in its history and sent out North Texas scalpers for hard-to-find tickets. Woods appeared publicly for the first

NCAA Competition

The 1994 NCAA Championship hosted by Southern Methodist University and held at Stonebridge Country Club in McKinney showcased the toughest course in

Texas at the time and demonstrated just how good the latest crop of Texas and other college golfers really were. Justin Leonard won the 1994 individual title with a pair of low-60s rounds and lifted his Longhorns to a close second-place finish.

The winner at Stonebridge was not the harsh course conditions, boasting the highest slope ratings in the state, but the top players who arrived in North Texas. Stanford, led by legendary coach Wally Godwin, won the NCAA team title with Cardinal standout and current PGA Tour member Notah Begay shooting a course-record 62.

It was the second NCAA Championship held in Texas following the University of Houston's successful tournament in the previous decade and came at the invitation of Hank Haney, the noted teacher and Southern Methodist head coach. He had already become fabulously successful as a teacher of both pros and amateurs, coaching the likes of pros Mark O'Meara and Hank and Kelli Kuehne, at his horse barn turned worldwide headquarters only a few miles from Stonebridge.

After earning plenty of success in the teaching world, Haney was looking for a way to give back to the game that had been so good to him since he moved to the Dallas area in 1980. He decided to volunteer his services as coach of the Southern Methodist men's team, forgoing his salary to help a proud program that had recently fallen on tough times. He guided the revived Mustangs to a conference title when the team had barely had a presence before and led them to the NCAA Tournament for the first time in school history. Haney showed he was a man who had dedication and a debt to repay for the many gifts Texas golf had given him.

Restored Lone Stars

One encouraging trend that began in the 1990s has continued into the 21st century and has the potential to reshape Texas golf for the good for years to come. This trend is the restoration of formerly great yet faded municipal golf masterpieces. "Showing their age" as they would say in polite company, but with a nip here and a tuck there, these great courses have been restored to their former glory. "When people talk about municipal golf courses, they almost spit out that word as in, 'It's just a muni course,'" said Houston director of golf operations Fred Buehler. "We're helping to overcome that image."

Houston's Memorial Park was the first to get the makeover treatment beginning in the early 1990s. The course, which opened in 1936, was declared his finest course by no less an expert than Texas golf pioneer John Bredemus. It opened on a huge plot of land just inside the center-city loop in Houston as part of a Works Progress Administration project. It was revolutionary for its era, but over the years the ravages of time, thousands of rounds of municipal golf, and less-than-stellar upkeep began to have an effect.

By 1993, the course was the place for golfers to avoid, not savor, and it took the vision of Buehler along with Mayor Bob Lanier and Memorial alumni turned architect Jay Riviere to turn things around. Lanier called for a special Memorial Park task force to look at ways to return the old course to top shape. Buehler was in charge of spearheading the project, and he turned to Riviere to do the restoration. Buehler admits that when the Memorial Park project was first discussed in the early 1990s, nobody wanted to play

Dallas' Cedar Crest, site of the 1927 PGA Championship, was one of many historic courses recently renovated. (Photo courtesy of City of Dallas)

there unless there was absolutely no other option. "The course condition had basically been status quo since it opened in 1936."

Lanier's committee recommended that the city spend $3 million on course improvement and another $1.2 million on a new clubhouse. The money was raised by selling on-course sponsorships. Memorial Park was closed for 13 months from September 1994 to October 1995. "We still have people saying they'll never play Memorial because we raised the prices, but most people can't believe how nice we made it," Buehler added. While the green fees were raised from $12 and $16 to $22.50 and $32, income to the city doubled

with revenues in the first full fiscal year at $2.5 million on a $2.2 million budget, compared to income of just $1.2 million before the renovation.

The project was a huge success for those who had grown up playing the course, visitors to the city, and those who appreciated great old-style golf. "To me it truly was a labor of love," Riviere said. "Memorial Park was our front porch," said Houston golf executive and former Rice quarterback King Hill. "We all played here and learned here." The Memorial team wrote a self-published history and even enlisted former president and Houston resident George H. W. Bush to serve as honorary chairman.

Just north on Interstate 45, city golf leaders in Dallas were paying close attention to the Memorial Park success story and decided to try much the same thing at the Tenison Park West Course in East Dallas. They called on Dallas-based Golf Resources, Inc., and the project became a mission for native and lead architect Steve Wolfard. "I grew up playing those courses and the condition was really shocking how bad it was, but we just didn't have any other options back then," he said.

Dallas parks and recreation director Paul Dyer said the project, budgeted for $5 million, had to receive city council approval, and initially there were plenty of skeptics. "Some people were reluctant to close the course to do the work," Dyer said—so much so that a group of citizens was able to get an injunction to halt the work for nearly a year. But after addressing concerns over tree removal, the environment, and prices, renovations at Tenison began in October 1999 and finished a year later.

Instead of a place or a stigma that Texas golfers were eager to avoid, city governments statewide became eager to put money into a real, live city service that people might use and enjoy. "When done right, it shows just what city government can accomplish," said Buehler. The latest city course to get a facelift is Dallas' Cedar Crest, which opened in late 2004 after Golf Resources, Inc., which had worked its magic on Tenison, was given the project for the course, which had hosted the 1927 PGA Championship and was the first A. W. Tillinghast design in Texas. "I made 30 to 40 trips to the site to get everything right, because I knew how special it could be," Wolfard said.

As Texas golf headed into a new century, there were plenty of special accomplishments to celebrate over the last 100 years and plenty of special events to occur in the first decade of a new century.

The 2000s
A New Century of Historic Firsts and Lone Star Surprises

5 Highlights of the 2000s

★ Annika Sorenstam becomes the first female golfer in 58 years to play in a PGA Tour event by competing in the 2003 Colonial.

★ Big-money private clubs emerge statewide with top-notch service, conditioning, and layout and a six-figure initiation fee.

★ Rich Beem comes from obscurity in El Paso to capture the PGA Championship in 2002, the first major championship won by a Texan in the new decade.

★ Fred Couples becomes the first University of Houston Cougar to win the Houston Open, capturing the 2003 tournament at the new Redstone Golf Club.

★ Longtime college rivals Texas, Texas A&M, Baylor, and Texas Tech all build premium golf courses connected to their colleges, students, and alumni base.

Story of the Decade: Madame Colonial Pro

Somewhere in the late fall of 2002 or the early spring of 2003, Colonial founder Marvin Leonard had to be smiling broadly. While Leonard passed away in 1970, there was little doubt that he was watching the world-wide scrutiny over the course and tournament he had founded, happy they had made it back into the national golfing spotlight, thanks to a pro Leonard never dreamed would one day play in his invitational PGA Tour event.

When the world's top-rated LPGA female player, Annika Sorenstam, became the first female in 58 years to play in a men's PGA Tour event at the 2003 Colonial, she attracted interest and attention from both the golf and the nongolf public worldwide. Tickets to the 2003 Colonial sold out in record time. Nearly 1,000 journalists from eight countries made their way to Fort Worth to witness Colonial and Sorenstam's historic bid to play with the best of the PGA Tour. "I don't think any of us had any idea how big this would become for the club and for golf," said longtime Colonial tournament committee member Scott Corpening—big enough to give the 2003 tournament the best financial year in the 50-year-plus history of the event Leonard founded in 1946 and focus the attention of the golfing world on Leonard's dream course.

The idea first started in the fall of 2002, when Sorenstam, bored with her annual domination of her fellow females on the LPGA Tour, announced she would consider playing in a men's 2003 PGA Tour event to test herself against the best male players in the world. When various PGA Tour events assessed the

publicity benefits of having the world's top-ranked female in their tournaments, the offers for Sorenstam to play begin to pour in. Colonial, though, was not one of them. Tournament chairman Dee Finley even went as far as to announce that the tournament was not seeking or even particularly interested in her. With the invitational format of the tournament, they didn't expect to invite the talented Swede to play in the 2003 Colonial.

Sorenstam's crafty agent, Mark Steinberg, who also just happened to be the agent for Tiger Woods, got together with Sorenstam and her equally media-savvy husband Davis Esch and decided Colonial would be a very good fit for her singular 2003 quest. The course was a classic, old-style design, which meant it was shorter than most used on the PGA Tour, a factor that would aid Sorenstam, while the many doglegs at Colonial would play into her strength with iron play. But instead of calling Finley first with a sponsor exemption request, Steinberg called Dockery Clark, who represented Colonial title sponsor Bank of America. Clark quickly saw the publicity value, signed on to the idea, and urged Steinberg to call Finley.

The call came to the longtime Colonial member and tournament executive at Finley's Fort Worth law office. Steinberg said that Annika would like to play at

Annika Sorenstam made Colonial in Fort Worth her stage as the first female in a PGA Tour event in more than 50 years. (Photo courtesy of Colonial Country Club)

Colonial in 2003 and that he already had the backing of Colonial title sponsor Bank of America.

His afternoon call put Finley and the Colonial executive tournament in a very tough spot. They have traditionally been one of the most familiar of tournaments, patterning their tournament after the equally tradition-bound Masters. Finley was already on record as saying he wasn't excited about Sorenstam coming to Fort Worth. On the other hand, the tournament's title sponsor, which supplied the majority of the total purse, was actively in favor of the move. Sorenstam's agent also represented the one player (Woods) whom Colonial had been desperately pursuing to make a return visit since he came in 1997.

Finley wrote his pros and cons of the decision, telling no one about the phone call except his wife. "Bank of America told us it was up to us, it was our exemption to grant, and they would have supported us," Corpening said. After thinking over the decision for several days and its ramifications for the club and the tournament, Finley called a secret meeting of past and current tournament leaders to get their opinions. They decided the one-time event would be good for the club and the Colonial tournament, helping to raise money and club publicity. "Of course it will be a media circus, but so what? I can't believe anybody doesn't think it will bring great attention to Colonial and Fort Worth," was the prevailing local opinion as voiced by Fort Worth native and golf writer Dan Jenkins.

When the announcement was finally made that Sorenstam would be coming to play in the 2003 tournament, the reaction was immediate but not totally favorable. "In a club this size, you could probably find people against motherhood and apple pie, but the majority of people are in favor of it as being good for the club and good for the tournament," Finley said. The first to sound off was Colonial defending champion Nick Price, who slammed the sponsor exemption. "It's not right," Price said of the Sorenstam situation. "This just reeks of trying to find publicity. Why? What's she trying to prove?"

The next to dissent was PGA Tour superstar Vijay Singh, who told a reporter two weeks before the event he hoped she missed the cut and then pulled himself out days before the Colonial tournament citing fatigue. The PGA players most critical kept their opinions to themselves to avoid the public censure given Price and Singh. Of all the millions of pre-Colonial words spoken, some of the best and most honest belong to Dallas' Harrison Frazar: "You know she's not going to finish last; she's going to beat some people. I just hope to God it's not me."

The pending arrival of Sorenstam at Colonial continued to swell interest in the tournament every week. She arrived for a practice round at Colonial a month before the tournament, quickly charming the membership and staff, happily signing autographs for anyone who asked. When introduced to the 14-time Colonial women's club champion, Donna Thompson, Sorenstam said she should be asking for an autograph from a local expert like that instead of giving one.

Corpening and Finley continued their preparations for her visit, readying the entire ladies' locker room for one player and arranging for security and media attention worthy of a presidential visit. The USA Network, which was responsible for showing early-round action at Colonial, announced that they would scrap their entire afternoon lineup to show Sorenstam's first round shot by shot, an opening-round viewing window never given another golfer, male or female. Scalpers moved into the Colonial area selling red-hot tournament tickets to watch a shot at history, making it the most anticipated Fort Worth golf event since the 1941 U.S. Open. Even Las Vegas chimed in, setting the over–under total for Sorenstam's first-round score at 76.5.

Sorenstam's playing partners for her historic Texas round were Aaron Barber and Dean Wilson, both relatively young and unknown players still looking for their first PGA Tour wins but caught up in the media and golf-attention firestorm surrounding Sorenstam. They both were given their own press conference Tuesday of Colonial week to explain their bit parts in the worldwide drama, and then Sorenstam held court for nearly 40 minutes to a packed gallery of media from around the world. "I'm doing what I want to do, testing myself against the best players of the world on a course I think is well suited for my game," she said.

Although the first couple of days of tournament week were rainy at Colonial, Thursday dawned sunny and warm with the drama and tension thick and heavy as Sorenstam prepared for her 12:20 P.M. tee time. The overriding question among the fans lined 20 deep along the wall next to the 10th tee was, after all the words spoken by Sorenstam and hundreds of others, how would the world's best female player fare against the PGA Tour's best on Leonard's historic course? With one mighty swing of her 3-wood, Sorenstam began to answer her doubters. Teeing off last in her group, she split the middle of the Colonial fairway, while her partners faded to the left and right. Sorenstam mock staggered off the first tee, clutching her chest while smiling, but it was clear she had not let the intense pressure get her down.

Her second shot of the day left her with a birdie putt on her first hole and began an amazingly consistent pattern. The sweet-swinging Swede had a putt for birdie of some length on all 18 of her opening-round holes on a layout she had only seen a couple of times and had never played in competition. After a couple of near-misses, she scored her first Colonial birdie with a 15-foot effort from just off the green on the par-3 13th hole to see her name briefly go on the leaderboard at one under par.

Her first-round one-over 71 left her well within the 36-hole cut line and within a few shots of the first round leaders. The praise was immediate and widespread for her heroic opening-round effort under the heavy pressure and scrutiny. "Ecstatic," said husband Esch, who left his hospital bed in Orlando to fly in for the first round. "Amazing," concurred agent Steinberg, who has seen plenty of top rounds in his career working for Woods. "Wonderful," added Swedish teacher Pia Nillisson. "I was so nervous on the first tee and all throughout the day, but I'm very pleased with the score," Sorenstam said.

She beat one playing partner, Barber, who shot 72, and tied another, Wilson. "I'll probably take a little ribbing for losing to her, but she'll beat a lot of people out here. She's an excellent player," Barber admitted. "I tied her, but I had work for it too," Wilson added. She missed only one fairway the entire day, the par-4 fifth. In fact, her only trouble came with three-putt bogeys on the fifth and ninth holes, missing her par putts

from inside five feet both times. "I should have bet on myself," Sorenstam said.

Her huge gallery consisted of hundreds of Texas golf fans wearing the green "Go Annika" buttons, which were the idea of a pair of Colonial assistant golf pros and turned out to be the hottest-selling items of the week. They quickly sold out at $3 each and went on E-bay for as much as $50 a button. "I am glad my assistants could make some money for their idea," said Colonial head pro Dow Finsterwald Jr. There was also Fort Worth golf fan John Harrell, wearing a self-made chicken hat with the name "Vijay" written on both sides. "Vijay Singh is a chicken for not showing up today, and Annika showed why," he said.

The second day was also warm, bright, and clear but a day where the famed Colonial links fought back to deny Sorenstam an extended run at history. Her quest came to an abrupt end Friday, missing the 36-hole cut in a blizzard of poor chips and three-putts on the baffling Colonial Country Club greens.

She shot a second-round 74 to finish at four-over-par 145, missing the 36-hole cut by four shots. She finished tied for 96th place but left with the sounds of seemingly endless standing ovations ringing in her ears as she headed up the hill past the 18th green to the scoring trailer. "I guess I didn't want it to end. I wanted to play here on the weekend," Sorenstam said of her heavy sobs, which continued in the media center. "I'm living a dream I want to live. I am doing what I want to do." The dream captured the attention and appreciation of thousands of Texans and jump-started golf's next century in Texas on a historic and high-spirited note.

Texas Rich in PGA Talent

The 20th century has already produced one Texas pro who moved to El Paso en route to a future star golfing career in Lee Trevino, and the 21st has already produced one more who followed Trevino's steps in moving to the far West Texas city to turn his career toward stardom by winning the 2002 PGA Championship.

Rich Beem had grown up in New Mexico, where his dad was the head golf coach at New Mexico State University. While he displayed plenty of golfing talent, it was not channeled into a positive direction until he moved to El Paso to work for Bill Eschenbrenner and Cameron Doan at El Paso Country Club. "Rich has just got so much energy that he's got to have a place to burn it off. If you look at all the great players that have got it all together in their personal life and their game, they all have done that," Eschenbrenner, the former longtime pro at El Paso Country Club, said.

Despite his well-documented string of wild off-the-course activities that mainly involved alcohol, Beem was able to pull his game together thanks to the help of the two teachers. Doan made perhaps the most important move by firing Beem as his assistant and telling him to get out on the range and practice his natural golfing ability. "Rich was never going to be comfortable folding shirts and giving lessons," Doan said. "I told him he needed to be out there playing and working on his game."

Beem took that advice to heart, playing in several minitour events in the area, then graduating to the PGA Tour. He won the 1999 Kemper Classic outside of Washington, D.C., as a virtual unknown like his El Paso role model, Trevino, and then after getting married, he rededicated to his golf game to capture the 2002 International outside of Denver in an exciting duel with Steve Lowery. "I'm a streak player, that's the way it was last year, and that's the way it's always been," Beem said.

But little could prepare him for the ultimate streak a few weeks later when he teed it up at the PGA Championship at Hazeltine Golf Club outside of Minneapolis, Minnesota. He shocked the major championship field by sharing the 36-hole lead with fellow Texan Justin Leonard and others, along the way charming the assembled media and fans with tales of his humble Texas roots, his career as a former cell phone salesman in Seattle, and his habit of chugging bottles of Pepto-Bismol to calm his nerves. "I didn't have any expectations because I had never won a major before," Beem said.

He was three shots behind Leonard going to the final round, two ahead of Tiger Woods, but outclassed both of them with a final-round 66 to capture his first major title, eagling the par-3 13th hole and rolling in a 35-foot birdie putt on the 16th hole to hold off another Woods Sunday charge. Beem closed his eyes and danced a small jig after his win, the first Texan to capture one of golf's major championships in the new century. "Rich wasn't the ball beater Lee was, but he had plenty of talent and a desire to win, which is what he had in common with Lee," Eschenbrenner said of his second West Texas golfing star.

Texas Super Clubs

Heading into the 21st century, Texas had gone more than a decade without a new upper-end, equity private club, a place where the initiation fee was in the six-figure

Vaquero Golf Club.
(Photo courtesy of
Discovery Land Company)

range, where the service and conditions were beyond compare, and where the bluest of blue bloods, the upper end of the golfing elite, the most successful of golfers, met to discuss their shared passion. Legendary clubs like that existed in almost every major city, but most had been there for decades: River Oaks in Houston, Preston Trail in Dallas, and San Antonio Country Club in the Alamo City. Fortunately, the opening years of the 2000s brought an exciting new crop of courses for the truly passionate and well-heeled golfer.

Almost every major city in Texas began an upper-end private club over the first couple years of the new decade—all tributes to great architecture, great passion, and great wealth. The first of this new breed came from the highly successful Redstone Company in Houston. It opened Shadow Hawk Golf Club in the booming suburb of Richmond at roughly the same time it also opened the Houstonian Golf Club. Already known for its landmark Houstonian Hotel in Houston, where former president George H. W. Bush stayed when he was in town while bunking full time at the White House, Redstone built Shadow Hawk as a private golf oasis in the mode of Champions, River Oaks, and Houston Country Club.

Rees Jones was hired to design the course, along with the slightly less exclusive Houstonian Golf Club, and Redstone snagged longtime Houston Country Club pro Paul Marchand as the new golf director at Shadow Hawk. "We want to have a special course with special service and a truly special place for our membership," he said. The first founding member was the 41st president and longtime Houston golf nut, Bush himself. He hit the first tee shot on the par-71 course when it opened and is known to bring an interesting mix of people to play, including former secretary of state and fellow Houston resident James Baker. "You can never tell who the president is going to bring," Marchand said. "It might be the prime minister of this or the president of that."

Next for this upper-end golf glory was Austin Golf Club and Austin's favorite son, designer Ben Crenshaw. "We don't have tennis or swimming or anything else, it's just a quiet place to play golf," Crenshaw said of his labor of love just over 20 miles from downtown Austin. Crenshaw and his longtime architectural partner Bill Coore designed the tough par-70 layout to fit their minimalist golf design philosophy. You won't find huge carries over manmade craters here or thousands of pounds of dirt moved to create a spectacular effect. Each hole is individually labeled with an appropriate title, including "Take Dead Aim," to honor his longtime teacher Harvey Penick, and "Innocence." Highly successful teacher Joe Beck was hired from Barton Creek as the new director of golf.

Austin Golf Club, like Shadow Hawk, appealed to the most successful of golfers with initiation fees of six figures and higher. Caddies were available to all who take part in this once-familiar golf tradition that is making a Lone Star comeback thanks to the new clubs. "What we tried to do is a little different in the sense that everything is done to enhance the game of golf," Crenshaw said. "Nothing distracts from that, and I've been very pleased with the final results and reaction we've received." Golf fans should not count on buying their dream home on the 18th hole or anywhere else at Austin Golf Club because the club maintains its strict golf-only atmosphere.

North Texas received the regal new private club treatment thanks to the vision of two men, Mike Meldman and John MacDonald. Both became highly successful in different facets of the business world, but both came to the same conclusion: that the Dallas–Fort Worth area was decidedly underserved when it came to upper-end, exclusive golf clubs.

Meldman and MacDonald, the principals of the Vaquero Club and Dallas National, opened their own private golf clubs within seven months of each other in 2002. Each required a six-figure-plus investment (unheard of for the North Texas area), both used the same architect, and each opened among some of the most challenging economic conditions this area had seen in nearly a decade. Vaquero opened at $65,000 plus a six-figure lot purchase required, while Dallas National started at $75,000 but quickly jumped to $175,000 and headed to $200,000, making it the most expensive club to join in the state.

Tom Fazio, renowned as golf's greatest living architect, was the architect for both courses, which feature over-the-top service, such as walking with caddies in the grand tradition of the game, unmatched course conditions, and lavish clubhouses. "Dallas, Texas, has not opened a true upper-end equity club since Preston Trail in 1964, so the expectations are very high," MacDonald said. "There are not a lot of high-end equity clubs in this area, and the good ones are hard to get into with long waiting lists," Meldman added. "We wanted to have the instant tradition of Brook Hollow, Northwood, and Preston Trail."

Par-71 Dallas National is golf only and sits on what MacDonald called "a miracle piece of land," a steep, hilly, tree-covered, 388-acre site better suited for Austin or San Antonio than traditionally flat Dallas. Par-72 Vaquero operates as a traditional family club and hired former TPC-Four Seasons golf director Mike Abbott, who brought a level of service not previously seen in the market. "It's simple services done right, but something most clubs ignore. We've made part of your daily life easier," Abbott said.

Despite their hefty initiation fees and tight membership caps, both were immediately successful, with Dallas National quickly selling out of its 350 memberships and Vaquero attracting more than a dozen PGA Tour pros to play and practice there when they are not on the professional golf road. Despite opening in challenging economic times, both professed to reach a limited but very avid golf niche. "The economic downturn is overstated for people at the income level we're seeking," MacDonald said.

Tom Fazio was also the designer at the San Antonio private golf haven Briggs Ranch, which also opened in the first years of the new decade. "We wanted to bring in a golf experience people in San Antonio have not had," said part-owner Buddy Cook, who also had a role in opening the highly successful San Antonio courses The Dominion and La Cantera Golf Club.

Former British Open Champion Bill Rogers came over from San Antonio Country Club to serve as director of golf at Briggs Ranch, offering his experience and expertise to the highly successful new project. In Austin, longtime Barton Creek golf director Brent Buckman left after 20 years to help start Spanish Oak, designed by Bob Cupp, a golf-only design that attracted Austin golf pros Joe Oglivie and Rich Beem, who moved from El Paso to Austin for the experience. Gentle Creek, a D. A. Weibring/Golf Resources golf-only project, opened in the growing North Texas suburb of Prosper to great reviews and success. Even Jack Nicklaus got into the act with the spectacular Carlton Woods club in The Woodlands outside of Houston, which was joined by a Fazio course in 2005.

The first few years of the new decade showed that legendary Texas golf passion, vision, and big dollars were still alive and well with a new crop of superclubs.

Cougar Houston Open

Sometimes it's not money and trophies that signify a PGA Tour victory. Sometimes it's just the tears. That was the case for Fred Couples at the 2003 Houston Open. For more than 50 years, the Houston Open had signified great Bayou City golf with champions such as Arnold Palmer, Curtis Strange, Hal Sutton, and Vijay Singh—but never a current or former University of Houston Cougar golfer, that is, until proud Cougar alumnus Couples did the trick in 2003 at the first tournament held at the beautiful new Redstone Golf Club.

Couples, a Seattle native who once lived near Dallas, dominated at the University of Houston, teaming with roommate Blaine McCallister to play for the Cougars. He also met suitemate and future CBS announcer Jim Nantz and star Houston golf professional Marchand while in college and has remained close to them ever since. Couples was an unlikely player to break the Houston Open Cougar jinx. The 1992 Masters champion hadn't won in five years and rarely played more than 15 or 16 times in a season because of chronic back problems.

Houston still held a strong attraction to Couples, and with the strong urging of his friends and former college classmates, he committed to the 2003 tournament along with a stellar field that included Singh, Ernie Els, and Phil Mickelson. Couples held the first-round lead and headed into the final day a single stroke in front of good friend Mark Calcavecchia, two better than Australian Stuart Appleby.

Texan Hank Kuehne, who shared the second-round lead with Couples, fired a six-under 66 Sunday and briefly held for the lead, but Couples fought back, hitting his approach to a foot on the par-4 16th for an easy birdie and another birdie on 18, reducing the usually calm and stoic Couples to tears on the 18th green. "To be the first U of H guy to win is—I don't think it's any different for any of the rest of the guys. It's different for me, and what a school, what a great, great school to go to," he said.

As he prepared to begin the public awards ceremony at the 18th, Couples was greeted by Nantz, who had just broadcast the event for CBS, and Marchand, who had closely followed the final holes. The threesome formed a tight, tear-filled circle, celebrating the end of the Cougar Jinx and victory for the former Houston star. "I am always emotional when nice things happen to nice people," Couples laughed, his smile highlighting the tears of a Houston Cougar champion with a most popular hometown victory.

Lone Star Travels to Victory

On the Texas map, the distance between tiny Andrews, Texas, and massive supercity Houston is several hundred miles, but the distance that Andrews native Chad Campbell covered to arrive at the 2003 Tour Championship at Champions Golf Club is a lifetime of Lone Star golf dreams and excellence. The soft-spoken, low-key Campbell had dominated every phase of his golfing career, from the generously named Andrews Country Club to a state high school title, Hooters Tour legend, and Nationwide Tour promotion to the PGA Tour for three wins in a single season.

He had already collected three second-place finishes in 2003 and eight top-10 finishes along with more prize money than most people in his hometown will make in their entire lifetime. But the one thing Campbell was missing in his first trip to historic Champions Golf Club was a PGA Tour victory. "I really don't know much about Champions," Campbell said a few weeks before the event started. "I know it's a famous course, but not much about Mr. Burke."

Burke, who built and carefully guided the course for decades, certainly had heard of Campbell by the end of the tournament. He stayed around the leaderboard for the first round, then blew past the star-studded field with a course-record 61 on Saturday, humbling the layout that had hosted more golf championships

Andrews native Chad Campbell made the Tour Championship his first PGA Tour title. (Photo courtesy of David Redwine/Redwine Images)

in Texas than any other course. "It was a great day," Campbell said of his record round.

But off the course, the news of the decidedly non-flashy Campbell's record round hadn't circulated far past Champions' gates. Campbell, along with his entire family, in town for the season-ending event, went to dinner at a local chain restaurant. Seeing the group

dressed in golf attire, the perky waitress asked, "So, are you in town for the tournament?" Chad's older brother Mike quickly answered, "'Yes.' Then I changed the subject as soon as possible."

A front-nine 31 pushed Campbell to a five-shot lead Sunday, and he cruised home to his first Tour victory in his home state before family, friends, and thousands of Lone Star admirers. "It's nice to get the first one under my belt and to especially do it in Texas makes it extra special."

Campbell became the first player to make the Tour Championship his initial PGA Tour victory and the first Texan to win the event since Tom Kite won the third such tournament in 1989. He validated the win with a follow-up victory at Arnold Palmer's Bay Hill tournament in early 2004 and earned a spot on the U.S. Ryder Cup team. The road from Andrews to Houston to nationwide golfing fame is a long one, but nobody has covered it more impressively than Campbell.

The Claret Jug Returns to Texas

Todd Hamilton didn't grow up or learn his golf in Texas, but Dallas–Fort Worth offered the only direct flight to Japan, so for the globe-trotting, dream-chasing golf gypsy, that was as good a reason as any to move to North Texas. Along the way, he became the fourth Texan in 35 years to bring golf's oldest trophy home to the Lone Star State.

Growing up in Illinois, Hamilton didn't know much about Texas golf history and legends until he was exposed to them while playing in the Big 12 Conference at the University of Oklahoma. When a college friend moved to North Texas and settled at the Pete Dye–designed Stonebridge Country Club in McKinney, just north of Dallas, he told Hamilton about the warm weather, great facilities, and top players to play and practice against. "He told me this was a pretty good place, and when we came down here, it was really nice. My wife and I really liked it."

With Hamilton achieving little or no success at PGA Tour Qualifying School, his chances to play at home were limited. "One thing I learned was playing with good players every day I was in Texas really helped me," he said. He joined fellow Texans Brandt Jobe and Brian Watts as part-time members of the Japanese Tour, winning four times in 2003 and finishing third on the Japanese Tour money list. "I was always getting ready for another Japanese tournament, and the DFW Airport was one of the easiest ways to get there," he said.

Encouraged by his overseas tour success, Hamilton finally received his PGA Tour card for 2004 at age 39, on his eighth try, earning the 16th and final spot in the 2003 PGA Tour Qualifying School finals. He ensured his stay would be a long one by capturing the 2004 Honda Classic outside Fort Lauderdale, but the journey didn't turn truly historic until a couple of months later at Royal Troon in Scotland, where fellow Texan Justin Leonard had emerged to greatness in 1997.

Hamilton missed the cut at the 2003 British Open playing on a Japanese Tour exemption but stayed near the top of the pack going into the weekend at Royal Troon in 2004. Hamilton's steady play, honed by years of success in Japan and months of practice with his new pro friends in Texas, molded him for the improbable challenge. "Day in and day out, playing with good players will help your game. I learned that there are a lot of good players in the state and all Texans are pretty good ball strikers."

Thanks to his lessons on ball striking and low-ball hitting, which would make any West Texas native proud, Hamilton emerged from 18 holes of grueling final-day competition in a playoff with former British and U.S. Open champion Ernie Els. That's when the unthinkable became reality as Hamilton used his short-game wizardry and clutch putting to defeat Els in the playoff and captured the 2004 Open Championship, bringing the Claret Jug trophy back to Texas. "I put in the tape the other night and watched it, because I still have a hard time believing what happened," he said.

Less than 72 hours after his landmark win, Hamilton returned home to a rowdy celebration at Stonebridge Country Club in McKinney, pulling up in a white stretch limo to 600 friends and supporters who lined up for hours to congratulate him and have their pictures taken with his new trophy. "I really think the Dye course had something to do with me winning the Open," said Hamilton. "The links layout is much the same, and often the wind is the same, plus all these people here standing behind me supporting me."

In the fall of 2004, Hamilton moved to the upscale Vaquero development in Westlake, between Dallas and Fort Worth, less than a pitch shot from good friend and 1998 British Open runner-up Watts and a good drive and 3-wood from fellow Troon champion Leonard. "I didn't grow up here, but I learned there are plenty of good players and good ball-strikers. I'm very grateful," Hamilton said.

So is Texas golf for another transplanted golf champion who chose to add his name to the ever-growing legacy of major champions.

Tiger Returns in Style

After getting an excused absence from tournament namesake Byron Nelson to skip the 2003 Byron Nelson Classic, Tiger Woods returned in grand style to the 2004 PGA Tour event at the fabulous Four Seasons Resort in Irving. The 2004 tournament attracted the best field in the history of the Nelson, with the world's top four players—Woods; Vijay Singh; Phil Mickelson, fresh off a Masters win; and Ernie Els—all entered together for the first time in a nonmajor that year. "It's great to have all of us together to see what's going to happen and be able to keep an eye on each other," said Mickelson.

Woods, the 1997 Nelson winner, came in after another disappointing finish at the Masters and with only one victory in the nearly halfway-completed season. "It's great to be back," Woods said. "The golf course has changed a little bit. The rough is up a little higher and it's very soft, but other than that, it's the same golf course."

With the Big Four all gathered in the same event for one week, the ultimate winner was another world-class player who had been somewhat overlooked since he burst onto the scene in 1999: Sergio Garcia. He emerged for a three-way playoff to capture his first Nelson victory and his first win in nearly three years since winning in Fort Worth at the 2001 Colonial. It also came at the site of Garcia's PGA Tour debut in 1999. "It is special, no doubt about it. As you all know, it's the course where I started my career here in the U.S.," Garcia said. "Byron has been such a great supporter for the game of golf and also for the Tour, and he's been very good to me, too. He's always said nice things about me."

While Garcia stuck around late Sunday night, buying drinks for his friends and fans at the Four Seasons poolside bar, the victory didn't come without the trademark Woods dramatics. He staged a huge rally on the back nine to cut Garcia's lead to a single shot but needed a birdie on the last hole to make the playoff. Woods pushed his drive off the 18th tee way right and couldn't find the fairway with his second shot from deep rough. Needing to hole his approach shot, Woods made an incredible recovery from the tangled grass, landing his birdie try two feet from the cup and a playoff berth. "I thought it might have had a chance," Woods said. As Tiger has proved on his many North Texas golf visits, he always has a chance for something special. Woods' 2005 visit to Irving for the EDS Byron Nelson Championship was even more memorable, but for a different reason. After a 1-under 69 on Thursday he shot a 2-over 72 on Friday at Cottonwood Valley, bogeying the par-4 18th hole from a greenside bunker, to miss the 36-hole cut for the first time in nearly eight years on the PGA Tour, more than 140 tournaments. It's another Texas first which will likely never be repeated here or anywhere else.

TPC for Texas

David Craig, a highly successful North Texas businessman, and Tom Weiskopf, a world-class golfer and former British Open champion, don't have a whole lot in common, but they were committed to one thing. They were both passionate about golf and determined that the North Texas area needed one more premium course with a TPC (Tournament Players Course) designation.

The result was the opening of the TPC at Craig Ranch in the fall of 2004, a private par-72 Weiskopf design. It took a budget of more than $40 million, spent on the layout, a massive clubhouse, and three years of working Weiskopf's architectural magic. "I think we took some great land and great views and gave people a very memorable course," Weiskopf said before the grand opening.

Former Dallas Cowboys legendary quarterback Troy Aikman was recruited as the celebrity member/host for Craig Ranch, which gave Texas three TPC designs at the time, joining the one in Irving and The Woodlands, the second most of any state in the country. "You can certainly tell by the success of the TPC courses in Texas, this has been very successful brand and a very good market for us," said PGA director for public relations/business Chris Smith.

With an opening initiation fee of $50,000, Craig Ranch was an early success in Craig's hometown of McKinney, just north of Dallas. The course wasn't initially scheduled to hold a PGA Tour event, but Tour Commissioner Tim Finchem, in town shortly after the opening, hailed its impressive beginnings as another winner in the always-impressive Texas Tour course arsenal.

Big 12 Conference Clash

Longtime conference rivals Texas, Texas A&M, Baylor, and Texas Tech usually can't agree on anything, but one thing they all came together on in the first decade of the new century was the need for outstanding golf courses for their students, golf teams, fans, and alumni. All four Big 12 Conference schools built outstanding golf facilities that are closely tied to their schools' golfing fortunes.

While Baylor University is seldom first in many athletic endeavors, it jumped to the top of the list when the Peter Jacobsen–designed Bear Ridge golf facility opened in late 2001. The semiprivate par-72 design is 20 minutes from the Waco campus and serves as the home for the highly competitive men's and women's Baylor golf teams along with Baylor supporters of all ages. "College golf is a big business now, and Bear Ridge will boost the Baylor programs into the top level for the next 20 years," Jacobsen said.

Working with longtime associate Jim Hardy of Houston, Jacobsen took a rolling piece of land that wrapped around the Bosque River on the back nine and crafted a highly enjoyable test of green-and-gold-hued golf. "We were provided with a beautiful piece of land," Hardy said. "This will be one of the top courses in Texas and will be reminiscent of many of the scenic, rolling, hilly-type courses you see in Austin."

Also included is an 8,000-square-foot indoor/outdoor practice center for the Baylor golf teams, including covered hitting areas, video monitors, practice holes, and a full locker room facility with space inside for the Bears' golfing trophies.

Texas Tech was next to get into the act with a public course on campus designed by highly respected architect Bob Cupp. He might have had the toughest job of all on the flat plains of Lubbock as he scooped several thousand feet of dirt on the par-72 Rawls Golf Course facilities to set the course below street level. The visually appealing layout is somewhat blocked from the winds and also has more humps, bumps, and elevation changes than you see in the surrounding West Texas landscape.

The green fees are low enough to fit into any college kid's budget and set the green-grass stage for Texas Tech to build a strong college golf program.

Baylor University was one of several Big 12 schools to open school-themed courses in the early 2000s. (Photo courtesy of Baylor University/Cliff Cheney)

The University of Texas has never lacked for a strong program or golf history, but the University of Texas Golf Club, which opened in 2003 at Steiner Ranch in Austin, was the first course ever dedicated to the storied program. The par-71 layout was designed by local architects Roy Bechtol and Randy Russell and set in the natural Hill Country scenery and beauty.

Each hole is dedicated to a University of Texas golf or sports legend, which means the school may need another 18 holes to get them all in, but the course with its orange and white golf carts and orange tees is perfect for any Longhorn lover. Head football coach Mack Brown serves as the chairman of the board of directors,

with longtime Austin golf professional Steve Termeer as the director of golf.

While Jack Nicklaus has also been known for green with his six Masters jackets, he slipped on enough maroon to design the outstanding Traditions Golf Club at Texas A&M, which opened in the fall of 2004. The private par-72 facility is a stern test from the back tees with dozens of hardwoods lining the course, natural creeks crisscrossing the layout, and plenty of bunkers to punish any wayward shots.

Nobody loves tradition more than the Fighting Texas Aggies, and the course should build a strong tradition of great A&M golf, which has already produced top PGA Tour players Jeff Maggert, David

Ogrin, and 2004 Walt Disney Classic winner Ryan Palmer. The greens are a challenge in themselves, as Nicklaus combined with his son Jack II to lay out his first course in the lush Brazos Valley area of Texas.

Building the Dream for the Twenty-First Century

Texas has always promoted the notion of golf's most historic state through wave after wave, decade after decade, of legendary golfers, places, and events. From Harry Cooper and Ralph Guldahl to Nelson and Hogan, Burke, Demaret, Trevino, Crenshaw, Kite, Leonard, and Campbell, Lone Star golfers represent an unbroken string of golf greatness worldwide.

What about the next decade, the next generation, the next century of Texas golf? What lies ahead for the state's nearly 1,000 courses and the players they will produce and nurture? Is Texas headed for a lull, a revival, or a new golden era of golf and golfers?

The view from those who know the state and its golf programs best suggests that Texas is poised to not even miss a beat as it moves forward into a new century. "I think there are a lot more opportunities today for success than even during the Age of Hogan because the players are better," says longtime Dallas golf pro Randy Smith, who molded Leonard and Harrison Frazar to PGA Tour success. "The tradition always filters down and serves as a stimulus for the kids now in the golf pipeline."

You don't have to look far to see the golf pipeline is bursting with the next generation of promising Texas golfers. Dallas' Matthew Rosenfeld, the 2000 U.S. Junior Champion, is now playing golf at the storied University of Texas program. McKinney's Hunter Mahan, the 1999 U.S. Junior Champion, was the second-youngest player on the PGA Tour in 2004 and regained his playing card with ease, earning more than $800,000.

Long-hitting Hank Kuehne, from McKinney, who captured the 1998 U.S. Amateur, has already won two international tournaments along with a two Tour two-man partnerships. San Antonio's Jimmy Walker came through Baylor to win Nationwide Player of the Year honors in 2004 as the Tour's leading money winner. "We will keep the heritage going and keep it even better across the board because we have even better, more athletic players coming up who are just as intent on being the best," Smith said.

Amarillo's Palmer was a lesser-known player at Texas A&M, playing the TightLies Tour with Campbell before spending a year on the Nationwide Tour in 2003 and making the PGA Tour as a rookie in 2004. Playing in the next-to-last full-field tournament of the year, all Palmer did was knock off the world's top-ranked golfer, Vijay Singh, to win the Walt Disney World tournament. "Growing up in West Texas watching Kite, Crenshaw, and Justin Leonard, I still can't believe it. Getting to hang out with friends like Chad on the Tour now is great, just like a dream."

For the past century, the next decades, and all golf millennia to come, Lone Star golf has and will always be about dreams—those fulfilled, those shattered, and those still to come.

Appendix
Major Championships
Won by Texas Golfers

Masters (12)

1937: Byron Nelson, Roanoke
1939: Ralph Guldahl, Dallas
1940: Jimmy Demaret, Houston
1942: Byron Nelson, Roanoke
1947: Jimmy Demaret, Houston
1950: Jimmy Demaret, Houston
1951: Ben Hogan, Fort Worth
1953: Ben Hogan, Fort Worth
1956: Jack Burke Jr., Houston
1971: Charles Coody, Abilene
1984: Ben Crenshaw, Austin
1995: Ben Crenshaw, Austin

U.S. Open (12)

1937: Ralph Guldahl, Dallas
1938: Ralph Guldahl, Dallas
1939: Byron Nelson, Roanoke
1946: Lloyd Mangrum, Trenton
1948: Ben Hogan, Fort Worth
1950: Ben Hogan, Fort Worth
1951: Ben Hogan, Fort Worth
1953: Ben Hogan, Fort Worth
1968: Lee Trevino, Dallas
1969: Orville Moody, Sulphur Springs
1981: David Graham, Dallas
1992: Tom Kite, Austin

British Open (6)

1953: Ben Hogan, Fort Worth
1971: Lee Trevino, Dallas
1972: Lee Trevino, Dallas
1981: Bill Rogers, San Antonio
1997: Justin Leonard, Dallas
2004: Todd Hamilton, McKinney

PGA Championship (15)

1940: Byron Nelson, Roanoke
1945: Byron Nelson, Roanoke
1946: Ben Hogan, Fort Worth
1948: Ben Hogan, Fort Worth
1956: Jack Burke Jr., Houston
1965: Dave Marr, Houston
1967: Don January, Dallas
1974: Lee Trevino, Dallas
1977: Lanny Wadkins, Dallas
1978: John Mahaffey, Kerrville
1979: David Graham, Dallas
1984: Lee Trevino, Dallas
1995: Steve Elkington, Houston
1996: Mark Brooks, Fort Worth
2002: Rich Beem, El Paso

LPGA Championship (7)

1959: Betsy Rawls, Austin
1965: Sandra Haynie, Fort Worth
1967: Kathy Whitworth, Monahans
1969: Betsy Rawls, Austin
1971: Kathy Whitworth, Monahans
1974: Sandra Haynie, Fort Worth
1975: Kathy Whitworth, Monahans

U.S. Women's Open (8)

1947: Betty Jameson, San Antonio
1948: Babe Zaharias, Beaumont
1950: Babe Zaharias, Beaumont
1951: Betsy Rawls, Austin
1953: Betsy Rawls, Austin
1954: Babe Zaharias, Beaumont
1957: Betsy Rawls, Austin
1975: Sandra Palmer, Fort Worth

Texans in World Golf Hall of Fame (18)

1951: Betty Jameson, San Antonio
1974: Ben Hogan, Fort Worth
     Byron Nelson, Roanoke
     Babe Zaharias, Beaumont
1977: Sandra Haynie, Fort Worth
     Carol Mann, Houston
1981: Lee Trevino, Dallas
     Ralph Guldahl, Dallas
1982: Kathy Whitworth, Monahans
1983: Jimmy Demaret, Houston
1987: Betsy Rawls, Austin
1992: Harry Cooper, Dallas
1998: Lloyd Mangrum, Trenton
2000: Judy Rankin, Midland
     Jack Burke Jr., Houston
2002: Ben Crenshaw, Austin
     Harvey Penick, Austin
2004: Tom Kite, Austin

Selected Bibliography

Anderson, Dave. "U.S. Open." *New York Times*, June 9–16, 1969, p. 1B.

Blair, Sam. "Texas Golf History." *Dallas Morning News*, March 2, 1997, p. 1R.

———. "Legends: Hogan's Trophy." *Private Clubs*, September–October 2000, p. 23.

Bradley, Jon. *Quotable Byron*. Nashville: Towle House Publishing, 2002.

Buenger, Victoria, and Warner Buenger. *Texas Merchant: Marvin Leonard and Fort Worth*. College Station: Texas A&M University Press, 1998.

Canty, Carol. *A History of the San Antonio Country Club*. San Antonio: Watercress Press, 2004.

Companiotte, John. *Jimmy Demaret: The Swing's the Thing*. Ann Arbor, Mich.: Clock Tower Press, 2004.

———. *The PGA Championship: The Season's Final Major*. Ann Arbor, Mich.: Clock Tower Press, 2004.

Crenshaw, Ben, and Melanie Hauser. *A Feel for the Game: To Brookline and Back*. New York: Doubleday, 2001.

Dalton, Kyle. "Golfsmith: More Than a Superstore." Travelgolf.com, July 15, 2002.

Davis, Martin. *Byron Nelson: The Story of Golf's Finest Gentleman and the Greatest Winning Streak in History*. Greenwich, Conn.: The American Golfer, 1997.

———. *The 25 Greatest Achievements in Golf.* Greenwich, Conn.: American Golfer, 1997.

———. *Ben Hogan: The Man behind the Mystique.* Greenwich, Conn.: American Golfer, 2002.

Dealy, Ted. *Diaper Days of Dallas.* Nashville: Abingdon Press, 1966.

Dedman, Robert, and Debbie DeLoach. *King of Clubs.* Dallas: Taylor Publishing, 1999.

Galloway, Diane Caylor. *Dallas Country Club: The First Hundred Years.* Fort Worth: Cockrell Printing, 1996.

Giordano, Frank, Jr. *A Chronicle of River Oaks Country Club.* Houston: Gulf Publishing, 1991.

Glenn, Rhonda. *The Illustrated History of Women's Golf.* Dallas: Taylor Publishing, 1991.

———. *Brook Hollow Country Club 75-Year History.* Dallas: Taylor Publishing, 1995.

Golf Courses of Texas. Austin: Great Outdoor Publishers, 1993.

Golf Magazine. *Golf in America: The First 100 Years.* New York: H. N. Adams, 1988.

Golf San Antonio. *2004 Valero Texas Open Media Guide.* San Antonio.

Hauser, Melanie, ed. *Under the Lone Star Flagstick.* New York: Simon & Schuster, 1997.

Hermes, Frank. *Texas Golf.* Dallas: Taylor Publishing, 1987.

Holmes, Jon. *Texas Sport: The Illustrated History.* Austin: Texas Monthly Press, 1984.

Horn, Barry. "Alvin C. Thompson." *Dallas Morning News,* August 29, 2001, p. 1B.

Houston Golf Association. "1996 Shell Houston Open Program." *The Woodlands,* p. 30.

Kelso, Margo. *Galveston Country Club 100th Anniversary.* Galveston: Minute Man Press, 1998.

Kite, Tom. *A Fairway to Heaven.* New York: W. Morrow, 1997.

Ladies Professional Golf Association. *2004 LPGA Media Guide.* Daytona Beach, Fla.

Luska, Frank. "Gus Moreland." *Dallas Morning News,* February 12, 1988, p. 3B.

Lynch, Eamon. "Raymond Floyd." *Golf,* June 2004, p. 188.

Nelson, Byron. *Byron Nelson's Winning Golf.* Dallas: Taylor Publishing, 1973.

———. *How I Played the Game.* Dallas: Taylor Publishing, 1993.

———. *The Byron Nelson Little Black Book.* Arlington: Summit Publishing, 1995.

Newberry, Kevin. *Shell's Golf Guide to Houston.* 3 vols. Houston: 21st Century Media, 1992, 1993, 1995.

———. *Texas Golf: The Best of the Lone Star State.* Houston: Gulf Publishing, 1998.

Pate, Russ. *Colonial Country Club, 1936–1986.* Fort Worth: Motheral Printing Company, 1986.

Penick, Harvey, and Bud Shrake. *Harvey Penick's Little Red Book.* New York: Simon & Schuster, 1992.

———. *And If You Play Golf, You're My Friend.* New York: Simon & Schuster, 1994.

———. *The Game for a Lifetime.* New York: Simon & Schuster, 1996.

PGA of America. *2004 PGA of America Media Guide.* Palm Beach, Fla.

PGA Tour. *2004 PGA Tour Media Guide.* Ponte Vedra Beach, Fla.

———. *2004 Champions Tour Media Guide.* Ponte Vedra Beach, Fla.

PGA Tour and LPGA Tour 2002, 2003 and 2004 media interview transcripts.

Richardson, William. "U.S. Open." *New York Times,* June 8–14, 1941, p. 1B.

Rule, Bob. *Champions Golf Club.* Houston: Graphics Unlimited, 1976.

Salesmanship Club, Dallas. "Byron Nelson Program." May 2002, p. 52.

———. "Byron Nelson Program." May 2004, p. 29.

Sampson, Curt. *Texas Golf Legends*. Lubbock: Texas Tech University Press, 1993.

———. *Hogan*. Nashville: Rutledge Hill Press, 1996.

Shipnuck, Alan. *Bud, Sweat, and Tees*. New York: Simon & Schuster, 2001.

Stewart, Tracey, and Ken Abraham. *Payne Stewart: The Authorized Biography*. Nashville: Broadman and Holman, 2000.

Stone, Jason. *The Texas Golf Bible*. Dallas: Fandango Publishing Company, 2003.

Stricklin, Art. *Southwestern Bell's Golf Guide to Austin–San Antonio*. 2 vols. Houston: 21st Century Media, 1993, 1994.

———. *Texas Golf Guide*. 2 vols. Plano: Republic of Texas Press, 1997, 1999.

———. "GCSAA Golf Course Management." Dallas, February 2001, p. 30.

———. *A History of Northwood Club: Thanks for the Memories*. Virginia Beach, Va.: Donning Company, 2002.

Stricklin, Art, and Kevin Newberry. *BMW Golf Guide to Dallas–Fort Worth*. Houston: 21st Century Media, 1996.

Trevino, Lee, and Sam Blair. *They Call Me Super Mex*. New York: Random House, 1982.

———. *The Snake in the Sandtrap*. New York: Henry Holt, 1985.

Trimble, Francis. "Fact from Fiction." *Texas Golf Magazine*, June 1990, p. 18.

———. "The Birth of the Texas Open I and II." *Golfiana*, Fall 1992, p. 13.

———. "The Symonses: Texas' First Family of Golf." *Golfiana*, Fall 1993, p. 11.

———. *One Hundred Years of Champions and Change: Austin Country Club*. Austin: Whitley Company, 1999.

Trimble, Francis, and J. C. King. *Golf: The Handbook of Texas Online*. Austin: University of Texas Libraries, 1997–2002.

United States Golf Association. "2004 USGA Media Guide." Far Hills, N.J.

Whiten, Ron, and Geoffrey Cornish. *The Golf Course*. New York. Rutledge Press, 1981.

World Golf Hall of Fame. "World Golf Hall of Fame Inductee Biographies, 1981–2004." St. Augustine, Fla.

Index

About the Author

ART STRICKLIN has written nine books on golf, focusing mainly on Texas, and has worked as a freelance golf and travel writer for ten years. His stories have appeared in regional, national, and international publications. He has been honored by five professional journalist associations, including being nominated for the Pulitzer Prize in Public Service. He is married with two daughters and lives in North Texas.